Oil Patch

Recollections of "The Way Things Were"

Compiled and Edited

by

Elsie Garstad-Rosenau

"A collection of Life's Happenings"
Elsie Garstad
#105 - 13104 - 132 Avenue
Edmonton, AB T5L 3R3

PH: (780) 451-2196
Printed by Quality Color Press Inc.

First Printing	May, 1997
Second Printing	July, 1997
Third Printing	December, 1998

This book is dedicated:

To my children, Lynda, John and Jim, whose support and trust fueled my enthusiasm for this writing project.

The memory of my mother, Magna Garstad, who, with her writing ability and interest in the 'way of life and living' as she put it, has always been an inspiration to me.

ACKNOWLEDGMENTS

I am indebted to Maureen Cadence, Valerie Pawluk and Eunice Scarfe for showing me ways to visualize and tap into my creativity to pursue a dream or two.

To Ford Bergwall who had belief and faith in me and my endeavors, I send my thanks. Ford gave of his time and talent by providing a drawing of the oil patch logo.

Thanks to Fred Dreichel, the man I married in 1952. If I had not met him, I would have missed a part of my life that was filled with happiness and sadness, hardship and reward, triumph and failure. I would have missed an opportunity to be involved in this special phase of the Petroleum Industry of Alberta.

A special note of appreciation to the many storytellers, who participated so generously. Without their interest, encouragement and recollections, this book would never have been completed.

I appreciate the many friends and relatives who gave me assurance and support when my courage flagged. I thank them for their assistance throughout this entire process.

I extend my gratitude to those friends who volunteered their time to assist me in completing the last minute details for the publication of this book.

Finally, I give special thanks to Valerie Perry, my transcriber and secretarial assistant, who worked tirelessly with me to complete this book within the required deadline.

Elsie Garstad-Rosenau
Edmonton, Alberta
May 1997

Table of Contents

The Children

Anonymous Anecdotes

INTRODUCTION

When thoughts first came into my mind that I might put together a book about 'the way things were', I wanted to forget the whole idea. But the idea persisted and I began to take the project seriously. Things fell into place very quickly. The interest and enthusiasm of the people I spoke with gave me confidence to take a step forward and begin my first collection of human interest stories.

The Petroleum Industry has a colorful history not unlike the fur trading, gold mining, road construction or railroad building. Ordinary, hard working, everyday people had to be tough to survive the working conditions and fast lifestyle that was the norm. They had to have a sense of humor and a strong sense of earning a day's pay by using their wits, agility and sheer, brute strength. A section of the book contains recollections of the men who worked very hard in a very dangerous occupation.

This book will appeal to all those strong, tough minded young men who began working in the oil patch in the forties, after Leduc #1. It will also appeal to the men of the fifties and sixties when the Alberta economy 'boomed' as never before. They were men who dominated the Alberta landscape with seismic rigs, drilling rigs, pickup trucks, mega-sized automobiles, private airplanes, skid-shacks and trailers.

I was a young girl, working in an office in a small town when I met a tall, blonde man, age 21, who had arrived in town with an oil crew. We were married the following year and I went into one of the most memorable experiences of my lifetime. Those of us who remember Alberta before the fifties, remember scattered amenities throughout the rural areas. Indoor plumbing and electricity were luxuries. Most people had been used to miniature size bank accounts that limited their perspectives. The oil boom arrived and this changed the picture and people's expectations dramatically.

This book is also for the starry eyed, hopeful young women who fell in love with these men, waited for them, moved around with them, or moved away from them. A section of the book contains recollections of the women who shared the lives of these nomadic workers. Life within the oil patch was not for wimpy women. It was certainly not boring and those who were part of it have a pocketful or two of memories. Another section of the book contains recollections of the children who moved around with their parents as they followed the rigs, or stayed in one place, waiting for Dad to come out on 'days off'.

At the end of the book, there is a collection of anonymous anecdotes. These are only a few of the many stories that are shared discreetly with others who are familiar with the life and times of the oil patch.

The majority of the recollections are drawn from taped interviews and are prepared in a narrative style. These are personal recollections from people who were involved. The recollections reflect, to a large extent, the storyteller's own words and style of speech.

Indeed all who were involved have earned a special place in the shaping of Alberta's history.

The Men

those strong, tough
minded men

who used their wits,
agility

and sheer brute
strength

all of which helped

the oil industry to
move foreward

Donald Adair

Donald worked approximately five years in the oil patch. In 1955 he began a career in Construction, working both commercial and industrial for many years and he is now enjoying retirement, in Edmonton.

I started when I was 20 years old. I will always remember April 13, 1951, the day I left home, in Athabasca, Alberta. I arrived in Lloydminster, Saskatchewan. It was a beautiful spring day.

The next day we left in the middle of a blizzard to go out to the drilling rig near Lone Rock which was just outside of Lloydminster. We had to walk the last two miles into the rig site to rig up for drilling to start on April 14th.

I worked on the rigs until the summer of 1955. Most of my 'rig work' was with J.W. Carroll Drilling on a Failing 2500, single stand, small rig. This rig was ideal for the drilling depth around Lloydminster (approximately 2200 feet) and later in the Bonnyville/Cold Lake area (approximately 1200 to 1300 feet). In the spring of 1952, some of my time was spent around Taber with Comet Drilling on a Carwell rig.

As a small town boy away from home, I was fortunate to work with Joe Carroll who was Jack W. Carroll's brother. Joe was my driller and he was a very caring and safety conscious person. I worked derrick most of the time. I especially enjoyed the "graveyard' shift when just prior to the dawning, I could climb the derrick and watch the sunrise. A very peaceful time of the morning!

I liked to sing and when I was up on the derrick platform, I could sing to my heart's content. Al Jolson was a favorite singer of mine at that time, and still is. Some of the songs I sang were 'Swannee', 'Red, Red Robin' and 'April Showers'.

The work was hard but work is enjoyable when you like what you are doing and you enjoy the company of your co-workers.

During my first year, we went to Bonnyville, to drill a gas well for the town. We hit oil instead, and then drilled many more wells a few miles out of town. As I said, we worked hard, working twelve hour shifts all summer until Christmas. We also played hard, involving ourselves in many activities after work.

Donald Adair (1995)

Edward (Ed) Brennan

He began working on the rigs in 1952, working intermittently to supplement his income from the farm. As the result of a car accident in 1971, he has been confined to a wheel chair ever since. A published author of three books, he continues to write and is active in fund-raising for the handicapped and assisting in the various organizations to obtain better housing and access to public buildings.

I started on the rigs in 1952. It was a winter job to keep the farm in Bonnyville going. My first job on the rigs was with High Tower Drilling and we drilled three holes.

We usually stayed at hotels and ate in restaurants or, if we were lucky, we found a place to room & board. I worked rough-neck, motors, and derrick. I was set up to driller and then I got hurt. I was in a car accident in the spring of 1971. Prior to that, I had worked in the oil patch, off and on, for about 19 years.

We were living in Hanna, working on a High Tower rig, thirty miles east of Pollockville. A blizzard hit and we were stranded at the rig for three days. The toolpush didn't even offer us a bloody coffee and if it hadn't been for the boiler-man and his wife, we would have been in pretty rough shape. They looked after us. They lived on the lease and had their trailer right there. We slept where we could get a little heat, in the change shack room.

Going home from the rig, back to Hanna, we saw cattle that had drifted with the storm until they couldn't go any further. They were in the corner of the barbed wire fence. They were stopped and some of them were frozen to death I can still see one of the cows, standing up and her hind quarters were against the fence. Her front end was still standing good but, she had froze to death, and still standing. There were others that were laying down, noses back towards their flanks, froze up.

That was the end of the job there, we tore out and came back to Edmonton. A few days later, I saw a truck, going through the city, loaded with cattle, their feet sticking up. They had to be the results of the storm; the stock that had frozen to death. In that storm, there were antelope that had been walking on the rail road tracks, their feet and legs had been frozen. Never seen a storm like that, before in my life, and probably never see another one.

One of the longest drives to work was the job in Hanna, where it usually took 1 1/2 hours to drive sixty miles to work. The morning shift began at 7 am until 4 pm. If we went straight home, we would be there by 6 pm.

These were long days. We had a short change when we worked "graveyards", finishing the day shift at 4 pm and back to begin shift at 11 pm, that same day. On long change we came off "graveyards" at 7 am, usually on a Saturday, then, returned to shift the next afternoon at 4 pm.

I worked in Swan Hills during the "boom". Swan Hills had a camp and that wasn't to bad. The camp cooks cooked good food and there was lots of it. We worked eight hour shifts, sometimes twelve to get longer weekends off. In the summer, cats pulled everything through the mud, in winter you could get through without much of a problem.

I worked in Hay River, Rainbow Lake and Zama. These were all camp jobs. At that time, there was just a trail, through the bush, to Rainbow Lake and Zama. I understand the roads are all paved now.

Once, in Hay River, the temperature dropped to 70o F below zero. It shut everything down, broke water lines, steam lines. We left the motors idling and kept the circulation going to see that the oil was up and every thing was in running order.

The toolpush went to town and we just laid around camp waiting for it to warm up. We played lots of cards. When it went up to 40o F below zero, everybody went back to work.

One time, one of the boys got his ragged coat caught up in some equipment on the floor. He was flipped over the pulleys and we took him to town to have him checked out. He wasn't hurt too badly. He took on a couple days booze, came back and put the same raggedy coat on and began working again. Safety measures weren't to much of an issue.

All the time I worked on the rigs, I never seen anybody get hurt to bad. Green hands, that is, the inexperienced, had to learn really fast and they did learn fast. Farm guys were strong, they were usually a good size. The boys out of Saskatchewan came off the farms in the winter time. At the end of March, they'd shut 'er down and go back home.

By 1955 a lot of the drilling was going on in northern Alberta. Out in isolated areas there were the camp jobs which was what we wanted in order to save money. There were the bunk houses and kitchens with excellent food.

Fort St. John had been proven when I was in there. It was a production field and not a lot of drilling was going on.

We were on a deep hole, slow drilling. Everything was all washed up and looking purty, as purty as it gets. I went into the change shack and went to sleep. I woke up and my work boots were painted BRIGHT YELLOW. It was an embarrassing situation. I couldn't say I wasn't sleeping. The derrick hand did it and I don't remember his name. Ken Hanson was the driller on that rig. He was the best driller I ever worked for and I'll never forget him.

Most of my time was on big rigs. I spent some time on a service rig out around Pincher Creek. Terrible situation, I thought. Totally different kind of ball game. They didn't want to kill the well to service it, because they had done that to another one and never got it back into production.

Pincher Creek, it is the windiest place in Alberta. Every time the wind changed, you had to change that bloody flare line a different direction. It was quite a mess.

Things were sure different then, than nowadays. I remember once, when I was roughneckin', the derrick hand had a new truck he was driving, the driller was with us, we hit the ditch. The driller just got out, took off walkin' to the rig. The derrick hand said, "Well, if that's all he thinks of his crew, were goin' to Edmonton. I said, "OK, I'm goin' too." We went. In those days you could go off one rig, go half a mile, and get a job on another one.

I worked for several companies. I did seasonal work because I farmed as well. In those days, when you wanted work, you went where the work was. Now, they seem to think you just sit at home and fill in a bunch of paper work and somebody is gonna come lookin' for you. Well it isn't that way!!

In the early fifties, if you were out of work, you could just go to the bar and you would get a job. The companies were crying for men. In the seventies, it became a little harder to find work and things just seemed to die in the eighties.

Ed Brennan (1996)

Leonard (Len) Brennan

Len began roughnecking in 1960 for High Tower Drilling Rig #1. Like everyone else working in the oil patch, he was away from home and family most of the time. He has written poetry, some of which is published. Two of his writings are printed at the conclusion of this story. He and his wife Doreen recently moved into Edmonton and are working in property management.

I started working around the rigs just after I got out of school. I worked in construction, in Swan Hills, at building sites and what-not. I remember the old forestry road into Swan Hills. There wasn't a tree around that wasn't all scarred up from vehicles winching themselves out.

I was catskinning, running a dozer for Brent Construction. I was sent out with two barrels of fuel and I was to pull the trucks out of the mud.

My instructions were to pull out the fuel trucks, which were stuck in the middle of the convoy. I was to make a road around the other trucks and leave them stuck in the mud.

You would have got killed if you tried to do something like that. There were so many trucks - guys had been on the road for two to three days with nothing to eat. I just pulled them all out.

The company man for the rig gave me those instructions. He didn't seem concerned about anyone but himself. When we towed those trucks through some of the pot holes, their headlights would be submerged. It was just unreal. No one would spend five cents to upgrade the road at all. Everybody used it and abused it and that was just the way it was.

Eventually everybody got there but they really suffered. When they did get to Swan Hills, there wasn't a whole lot there. The Hilltop Cafe was there, in the old town site. It was run by an old fella named Jack Cameron. When you came to the door, he would say "Hello, my friend." And when you left, he would say "You know that no-good." He would have a really good description of you, especially if he didn't like you. Yet, he was a good man and he fed a lot of people; no one left his place hungry.

He didn't live too many years after that. He left a box full of bills that people hadn't paid. I guess they didn't think it would hurt him too much

Then there was Swanie's Inn. Big Town Clothing started by just setting up a trailer. Hodge Propane was situated right on the shore of Edith Lake. The new town site was being developed. I was working on a dozer and I cleared the second location for the town. After that, contractors became involved and then things really began to happen.

I went to work roughnecking for High Tower Drilling, the day after Christmas in 1960. I was 21 years old, married and my wife lived in Edmonton. We never moved around in a trailer or that sort of thing.

There were lots of memories but the muddy roads stand out. They were horrendous. You could very seldom drive up to the rig. Most times, you would have to leave your vehicle and walk a half a mile to a mile in. The camp was good, although I guess they were quite crude compared to what camps are today. They were good in those days, compared to lumber camps and this sort of thing. You could never complain about the food in a rig camp. Forthier-Northey Catering was very popular and supplied the food and the cooks.

Most memorable recollection: The experience of Swan Hills stood out too. I went in there in the fall of 1958 and they were just building roads. When I first arrived, they were putting in a big culvert at the river and a network of roads. I think it was probably that winter when the rigs really started coming in large numbers. That's when the action really got started in the Swan Hills area.

I stayed on High Tower Rig #1, going back after spring break-up. It was really, really tough to leave my wife in Edmonton and go to work. One particular day just stands out in my memory like it was yesterday. I was going back to work after break-up in 1961. My wife was expecting and the crew came around to my house to pick me up. We were standing on the street in front of our house, saying our good-byes. It had been so hard to leave. I wrote a poem about that experience, much later, while I was working in Pakistan.

I had worked a 16 hour shift. It was noon and I had come in for a change when I saw the old dreaded police wagon, the R.C.M.P. I knew right then what it was all about. They said, "We're looking for Brennan." I said, "That's me." They told me, "Your wife is in the hospital." I got all excited, this was our first baby, and I went running up the steps to the dog house. I don't remember the driller's name. I was so excited but all he said was, "Don't get so excited. It will probably happen another 12 times in your life." Fortunately, it didn't.

When I saw my little baby looking at me with her big blue eyes, I melted. I quit the rigs then. I was so homesick that I couldn't stand it. Two years later, our second daughter was born.

I quit the rigs in 1961 and I didn't go back until 1966. I went to work with Big Indian Drilling up by Fort Providence. From then on, I just worked for different companies.

We adopted two boys after that. When we got our second son, I was working at West Carson Field, just past Whitecourt. We were about eight miles off the highway, on a bull-dozed trail, just off the first gravel road.

When we were to pick this baby up, I finished my day's work and I was coming home. About three miles from the rig, I got stuck. I waited and waited all night long. Finally, in the morning the fuel truck came, tearing up the road behind him. He had chains on. He pulled me out and I went back to the camp. I just couldn't make it out and I had to wait for two more weeks before I could go home.

About that time the whole Alberta experience in the oil patch changed. I went with Westburne to Norway in 1971 and again in 1972. Actually we went to Oslo, Norway and went to Tromso, where we caught up to our rig. Then we went to Edge Island, which is just a dot on the map. It's situated about 600 miles from the north pole behind Greenland.

After that, I went to work for a year at Farris Engineering in the Gulf of Suez. I took my family with me to Israel. When we came back, I was home for about a month before I went to work in Libya in 1977. Next, I went to work in Pakistan. I worked for Southeastern, a company out of Dallas. I also worked in Algeria. It just seemed for a while you couldn't pick up a Calgary or Edmonton paper without seeing overseas opportunities for rig hands of some sort.

Overseas employment was a different way of life but it was good, very good. If it hadn't been for the oil patch, a lot of people, including myself, would never have seen as much of the world as we did. Through it all, I passed through about 20 different countries. On the other hand, you just did what you had to do, you went where the work was. There were thoughts about quitting but it wasn't possible to make that kind of money anywhere else. It didn't take too long before you knew that this was the work you knew best. The better you got, the better another chance for promotion and another raise. You wound up being glued to the industry.

The last overseas job was in February 1983. By then I had worked for Southeastern for five years and overseas employment in the oil industry fell apart. When we left Pakistan, Challenger Drilling took over our office and bought a couple of trucks from Southeastern.

In 1983, the oil industry in Alberta began to fall apart. Rigs began moving to the States like there was no tomorrow. The industry fell apart, it didn't slow down, it simply fell off the cliff, as it was. People were saying, "Had I known, I wouldn't have bought that new truck. Hang onto your money because we don't know what's happening."

When I lost my job, as a whole lot of others did, I still wanted to stay overseas but I couldn't get lined up with anything. I phoned all over the States and then I phoned Challenger Drilling. They said to call Athens. When I did, they said "We have no less than 600 applications and we're hearing from guys that are just dumped all over the world the same as you are." In 1983, my wife, two boys and I were living in Barcelona. We just packed up and came back home. My ticket was paid but my family's fare was not. Both girls were married then, and living in Canada.

All things considered, I have no regrets. It was different. I worked up in the Arctic for Westburne, who in turn worked for PanArctic. That was an experience in itself. Everybody knows there's nothing there, but seeing how nothing is, is quite something.

I worked on King Christian Island in 1971. That was the rig that blew up and caught fire. Actually, I was going out on shift. I was just waiting for supper. Our kitchen was on the rig side. There was a hallway and a recreation area there. I was sitting on a chesterfield having a coffee when the electrician came running in and said, "The well blew in, the rig is on fire." I ran out, grabbed my clothes that were hanging on the wall outside of the camp. I couldn't believe only minutes had gone by and all this had happened. The tarps were all burned off the rig and I died a thousand times before I got over there. I just knew our escape line for the derrick man was up but our buggy wasn't on it yet. It was sitting down at the end of the catwalk. The derrick man had just got to the bottom, when the fire blew. Everyone was OK, no one got hurt, but it was a real long, long day.

The rig burned for three months until they drilled a directional well to put the fire out. The rubbers from the blowout preventors were taken to P.I.T.S, the drilling school in Edmonton. They were still there several years ago.

In 1985 I ran wire line for Shorty's Oilfield Services. I worked for him for five years. I was in various places, including Red Earth, doing plugs and abandonments.

When we were working up in the Arctic, our toolpush was a guy by the name of Jerry Korth. He was from Rocky Mountain House. I think he's one of the most respected men in the oil patch. Actually, I guess I would take my hat off to him. He was a prince to work for. He could get more work out of his men by being civilized and decent than most people could by walking over top of them.

Jerry liked to play jokes on people, just nice things, so we did one on him one time. We were moving the rig and we saw this fox run into a pile of casing. We pushed the fox out, caught it and turned it loose in Jerry's bedroom.

The next morning as we came in for breakfast, the crew coming out to work told us, "Jerry is really upset about this fox in his room." Of course, no one knew a thing about it. We came for breakfast and we all sat at the table enjoying our meal. Jerry was sitting there just talking to the guys trying to let on nothing was wrong. Everyone was just trying so hard to keep from busting out laughing. Then he said, "So OK you guys, who put that fox in my room?" No one knew anything about it. He went on to tell us, "I didn't mind the fox. I got up and went to shave and came back and looked and there was this fox under my bed. I didn't mind that until I got looking around some more. That fox of yours had climbed up on my desk and messed my papers all around." He was an OK guy. As far as I am concerned, Jerry Korth and Al Bunn were probably both kings of the oil patch.

One time, when I was working in Pakistan, we were drilling a hole between Islamabad and Lahor. We had been drilling for 280 days; 11,000 feet at $13 million dollars. There had been trouble from start to finish. We started out with a 36 inch hole, then ran a thirty inch casing. We went down 250 feet.

In this particular case, when we were finished drilling the hole and it was all cleaned out with a cellar jet, there was a lot of mud and crap to clean out of the cellar - rocks and cuttings and all that. The roustabout crew was cleaning the hole out. When the rig crew was done, we went down to make it go a little faster. One guy, a native fellow on the roustabout crew who had been working there for four to five hours, crossed the cellar and walked right into the hole. I saw it! The hole was 36 inches wide and 250 feet deep! Amazingly, he was pulled out by his fellow men before he sunk.

I just flew down those steps. It was all over when I got down there. He was mud right up to his armpits. I'm sure that was the closest I ever came to having a casualty on the rig. The guy wasn't hurt. He was shaking pretty badly and I told him, "That's OK, you can just take the day off."

Another time, when I was working for Westburne in Zaire, a guy was electrocuted. He was bleeding from his ears, nose and mouth. We just put a mattress in the back of a truck and drove him down to the military station, which was about 40 to 45 miles away. He survived. And the irony of it all was that, in that country, it didn't even merit an accident report. It was considered uneventful.

Memories. They're not all good. They're not all bad.

If I could do it over: I'm not really sure if I would do it over again. That's something I can't really answer. The only reason I did it at all was because I had to make a living and the money was good. It wasn't because I appreciated being away from home and family."

Len Brennan (1997)

The following is a footnote to Leonard Brennan's poem "Parting - To My Wife"

The Airport
While waiting for the plane..

Just before entering the departure lounge at the Islamabad airport in Pakistan - I saw a scene so heart warming and beautiful, it prompted me to write this poem. The young couple were parting - a Haliburton employee from London was visited by his wife and two little children. They were parting at the airport - she was returning to London with their two kiddies.

In that fleeting moment, I saw the years of my life as in their mirror image. I knew the emotional tugging on their heart strings - for that was the story of my life. They stood out of the traffic flow, holding each other; she was looking steadfast into his face. Not one to make a scene, but the tears - she couldn't hide - and hanging onto daddy's legs were their two little kids. To me - my Shawnna and Tracie.

For some reason, it caused me to reflect on my past years - remembering when my wife Doreen was pregnant with our first child. I was working in Swan Hills in the spring of 1961. We were returning to the rig after spring shut down. As we stood on the sidewalk, ready to drive away, we held each other in our "say good-bye." I'll always remember her trying to be strong, but the tears rolled down her cheeks. I tried to find comforting words and said, "It won't always be like this - things will change.

Little did I know then that this would be the story of my life for quite some time. Things did change. Now I was nineteen flying hours, 10,000 miles, twelve time zones and half the way around the world from home.

After pondering for a while, I found it comforting to know that things really had changed but the things that really counted hadn't changed at all.

Parting - "To My Wife"

Crowding through the airport
In Islamabad -
I saw a family parting -
It made my memory sad.
- "Sweetheart"-
I know we love each other
dearly -
Would for each other die;
Yet my many times in leaving -
Has changed our -
"Say Good Bye."
I remember - just a while ago -
When our kids were small,
Oh how we'd hurt in parting-
But time has conquered all.
No longer do we linger
And share a last embrace.
To hold each other tender -
And share each others face;
It seems our time in parting
Is just another phase -
Of the way we live together-
Across ten million waves.
Or could it be Sweetheart
We've grown a little cold -
Or just a little wreckless
With strings of love we hold?
These are haunting questions -
That Darling - I won't hide-
You're only mine forever -
The answer's still inside.
Goodbye could be forever;
Let's not hasten till I'm late -
If it takes from now till never -
Let the big bird wait!

Excerpt from:
Strips Off My Heart
by Ed and Len Brennan
Edmonton: Beartrap Publishing
and Distributing Ltd.,1981
Page 47

A poem written by Len Brennan during the time he worked in northern Pakistan 1979 - 1982.

- Reminisce -

I was raised on Bonnyville
On a rocky-poor land farm
Went to School in old Fort Kent
Years that done no harm.
I set four rules:
- Steer clear of fools
- Don't labour with my kin
- To set my eyes on yonder skies
- And travel like the wind.
So it's been for quite some time
The years have come and gone -
I've raised a little brood of four -
Time I can not shun;
Now they're slipping out my door
For I am forty-one.
I've travelled a lot -
I feel I've seen my share.
I've set my foot in twenty lands
And found some things most rare.
Now - I'd like to take a moment
And - sort of - Reminisce -
I'll tell you of some places -
And folks I sure do miss.
I've seen the Fjords of Norway
And Vieglands Sculpture Park -
Copenhagen's Tivoli Garden -
In Stockholms - King Gustav's Sunken Arc.
I've been to Holland many times
And Brussel's Seven Hills;
These are lands I'll not forget -
But others held more thrills.
I stood on the Shore of Galilee
Where the River Jordan flows -
"This could well be a place
where Jesus stood"
I solemnly supposed.
I've been to old Jerusalem
Half dozen times or more -
And in a place called Garden Tomb
I set old thoughts aside -
For this is said to be the place -
My Christ - was crucified.
We viewed the mosque of Omar -
It's glittering golden dome -
A Moslem sacred Holy place
Where weary pilgrims roam.
And rested on a mountain
My wife and little brood -
As-through Jewish eyes -
tried to surmise -
Masada's mortal feud;
As Roman camps built the ramp-
They waited - Horror's doom!
I've seen the Sinai Desert
It's rocky - barren hills -
And in the Town - "Abu Rodies"
Saw Egypt's Bitter Pills
This is the sore - that paid the score
By Egypt's troubled land -
Though this my friend was not a war.
T'was just a reprimand

The battle yet - To not forget
Is surely - sure at hand!!
We splashed in the Dead Sea
Near Quamran's Ancient Scrolls-
And made a trip to Gaza town
Beside its sandy beaches -
Where palm trees gently roll.
Made a trip to Bethlehem
Birth place of Christ My King-
And heard the tolling bells -
That made the valley's ring!
I've been in the raw Sahara
It's countries on both sides;
In Libya's land of shifting sand -
Algeria's rolling hills -
I've been to Spain and the
Pyrenees
And France a couple trips -
Made my home on Mallorca's
Stone -
And saw its awesome caves!
I saw the mighty Congo -
A river so vast and wide -
From Kinshasa's shore to
Barasaville
It's waters gently glide.
I've worked with men - In Zaire
land
Who's skin was black as coal -
With a desperate need -
Themselves to feed -
Yet - They smiled with a heart of
Gold!
Now - I am in Pakistan
Trying to drill some wells -
With a score of downhole
troubles -
This place is drilling hell.
But I hope to pause and linger
For a year or maybe more -
And meet some real fine people
In a land I've yet to explore.
Through all my many journeys
I feel that I've been blessed-
With a host of pleasant thoughts -
For memory's treasure chest.
- And Yet - Things I'll not forget -
Are the carefree ways of my
boyhood days
And Dad's old Ford - oh - How it
roared -
When I drove it like a jet!

Excerpt from:
Treasured Collections
by Ed & Len Brennan
Edmonton, AB: Beartrap
Publishing and Distributing Ltd.,
1982
Page 49 - 52

Thomas D. (Tom) Brown

As a young man, 18 years of age, Tom was hired on in Edmonton and sent directly to the bush with no training, but equipped with a warm jacket, long underwear and rubber boots. He worked in northern Alberta and northern British Columbia on short term contracts for seismic exploration. He currently resides in Lower Sackville, Nova Scotia.

Beginning in 1957, I worked in the oil patch on and off, usually on short term contracts either in the fall or winter of the year. I worked mostly on seismic exploration or service rigs, and usually just long enough to make some spending money. Northern Alberta and B.C. were the areas being worked at that time.

Living conditions were anything from a tent to a trailer. Sometimes, if we were lucky we got a hot-shot deal, which meant living in a motel or hotel with meals included. When entering a set-up camp with trailers, the experienced claimed the lower bunks, otherwise you roasted to death in order for the guys in the lower bunks to be comfortable. Also, the experienced stayed out of the inevitable poker games, unless they were expert players. Initially, if you were really slow, you came out of the bush almost broke with the knowledge that you had involuntarily contributed to another's vacation, new car, etc.

An incident occurred in October of 1960 while working on a seismic crew that could have been disastrous, but like a lot of things that seemed to shelter the "dummies in the bush", it came out all right.

We had finished on a short line of shot holes and having left the rest of the vehicles on-site, were heading back to camp with all the crew on the recording truck. If I recall right, there were five or six of us, two in the cab of the Nodwell and rest on the open deck behind.

As sometimes happens, the safety rules were overlooked and the open box of powder (60% nitro) as well as the open box of caps were tossed up on the rack with the jugs and cable reels. This particular Nodwell was one with an automatic transmission that was notorious for jumping out of gear at the most inopportune times.

A couple of miles from camp was a hill about a half mile long with a steep grade, maybe 30° - 35° F, which we would be descending, and yup! the Nodwell did it's thing! About halfway down the hill, as we picked up speed, we noticed the cab doors fling open. The Observer and Shooter sail past, informing us that, "She's outta gear, boys. Bail out!." This sounded like good advice and it didn't take any of us too long to find a comfortable spot to do a two cheek skid.

The vehicle continued on down the center of the trail and we were just starting to think that maybe this was another trick to get us to walk back to camp when it veered off the trail to the right, bouncing with one track on the tree trunks and bush pushed to the side of the trail by the bulldozer, sailed a short hop in the air, and impacted a couple of good sized trees!

This did the job of fetching it up that the driver couldn't. However, as we stood gazing at it from our relative safety up the hill, a thin wisp of smoke trailed up from what appeared to be the front of the cab. Us younger ones, who were logically impaired, started running down the hill to put the fire out with the extinguisher in the cab, when it dawned on us that the older guys were telling us to slow down.

When we did stop, they pointed out to us that we were running through a scattering of blasting caps and ground up powder that with the smack of a work boot could have placed parts of us in camp a lot sooner than it would take to do all that extra paper work.

We walked the rest of the way with our heads bowed, intently checking the ground, hoping that our neighbour was doing the same, and hoping that if there was a boom it would be caused by someone a good distance away.

We got the fire out without incident and then removed a couple of sticks that had become wedged between the cab and the exhaust pipe. While this was being done, the rest stood around the volunteers with both fingers in their ears.

Another incident comes to mind on the first seismic crew I worked on. The greenhorns stand out like a spruce tree in the desert and it doesn't take long for the wags to set them up.

In my case they used my lack of knowledge of the bush and the naiveté of a know-nothing city boy to set me up. First let me explain that I was hired as a first time Junior Observer and was oblivious to the fact that there just might be some resentment held by a couple of the younger native Indians on the crew. Anyway, coming back from the field to camp this one day shortly after our arrival, I thought nothing of the fact that I was asked to sit up front with the Observer and the Shooter, who was a native Indian and a second World War vet, and a man that I had an instant respect for.

The conversation, right on cue, turned to how fast I could maybe run and if, in fact, I could beat the Indian fellow on the crew as we were about the same age. To my amazement, the Shooter stood up for me, and the Observer was indicating he was more partial to the other fellow.

I, of course, bragged that I could pretty well beat anything on two legs in whatever contest that was being considered. Now that the bait was fully swallowed, the conversation turned to how much of a monetary bet should perhaps be wagered, just to make it more interesting.

Again, to my amazement the Shooter heatedly told the Observer to put-up or shut-up and wagered $50 on me, on the spot. He suggested that I do the same because it would be easy money for both of us. No sooner said than done, the Bombadiere stopped, out popped the native fellow, and we were to race from that spot to camp. To make it fair, it was suggested that we line up at a start line - like a real race - and take off on the ready, set, go! Which is just what we did. However, the other fellow only went down the trail for about 50 feet or so (I had a handy jump on him but he was making me work for it) and then cut off into the bush! Hell, no one had said anything about not running down the road! Why, he'll be disqualified, I laughed to myself!

The Bombadiere had, of course, taken off and passed us both just after the start and I was left alone to run down the trail as it got darker and darker, wondering just where the hell camp was, anyway. I got into camp later, after supper was over and everyone was sitting around snickering and talking about the nice steak they had for supper. I took it with good humor as I was left little choice, and found out later we were almost opposite the camp at the start of the 'race' and my able competitor had just trotted about 100 yards through the bush while I took the longer U turn of the road into camp.

And by the way, I was the only one to shell out any money. I think the split was $20 - $20 - $10. Live and learn, so they say.

T.D. (Tom) Brown (1997)

Chester Calvert

Chester operated a two-way radio, working night shift, putting calls through to the drilling sites, providing contact between the workers and the management or their families when there was no other means of communication. In 1963, he went on to other jobs. He worked for 20 years as a millwright at the Celanese Plant in Edmonton. He retired in 1991.

In the fall of 1952, I began working on seismic rigs near Athabasca, out of Baptiste Lake Then we went south of Calling Lake, and drilled nine holes, These were 1,000 foot holes and we electrologged them. We drilled there all winter, then moved to Camrose. The next summer we were west of Ponoka in the Rimbey area. Near Hoedley Hills we went down 2,600 feet In 1959 I started working with Peter Bawden Drilling I worked a year or so, hauling equipment and doing yard work.

Two-way radios were set up at all the rigs. The company wanted someone to take these over at night. I started the job at 6 pm and finished at 8 am I always worked this night shift alone. There were quite a few calls during the night until about 1 am or when calls stopped coming in from head office or the field.

If emergency calls came in, I would call the Field Superintendent at home, sometimes waking him up. At times, the geologist would talk in code to the oil company involved. With a tight hole, they had codes to communicate so others wouldn't understand the message.

The locations that most of the calls went through were Swan Hills, Wrigley, Fort Nelson and Melville Island, but all Peter Bawden rigs were equipped with radios and were contacted periodically.

The calls I put through were mostly business calls, but on the odd occasion there was an emergency. When family members wanted to get in touch with the men who were working on the rigs, they had to call to the Peter Bawden office. The men would receive the message and come into the rig's radio shack to return the call.

I rigged it up so I could phone their home number if they wanted to speak to their wives or girl-friend, I would put the receiver down to the microphone and it would go through the microphone to the rigs. I'd let the receiver up and whoever was on the rig would talk back to them. There was no privacy, I had to listen to them because

I had to keep switching over. I got so I could read the paper while I was doing this.

A guy wanted to talk to his girlfriend, called in on the radio and when I reached her by telephone, I told her, "Be careful what you say, you are on the radio. The Department of Transport may be monitoring this call."

At one point, during the conversation, the guy said something and she forgot she was on the radio, not the telephone, and answered him with a comment about the condition of her *#!$+%*, or some such thing. I broke in then, and said, "That's it." Bang !! I cut her off right now.

Censored? You bet it was! You were given a call number (e.g., CHQT) and you gave that number when you put calls through. The Department of Transport could listen in any time so you had to be very careful.

They told us that the Queen had come to Banff at a time when they were putting a pipeline over the mountain. She was preparing to make a radio broadcast and it was announced that the broadcast would follow shortly.

The radio was unpredictable, as always. Suddenly, just before the Queen was about to speak, a voice came on the line, asking, "Where is that *$#&%* toilet paper roll?" You can be sure there were precautions made, from then on, to keep that embarrassment from repeating itself.

One time a guy from up there called his wife, through the radio. Half the time you couldn't get through on the telephones since the night-shift operators were sleeping on the job, and didn't wake up a lot of the time. Anyway, he said something about buying a big car. That's the time when "the tax" came through on Buicks, the high priced cars. His wife kept asking, "why? why?" He hemmed and hawed but wouldn't tell her. Later, he got a letter from the Department of Transport with a strong warning.

One time there was a call from one of the guys up there in Swan Hills. He said, "You'd better get some grub in here or I'll "set it on the bank" (shut down the drilling). The fellow in Edmonton answered, "What kind of a hunter are you? Lots of bear roamin' around and pretty tasty too. I hear the sweet breads are pretty good."

The next day or two, along come a letter, from Edmonton, word for word of every thing said during the conversation. This warning came from the Department of Transport, who had been monitoring the calls.

I believe the two-way radios were set up in 1959. They were still in use in 1963 when I stopped working for the company.

Sometimes you couldn't get through on the radios. One time a call came in from Melville Island. We had a four different frequencies and the call came in clear. It was late in 1962. One of the guys flew to the rig in a DC-3. It was a white-out and they couldn't find the rig. I radioed the rig telling the toolpush, "They should be over your head right now."

They used to light up flares with a barrel of fuel by the landing strip but the pilots couldn't find the airport and they turned, trying to find the landing strips. They hit a storm, ran out of fuel, bellied the DC-3 down 200 yards from the radar base on the mainland and walked in at night. That was the night that someone had predicted that the planets would line up and the world would to come to an end.

The pilot's wife came into the Edmonton office and said, "He's in trouble." I said, "No, sit down, have a drink, it's Christmas time."

She did sit down and had a drink but when she left, she said, "If you hear anything, telephone me. He was in trouble once before, by an airport. I knew it then. He's in trouble now, and I know it."

The next morning a message came through from the Dew Line that the 32 foot plane was 200 yards north of the radar base. They had several lengths of drill pipe and groceries on that plane, approximately 6,000 pounds altogether. The plane was brought out later but in the meantime, the men at the rig still needed drill pipe and groceries.

At the camp, the wind was howling and a blizzard was in full force. A rope was tied from the rig to the camp so the men could get back and forth.

One night—took two Eskimos up to Inuvik and over to Melville Island to trap for him. He put them up in Perry's Cabin, Perry Bark was an Arctic explorer in earlier years. The Eskimos would take off in a howling blizzard, come back two weeks later and go on their trap line. They had trapped an Arctic White fox once and they brought it in to show us. Once, they were getting low on fuel at the cabin so they took a Nodwell, a track vehicle, out, but turned around and came back, afraid they'd get lost. Those Eskimos would disappear and come back, sometimes on land, sometimes on water.

Once, on the DC-3, the meat mush for the dogs upset. One guy complained all winter and said he'd never forget the stink of that dog food. In the spring of 1962, I was asked if I wanted to help tear the rig out at Melville Island. I told 'em, "No, not a chance." I wasn't going near the place.

They went up to Resolute Bay, which was a couple hundred miles east. They flew with the Beaver plane to the drilling site. The snow up there is just like sand, hard to push, even with a cat. It drifted in and covered the whole substructure of the rig, only the gin poles, on the cat, were sticking out.

The toolpush went in there, got the light plant going, started the radio at one o'clock in the morning on June 22. It was 40° F below zero. The crew then went in to tear the rig out. It took one day to dig all the snow away using cats. They took it the bank and left it there so when the ship came in they could load it on. Late in July and August the snow started to melt. The sun was just hitting the horizon and coming back up in the summer time. The sun don't go down up there.

One guy was badly hurt up there. They were changing shifts and the DC-3 was warming up. The driller told the derrick-hand to come on down. They were waiting in the doghouse and they heard this thump on the roof. He came down all right, landed on the doghouse roof, then on the frozen ground. He must have fallen off the ladder. No one knows what happened. Things were pretty risky in those days. Safety measures were looked into after that. This man's hip bones were driven right up into him. Damaged him a bit.

It took ten hours flight time and 1,600 miles later to reach the University Hospital in Edmonton. Three months later, this man came into the office in Edmonton. Drove up, riding motor bike! Tough guy. A tough guy, this 22 year old was.

Chester Calvert (1996)

Douglas (Doug) Dunn

Doug has worked in the oil patch since 1948 with the exception of four years. During that time he worked in the transportation industry, hauling oilfield equipment. In 1974, he returned to the oil patch and worked overseas until 1979. He worked in the following countries - Libya, Australia, the Philippines and Indonesia. Doug is consulting on a part-time basis and enjoys country living on an acreage near Wabamun.

I started roughnecking, at age twenty, in January 1948 for Young Drilling. It was an old conventional mechanical rig. While working there, I used to tag along behind the derrick bandit, a pretty good guy. We were going down to the pits, at that time there were earthen pits and no steel tanks for the drilling mud. Just as we got down alongside the pump, there was a hell of a roar in the air chamber. The air chamber sits on top of the pump and when the fluid comes in, it expels air. This air chamber went right up through the roof. That happened in 1948 and we haven't seen it since. That was quite an odd thing.

I worked my eight hours on the rig and after work, I drove a truck, hauling oil. They had dug a ditch and run it down to the corner where the Devon-Nisku road now runs. There was a big pit down there and oil was hauled from that into the old Imperial Oil refinery that had been hauled down from Whitehorse. Another way to earn extra money was to haul bagged cement up close to the rig. We would take it up by wheelbarrow, dump it off and then go back to haul oil.

The smell of gas was all over the country. There was an outdoor biffy quite a ways from the rig. There were signs of "No Smoking" in English, French and Ukrainian. A fellow went into this biffy one day and he decided to have a smoke. Well, the commotion that followed was an unforgettable sight. I didn't see it but the guys that did, and I'm sure they embellished the story a little, said they'd never seen anybody run so fast, never mind with pants down around the ankles, as what C— C— did. His nick-name after that became 'Shit House C—'. This guy married shortly after, left the country and never had any kids.

I remember Atlantic #3, I was there! I was working for Young Drilling at the time and living with three other guys in an old house with a coal and wood stove near the site. Two of us had just come home after working afternoon shift. We fixed a bite to eat and went to bed, leaving dishes, and pots and pans out on the table. All of us came awake in the morning like we'd been shot from a cannon. We heard this awful roar. Everything had fallen to the floor. A couple of us went into Calmar and heard about the rig blow-out. We drove up as close as we could. Oil was spewing all over the rig.

I left Young and went to work derrick for Cantex Drilling. It wasn't unusual in those days to go from one company to another. A rig could be down for two to three weeks and if you had a family, you went where the work was. The starting wages for roughnecks was $6 a day, with no fringe benefits. The job was dirty. It was wet and the rigs weren't encased the way they are today. There was a camaraderie of the guys, that kept you there. You swore after the second or third day you were there, that you would quit. Forty or fifty years later you're still there. It was hard work but it was enjoyable. Then again, payment of income tax was next to nil.

When I started in this industry in 1948, there were some rough, tough guys. Lots of drinking. Lots of partying. I remember one time when I was drilling a well, I went to four barn dances and a beer-fest/chicken-roast in one week. That wasn't unusual. There were guys who spent every night in the beer parlor. They would go in there as soon as they finished work or had supper, and they would be in there until the place closed at 11 o'clock. They always showed up for work the next morning even if they had been in a fight and been stitched up. As long as they could walk and were mobile, they were on the floor.

One of the things that happened when I worked for Cantex Drilling was sort of funny. We were drilling a well just a mile south of Devon. We were attempting to run surface casing and it wouldn't go down. The driller was trying to get it down and it wouldn't go. We had a toolpusher we called Frenchie. Frenchie lived on the lease with his wife and two or three kids in a little trailer. He came up and asked, "What's the matter, Doug?" I said, "Just won't go Frenchie." He said, "We'll see if we can make it."

He went over, took the brake from the driller and he took the blocks right up to the crown. Then he said, "It's your go Doug." He put the handle back and it was something that I'll never forget. My feet were doing 100 miles an hour and my body was standing still. When my body caught up to me down on the cat walk, he had laid the blocks down behind me. When I was out of danger, I started shaking my fist at him. He just said, "Get up here and go to work Doug. When you get off the brake, I'll come up and go to work." The casing went though.

I left Cantex and went to work for a firm called Canada West Drilling in 1979. A bunch of oilfield fellows, a lawyer and an accountant got together, raised some money and bought three rigs. One was a steam rig and a couple of hauler rigs. I went to work on the steam rig. On one of the holes that we were drilling, we twisted the drill pipe off. It was stuck in the hole and we had got a set of jars. With these jars, you could either jar up or down so you're going both ways. When they were jarring, it wasn't safe to stand on the rig floor because this was again an old conventional rig. There were bolts popping all over the yard, popping out and zinging all over the place. We would jar for a day and then shut down for a day, putting bolts back in the rig.

There were different times, to keep men working for them, that they had to go to the General Store in Calmar and OK credit for a line of groceries. They would miss a payday and maybe catch that payday up the next payday. Most people stayed working for this company as long as they could because these men were good guys and out there working just as hard as everyone else, but they eventually went broke.

I went to work for Loadstar Drilling in 1949. We went to Three Creeks, a place east of Peace River and drilled a wildcat well there. When the rig moved out and shut down for break-up, I went working derrick for a firm, called Manning Drilling. I only worked derrick one hole I think and then went drilling for them. They were wildcatting and we worked all over the province of Alberta that year. Rigs were starting to move out all over, out to Fort St. John, British Columbia and into Saskatchewan. I remember one break-up, I was out of work so I went down to the unemployment insurance office. When the girl started asking me all kinds of personal questions, I asked if I could use the phone. The company I phoned said, "Yeah, we let this guy go and if you're out there by 4 o'clock, you've got the job." The job was out of Camrose and I said, "I'll be there." I ripped her little sheet up and have never been back to the unemployment insurance office since."

I worked for Shell Oil, swing drilling, working derrick and worked there all of winter, summer and early fall. I went to work for Cascade Drilling. I drilled one well and then began pushing until spring of 1952 when I went to the States. I went down to North Dakota with Regent Drilling. The company could only take one Canadian down there. I was a dual citizen so I went down. I ended up in hospital with polio. By the time I had got out of hospital, they had left and gone back to Canada.

I worked at the Garrison Dam in construction, drilling the cans in the tunnels for about ten months. I went back to the oilfields until 1961. In the meantime, I was divorced and I remarried and we now had seven children, four of them teenagers. The big reason I left the oilfields then was that my wife phoned for me and when I phoned home she said, "You get home and tune some of these Dunn kids in or I'm going to divorce you, kill them, and then I'll be in Ponoka."

I went into the trucking business, moving rigs, hauling heavy equipment, logs, and pulp until 1974. Then I went working overseas in Libya, Indonesia, Australia and the Philippines. I worked in the Bass Strait. We rigged up a rig on a platform off-shore in the Bass Strait. Bass Strait is between Sydney and Melbourne.

Every second day while we were there, we had to do an evacuation drill. Everyone, on the rig and on the platform, had to know how to get off the rig if there was a fire or a blow-out. They had four round balls, all different colors. They were diesel operated, they had a steering wheel and seats inside. There was a fin underneath. Four people were in charge of designated colors. One time, I was in charge of one and the alarm went for evacuation. There was a blow-out. We all headed for it and climbed in.

When the alarm went, we had to go out a quarter mile from the rig and sit there until 'all clear' and then come back. Well, we went out to a quarter to a half a mile but we had to open the hatches and paddle back because someone had forgotten to put the fuel in them. There was a little hell raised over that one. In fact some 'big-wigs' came out in a chopper in the late afternoon and some of the people went back, with that chopper.

There were a number of Canadians working there in Bass Strait. When we went to Australia, we were in a group of fourteen Canadians. Within six months there were maybe three or four left. The agreement was that for the first year you were given a set wage and after that, a year end bonus. The second year was higher wages and a higher bonus, plus a cost of living allowance. If you didn't last a year, then you paid your own way back to Canada. I was the only one out of the fourteen that was paid full wages during the time we were there. I found that it was very important to write down how the work time was used in order to get paid full wages.

It was very enjoyable working over there when we had time off. We would rent jeep-like vehicles and just drive around visiting with the people. We worked and drilled two really deep wells in a place called Iniminka which is in the out-back. It was just a little post office, a bar, a little motel, and a grocery store. I was given a plaque appointing me as the honorary toolpusher in Iniminka.

On one of the wells that I drilled, southeast of Manila in the Philippines, we were drilling some distance away from a mountain that was volcanic. When it blew up, what a sight! We were far enough away that it didn't bother us and we were as high up as the mountain so we could look across. Before the mountain blew up fifty thousand people, who lived around this mountain, were given plenty of warning to go. When it blew up, they just left, all at once.

I went to Libya, as drilling foreman from 1974 to 1975. Then in 1976, I went to Indonesia and Singapore. In 1979, we came back to Canada. My wife had made her mind up. She had been two years away from her grandchildren and wanted to return home. I began consulting and have been working at that ever since I got back to Canada. I hadn't worked in Canada since 1961 and to come back to what was going on here in 1979, it was quite a change.

When I drove out to the lease, on my first consulting job, there were four pickups parked next to the camp. Under each pickup was a case or two of beer. Some 'wacky tobaccy' was floating around as well. I wasn't used to this. When I was roughnecking, drilling and pushing tools, we did our drinking and our partying but not at work. Now they were doing it at work. There were a lot more accidents now than we used to have. It was a whole different ball game and there wasn't too much fun. It's a good thing I came back as an oilfield consultant. If I had come back as a driller or as a toolpush, I'd never have made it. I probably would have killed somebody.

After I came back from the States, I drilled a well out on one of the gulf islands between Vancouver Island and the mainland. This was with Boyle's Brother's drilling. I had all ex-diamond drillers working for me and they were used to a different type of drilling. We finally got the well down to 2,700 feet and then the Pacific Ocean came in. It just came in!! We had five or six inch round pumps to pump mud down the drillway. When all the water came in from underneath, we didn't have the pressure to stop it. It just came out of everywhere.

I phoned Calgary to tell them this. They thought I had really gone bonkers, "Yeah, we'll forgive you. But you see, you've been out on the island too long." I replied, "Hey, the water's coming in and I've got a ditch back down to the Pacific Ocean." The water was coming up the wall, out the ditch, and down to the ocean.

Finally, I had a guy to fly out. He phoned Calgary back and told them, "He's right." We ordered a pumper truck out from Alberta. It came out on a barge. We loaded it with a bunch of cement. We got out to the bay, got to the island and then it tipped over with both of us in the pumper truck. We finally got some more cement and pumper trucks and pumped it off. We built a derrick right there, a single high, which was a twenty footer. They brought the drilling rig out and we finished the well. We went down to 3,900 feet and there was no gas, no oil, no nothing. I went back to Alberta and worked on the drilling rigs until 1961.

If I could do it over: I would have stayed in it. Like a lot of fellows, I would have gone to work for one of the service companies. Horizontal drilling, directional drilling or something like that. It would have been great to have been in a permanent place, because there was something missing. There was definitely something missing for the wife and the kids with all this moving around. I did get out and went into transportation for a while.

Some of the changes in drilling: It has changed tremendously because we had bang, bang, clutch rigs run by steam or power. Everything now is air. Bits have changed tremendously. The drilling procedures have changed. In 1953, I remember a mud-man in North Dakota tried to get people to drill copper with water and nobody would do it. The fellow stayed out at the rig, watching while I tried it. We didn't tell anybody. Nobody knew except the guys on the rig and when they were asked to be quiet in lieu of death you know which choice they made. We drilled it with water and did that with two wells before anybody knew. We didn't even tell Regent Drilling. The procedure was a success, we went to other oil companies, and said, "Hey look, here's what we did." That started water drilling in 1953.

I'm still working, as a matter of fact, I'm out in the morning for a week. I work for only one oil company. The deal I have with them, and I've done this for five years, is that I'll go out and relieve somebody for a week; if they get a well and have trouble; they bring someone in to get it going again. I've worked two to two and a half months a year. Gerry comes with me, because we all know if she comes out and if it's not a camp job, she does the cooking and also types my reports. I think I'll keep her.

We live a mile and a half north of Highway 16 and the phone rings and it's a guy that I worked with, driving by, "Hey, coffee pot on?" He'll stop in and we'll sit on the porch and shoot the breeze. You know, it sure is nice to keep in contact with those guys.

Doug Dunn (1997)

Glenn Edwards

Glenn recently retired in Edmonton. He worked for 41 years, and 35 years were in the oil business. He worked in Drayton Valley in 1955 and recalls what it was like in a typical oil town. There was mud and skid-shacks, and rubber boots were the order of the day.

In September, 1955, I left university in my second year of engineering and took a job as a draftsman with Mobil Oil in Drayton Valley. At that time the name of the company was Siconi Vacumn and the symbol was the big flying Pegasus horse.

The conditions were quite interesting when I went out there. Living accommodations were in a camp, just outside the town of Drayton Valley. The boom had started in 1953 and the town was quickly being developed but it was still very small. I remember the bunkhouses. They were about eight feet by ten feet, with four double bunks on each side. There were four guys to a shack and not much room for anything else. There was a central tent or shack. Our work day was an eight hour day. Those of us who worked in the office lived in this camp and the office was attached to the camp.

I went into the office environment and was involved with production and drilling. A lot of my work was correlating the logs that we had on each well. This had to be done for each well and it would determine where the pay zone was for the oil producing zone. This information was used for the whole field and I followed this procedure for all the drilling activities.

I stayed out there for four years, working mostly on the drilling end of it but some of the production/technical work as well. I assisted the engineers, training them on some of the field applications. At that time, their whole production was all brought to the surface with pumping units, which we called pumpers or horses heads. They didn't have any flowing wells like they did in the Turner Valley field. Even the Redwater field was free flowing then.

I remember the road in from Highway 16. There was a two lane paved road going west from Edmonton, with lots of curves and small hills. Drayton Valley was 90 miles from Edmonton. It was great until we left the pavement and then we had a new experience.

The twenty-six mile road from the highway into Drayton was being built at that time. It was all gravel and it was being built through muskeg country. Basically the gravel was 3 to 6 inches in diameter on average (very coarse). When you drove over that it was like driving over a washboard. It was bangety, bangety, bang, none of this business of taking it easy, because you had to keep moving to keep going.

Driving conditions were bad all year round. The road into Drayton Valley from the main highway wasn't finished. For the last six miles we usually drove in the ditch or on the old dirt road between Rocky Rapids and town.

The town of Rocky Rapids still exists. I remember driving through the ditch because it was a little better than driving on the road. It was a challenge to get in there. When you got there you had to have your car checked over to see if the wheels were still on all four sides.

We used to take turns driving when we would come out on weekends to go to Calgary or Edmonton. We would all get together in one car to save wear and tear on the vehicles. If we could get a company car, that would be much better for us.

Driving in those days really did test the spirit. Getting stuck in the mud was an everyday occurrence. You had to be prepared to spend a lot of time digging yourself out of the ditch.

Things improved over the years. A bridge was built above the North Saskatchewan River in the fifties to complete the road across the river into another oilfield in the area. I can't remember the name of it now, but if you go down towards Rimbey you may see a paved road that comes out through Calmar and into Leduc.

A car would average about 25,000 miles and its life would be ended because of the roads. We used to get out as often as possible because Drayton Valley didn't have a lot for entertainment.

The town had the largest bars in Alberta at the time. I remember we had the sign for the beer parlor hanging on the bunkhouse living room wall. The sign announced, 'There is seating for 325 people in this bar'.

In those days bars closed at 11 o'clock. The lights flashed at 10:30 to warn you it was time to close. Ninety percent of the bar was for men only and the other part was the mixed section. Women couldn't get in there without a male escort. The women usually would find some poor soul to accompany them and they would all go in together. The bar was an L-shaped room and the women and escorts sat in one end just off from everyone else. They could still watch all the fights and everything. That was the entertainment.

The roughnecks would get in off the rigs and be bragging about their big strike. Someone else would challenge them and there would be a big fight.

There would be beer glasses flying, along with everything else. When the fights started, the first thing you did was grab your beer when the fights started because that would be the first thing that would get spilled.

This was the big thing for entertainment in that town. It was basically the bar unless you left town and went somewhere. We had dances at the community hall and we had a social club. We would have barbecues, dances and visiting, but for the most part, I guess I'd have to say the bar was the central entertainment point. You met there and then you wondered why you were there.

There was a bowling alley in town, but no curling rink. There may have been a community skating rink there, and of course, schools.

The town was beginning to grow. Basically it started out as a little village with very few retail buildings. Clothing merchants set up new businesses. Some of these were people who had been around the oil patch who moved on and set up in many of these small towns.

One of the two main oil companies in Drayton Valley was called Stanland. They later became Pan American and then eventually Amoco. The other company was named Siconi Mobil Oil of Canada Limited, when I left there 1959.

The office itself really never changed too much over the years. In 1959, I was really tired because progression was slow and my wages were low. I hadn't gone ahead too far in the four years I'd been there.

I left Drayton Valley and went to northern Manitoba in June for a three month stint with a survey crew. I wanted a change in my career and I wanted to get out of the oil business.

I ended up on a survey crew staking mining claims up in Thompson, Manitoba. The first thing they gave me when I arrived in camp was an axe. I was told, "Here you are, go make your bed." The living conditions were pretty primitive compared to what I had experienced. The mail plane came in once a week and landed on a nearby lake.

I stayed three months. That was hell, but it was quite an interesting experience. We got up at five in the morning and left camp for work by six. It was a twelve hour day and $10 a day was the flat rate. If you only worked a half day you got $5.

When I arrived in June, we had to break the ice on the lake in the morning so we could wash up. It was pretty cold and showers were unheard-of out there.

My foot was injured in an accident. I had to go out, not for stitches, but because I got infection. When I was out of there, I just kept on going. I said to myself, "that's it, I've had it."

I was tired of eating terrible food. We couldn't keep it in the pits because the bears would get it. It was all put in a sack and hung in the water at the end of the dock, out in the lake. We ate boiled steaks, boiled roasts and boiled pork chops.

There wasn't much future in this type of life and I left for Alberta in the latter part of 1959. I began working for Shell Oil and settled in Edmonton.

I worked for them for three years until 1962. I was in the explorations/seismic end of it and worked in the office doing the budget work and the planning work. I also kept the files and records in order. These were the seismic records that were run off during the explorations out in the field.

At that time we were working in northern Alberta and the Northwest Territories. We were also working off shore on the west coast. We were doing seismic work in the ocean between Vancouver Island and the mainland. There was some work going on in southern Alberta, down near Pincher Creek. I was with Shell Oil when they built the sour gas plant down there. This plant became very controversial years later.

I felt that Shell was an up and coming company then and I liked it but my opportunities were somewhat limited. I was still in an office environment and I wanted to get out and do some work in the field.

I got married in 1961. When our first child was born in 1962, I left the oil business again and joined the Edmonton City Police Force. I was quite secure there, pounding the beat and working patrol.

The shift work was disruptive to family life so I left the Police Force in 1968. By that time, we had three children and were expecting the fourth.

Returning to the oil industry, I went to work a second time for Mobil Oil in Edmonton. I was back into the office environment, working in the accounting end of it. I worked on the drilling contracts for all the drilling development and exploration that Mobil was doing. Rainbow Lake field was discovered. A lot of exploration work was being done with respect to that field. Mobil was one of the two big producers up there.

There was still work out at Drayton Valley and Whitecourt. I worked on construction in Whitecourt for a six month period.

I had originally worked for Mobil Oil for four years. The company reinstated that time and I worked another eight years for them. During the construction period at Whitecourt, I commuted from Edmonton. When I finished that, I got a promotion and was sent to Drayton Valley.

Drayton Valley hadn't really changed. The one thing going for us was the company housing that was available. We sold our house in Edmonton and moved into company housing, paying rent at a flat rate. The plan was to stay there five years, to give the kids a chance to get settled and into school. Three of them were in the elementary grades at that time.

We only stayed a year in Drayton Valley and then we were transferred to Calgary, where I worked in accounting for four years.

I left Mobil Oil in January, 1976 and joined Alberta Gas Trunk Line.

This company had started in 1953. It had been set up initially by the Government of Alberta as a Gas Transmission Company. They had just started to diversify and grow bigger in the 1970's. Everyone in Alberta, including the children, were allowed to purchase twenty shares at $5 a piece. I did not take advantage of this opportunity but some people I know still own some of the original shares. This was one way to get a public company started. The Government of Alberta had four representatives on the board of directors, one of them was Don Getty.

During the time I was with Nova, my job changed five or six different times. When I started with Nova, I was ordering pipeline materials for various pipeline construction. We had stockpiled a lot of pipe at various locations within Alberta. Our main job was ordering the material up, making sure it was on site for the beginning of construction time and ensuring that the material was there during the construction time to support the activity. It was a busy time and I worked there two years.

I transferred into a Technical Section. Basically, what I did was work at the pipe mill, overseeing the actual production of the pipe. I spent my time in the pipe mills in Regina, Edmonton, Camrose at Stelco, and in Calgary. I traveled back and forth as Quality Insurance Inspector. This was a little diverse from what I had done before.

Another field in which I worked was when the Alaska Highway Pipeline was built. This was to move gas out of Alaska, across the Yukon, northern British Columbia, Alberta, Saskatchewan, Montana and further.

During the two-year period I was there, we built the section from the western side of the province, around Sundre, Alberta, across the Old Man River and down to the border. After that we went east to the Saskatchewan border, near Empress, Alberta. From there we went down to Monchy, Saskatchewan which was just a border point into Montana. It was an interesting time.

Now we were just getting into the early eighties and downsizing. I kept on working with Nova. Our department was transferred to Edmonton in 1983 and I continued working until retirement in the fall of 1996.

The last ten years I was with Nova was probably the most interesting part of my career. The job I took then was geotechnical work, which involved studying landslides and soil erosion on river banks and hills where pipelines crossed. It was a constant battle. There would be flooding which would wash pipes out. We would have to put them back together and then re-bury them. After about six years, I trained another young fellow to do the work in the office so I could go out in the field.

We would fly into remote areas in the bush by helicopter. We were dropped off and picked up later. We spent a lot of time on our own in the bush working and flying in all kinds of weather conditions. It was dangerous but it was exciting and I enjoyed the job.

I spent my last two years in the field, investigating pipeline explosions. It was the most interesting point of my career. I got to travel a lot, which was interesting. We stayed in different towns and villages all over this province. I think I've eaten in every restaurant in Alberta.

If I could do it over: I would have continued with Mobil Oil. In 1970, they were beginning offshore drilling near Sable Island. This was a different technology in drilling and I would have found that very interesting.

Over the years, there have been many challenges, all of which have certainly made my working career interesting and enjoyable.

Glenn Edwards (1997)

George Fyfe

George worked a total of 43 years in the oilfield industry. Most of that time he was employed with Imperial Oil. His work provided him with the opportunity to travel to many locations including the Middle East. He is now retired and he and his wife Irene, live in Edmonton

I was born in Calgary in 1914. I attended public and high school at Okotoks. I had aimed to be a district agriculturist. I took the two-in-one course at Olds Agricultural School in the winter of 1935 to 1936. That was the cheapest way to get first-year university. The room and board was $35 a month. My Mother and Dad couldn't feed me at that rate. At Olds I was the assistant editor of the OAS yearbook.

I started roughnecking in the fall of 1936 for Bert Banister on a Schneider, drilling Grandville #1 in Little Chicago. Little Chicago is on the south end of Turner Valley. I worked on a wooden derrick combination rig. The combination rig came about from converting from cable tools to rotary. These rigs had one Saunders steam engine. They always referred to it as 'old Maude'. The pump had walking beam and rotary equipment as well. With the calf wheeler, this pool hall and drilling lines on the calf wheel. And you feed it off from that to the rotary. Drilling fluid was mud made by boiling natural clay in mud tanks with water. So if you weren't tripping and doing other things, you'd be out shoveling clay. The well was completed and then there was no work.

I picked up odd jobs and I got a job working for Diamond Bolar. One days' work for three days' pay. This was a dirty job, adjusting tubing with the well blowing. The industry would sure frown on that now.

In those days, for drilling fluid, they used combinations of mud and oil or air. It was only in Turner Valley that they had to cook mud. And Bolar knew that I was around so he gave me a job as a separator man on Royalties' #1 on the south end of Turner Valley, almost right near little Chicago.

As a separator man, he taught me lots of things. One of the best jobs was to roll the oil tanks with wellhead gas the night before the tanks were being gauged to put into the shipping line. This raises the specific gravity of the oil and you got a better price.

Next I worked on a cable tool rig as a 'tool dresser' for a four months. It is a job that isn't much referred to now because cable tool rigs are seldom seen now.

When I was working as a 'tool dresser', we had to tin up the roof over the forge house. I was working up on top with a sheet of light corrugated tin and the chinook wind caught it and pulled the tin through my hand. It cut right through my glove and cut the tendons in my hand. They wanted to cut the finger off. I said, "Oh no, I can fill out a glove this way." I learned to pull the glove over with the other fingers.

At that time I was still living with my Mother and Dad on the farm at the Half-Way This was called Half-Way because it was half-way between Black Diamond and Okotoks. There used to be stables there. When they hauled out equipment from Okotoks, they would stay over night there. A famous character at that time was 'Half Way Eddie'.

I was using my Dad's car to go back and forth to work. He gave me hell for bringing it home all muddy. When I broke over the home hill which is part way between Black Diamond and 'Little Chicago', I had hit a chinook and from there on it had been muddy. Funny things happened with the chinook. Up the derrick the snow would be melting and dripping down and on the floor it was still 20o to 30o F below.

The work was interesting. Lots of new terms to learn about the rotary cable tool. One of the first terms that confused me was when the rig builder who was setting in the timbers for the base of his cable tool rig sung out, "Cut a key 48 inches long by 6 1/2 inches by go to hell." I didn't know whether he was telling me to go or what but it was a key that tapered off. The rig builder would drive it in between the timbers to hold them tight.

By this time I had forgotten about the University of Alberta and my wages went to help Mom and Dad on the farm instead of being saved up for tuition at the university.

In our working, Bert Banister who was my first driller had told me that if I was going to stay in the oil patch to try to get on to work for the largest company. So whenever I was out of work I would try to get on with Royalite. They were the Turner Valley drilling branch of Imperial Oil at that time. I finally made it in 1940. I worked on steam rigs in Turner Valley in 1942 when I was sent to Tilley to work on a Franks Jackknife rig. About that time I was also propositioned, "Would I go to Norman Wells?" But this blew over when CanOil and Norman Wells were shut down. With the Franks rigs we drilled around Tilley, Rolling Hills and Vauxhall and Truax, Saskatchewan.

While in Tilley, I got married to Irene Carron who has stuck with me through thick and thin. We will be celebrating our 55th anniversary this September. She came to Tilley to live with me in a 16 1/2 foot home made trailer which we towed up the river valley hill and at Vauxhall on the way to Regina. Going past the hills at Swift Current the model A would power out. Irene would run alongside the model A with a piece of 4 by 4 and put it under the car's back wheel whenever I had to rest the Ford.

It was chinooking then. By the time we got to Regina the chinook had run out and a heavy snow came in. We were trapped in Regina for ten days. We had to stay in a hotel because it was pretty cold and mean. The trailer wasn't too good for touring. The road to Corinne was finally opened and we made our way to Truax which was a little hamlet southwest of Regina. There were more oil crew members than locals in Truax but they rearranged themselves and accommodated us. We got the rig set up on a coulee below Dan Bolie's house. Old Dan Bolie would go around humming 'My Little Girl of the Prairie'.

Then we had a Saskatchewan blow. This was a snow storm after drifting snow. This coulee drifted full right over the light plant and the boiler house. We had quite a time finding things. We had a bundle of ten foot conduit and each of us took a piece of conduit to probe until we hit something and then we would dig down to see what it was.

One crew was stranded at the rig for 30 hours and we finally got drilling. Getting to work was a chore. There were no bull dozers in the area to push a road. We sometimes traveled 15 to 20 miles hitting the hit spots to get to the rig. Finally, George Kirkpatrick found a gas powered bull dozer. They got it going and they plowed out a road to the rig.

Spring finally came and we got the hole drilled. In Truax, the oil wives got a softball team going. Their big event was entered in the Ogena Baseball Tournament. The drilling rig was quite a novelty in the area. On Sundays, we had a whole bunch of country folk visiting the rig. They brought their lunch and their families.

The hole was finally completed. Another Imperial dry hole. We moved the 13 ton draw works into Truax to load onto the flat car with two five ton trucks backed together. This was a big weight on the trucks. The weight was right down to the rims of the tires. The tires were outside of the rims. We expected anytime that they would blow.

We finally made it and moved the rig back to the Taber area. We drilled several holes around Taber, Vauxhall and Raymond. In Taber, the town wanted us to put our trailers on what they called a trailer court. We were all squeezed in so tight that we couldn't move at all. I finally got permission to move out to the MacDonald's farm which was adjacent to town. We had a nice shade of some big cottonwood trees.

Mr. MacDonald had rented out the tillable land in connection with his holdings to Japanese market gardeners. With their reservation, he could use all of their products. Lots of times when I would be coming home from work, Mrs. MacDonald would catch me and say, "George, I need potatoes, peppers and such and don't go short." With the results, I had the best market garden in southern Alberta.

We completed drilling in that area and then we moved to Kinsella to drill on Amber's ranch. They were cattle raisers and cowboys and we used to drill right on their land. At that time when gasoline was short, Imperial Oil proposed to break down natural gas into its component parts and to break down water from the Saskatchewan River into hydrogen and oxygen. These components would then be recombined to make gasoline. But they discovered Leduc about that time so this wasn't necessary.

The wells that we drilled were sold to Northwestern Utilities to supply gas for Edmonton. I guess that would be the same gas company operated from Okotoks.

We were drilling at Morinville when Leduc oil activity started. We could see the smoke when the fire caught on. Quite a few of our men went over there. When they were fighting the Atlantic fire, our mechanics were there most of the time on pumps and pumping water out from the river.

Next we moved to Tilley. This was quite an expedition for the old Model A Ford and the trailer. We did have a little bit of trouble pulling up the Gwynne hill but we made it. We drilled the first gas wells south of the ranch. Then they established a camp at Minburn we moved over there. We were still living in the trailer at Minburn.

We bought an army type pre-fab and lived in it for a while. We made one big room heated with a space heater that burned wood and coal. This heated this one big room. We had a Findley Arkland cook stove to cook on. Our oldest girl was three years old and she thought that this was wonderful because she could ride her trike all around the stove in her snow suit. And then on bath night, Irene was bathing our daughter and trying to keep her warm. She backed her little backside up against the Findley Arkland stove and for some time wore a brand with the letters A.R.K.

We turned this army pre-fad into a 12 by 24 skid shack. Lots of skid shacks were wider than that but this was construction limited at that time. We loaded the skid shack onto the back of the truck and trucked some of the ways. Sometimes we loaded and shipped the it by train. We finished at Minburn and we loaded the skid shack on a flat car and shipped it by N.A.R. train to Girouxville in the Peace River country where we drilled some holes.

We drilled a well just east of Girouxville. Then we moved to Spirit River and drilled a well at Royce which is northwest of Spirit River. We were there during the forest fire scare. I forget what the year was but they had to have Royce ready for evacuation. The fellows all had logs cut and rope and wire ready to make a raft so that they could go down the Peace River away from the fire if it came too close.

After Royce, we moved to Keg River. The fire had gone through there. All the trees were just ghosts. During the cold of the winter time, you would hear bangs like rifle shots with the frost cracking these dead trees. They were dead but rich in sap yet. That's the first place that I saw a rabid fox, at Keg River House. We were having lunch at Keg River House and a fox outside tried to break the window. He tried to get in, hitting the window a few times and then he walked over and laid down and died.

After Spirit River, we moved back to Wanham and drilled a couple more holes there. Next we loaded the cabins on the N.A.R. truck and shipped them to Camrose. The cabins came through fine except one. And this lady had packed everything in the fridge. It didn't stand up to the shunting. We drilled many oil wells in Camrose. We were in Camrose in 1952.

We bought a house and sold the trailer while we were in Camrose. So Irene was elated. We had hot and cold running water. By this time we had three children and they went to school in Camrose.

From Camrose, I was called into the Calgary office to set up a training program for the crews. We sold the Camrose house and bought a house in Calgary on 3219 Kenmare Crescent where I visited the family whenever I got time off. I traveled to the rigs with these training programs. I visited all eight of the Imperial Oil rigs. And one crew messed up and I was sent out by Charles Visser and Floyd Welker to supervise the crew and stay toolpushing.

In 1956, ice had sheared off a wellhead at Bear Island at Norman Wells. I was sent up there to control the well. While I was there, we took a Franks rig out of the deadline and rigged it all up and drilled four wells on the mainland out under the Mackenzie River. One well was horizontal. That's the time of testing either to drill two wells in Goose Island and some on Bear Island. These were out in the river south of Norman Wells. By this time, Imperial Oil was barging rigs and equipment north of Tuktoyaktuk.

In 1965 and 1967, I was loaned to Exon to supervise drilling wells in Libya. I spent two years over then in the heat. When I came home the work was in the Arctic so we moved the family to Edmonton. And they worked out of the rail head. They had a warehouse there. In the Arctic I drilled two or three wells on Atkinson Point. One hit a pocket of hydro-carbons and we had oil and gas. This one well, we left it so it could be producing and run casing and tubing. It started to leak around the wellhead. I was sent in to properly abandon it. Because the perma frost had collapsed the tubing, I spent the whole summer drilling out the collapsed tubing in order to get to the bottom. In order to properly abandon a well, you have to cement it off.

Due to health problems, I took early retirement took early retirement December 1, 1976 after 36 1/2 years with the Esso organization. I was in the drilling field a total of 43 years.

If I could do it over: I wouldn't change the way it was. I don't think I would change anything. It was a matter of you working where you got work and doing what had to be done.

George Fyfe (1997)

David (Dave) Garstad

Dave began working as a roughneck. He combined oilfield work with a rodeo career in the late 1960's and 1970's. Dave still works in the industry. He is a well site supervisor under contract with various oilfield consulting firms. He and his wife, Linda live on an acreage near Big Valley, Alberta.

In the winter of 1963, I was working for a farmer for $175 a month about 18 to 20 hours a day and I ground feed on Sunday. Go to town and get liquored up once and you couldn't put a coil in the car. You got to have more money. Mud mills had it but conditions weren't as good. The first three days that I worked there, I had $225 in the bank. But I had more space between my ears than my eyes so I only got to roughneck for four days then I was working motors. The rig I started on was rig 11 of Cambridge Drilling. Orvell Smith was the driller. He was good to work with. He's still alive, living in Lacombe.

The rig location was down around Compeer. It was a double rig. They were a telescopic double but that doesn't reflect on what they call that same kind of rig today. This rig burnt down at Brooks about twenty years ago.

I was 19 or 20 years old, and it changed my lifestyle. In fact I could buy gas for my cars. I could even buy insurance and another car when the current one wore out.

I wanted to be a rodeo rider. But to do that I had to have some start-up money. You had to pay your dues in the business for about three years before you won enough to make you independent. But if you did other work, you had your own money without waiting for winnings.

I did seasonal work, mostly in winter. There weren't many rodeos on in the winter but the mud mills run steady then.

Most of the time my working conditions were marginal because I would go to the rigs and get hired on. I didn't know anybody there and I had to do my job and more or else I didn't keep it. I always thought it was that way for everyone, but maybe it wasn't.

I didn't like any tricks being played around the rigs. If you're sweating and some jackass pulled a boner, you'd kick him in the ass or get him out of the way somehow. You didn't have time for funnies.

But I didn't mind playing tricks. Some people got wet once in a while, but I made it look like it wasn't on purpose. A guy came up the ramp stairs once and we didn't see eye-to-eye. So I rinsed him down on to the cat-walk, but he didn't know who had done it. I guess you could say that was a trick.

The hotels were all full and if you were lucky you could get a so-called ham sandwich. It seemed it was just pig fat between bread. They charged about three bucks for it, and that was about ten times more than what they should have charged. There were some people who were really good too. We were fed well and usually stayed in a hotel. People caught a ride to the rig with the guy they were working for, usually because he wanted to keep us together and know that we got to work on time.

I never stayed with a company steady enough to get room and board any place. It was like being sent to jail. Every time I went to work on a rig, it was usually for 30 days. That's the way it seemed to happen. I could make enough money in 30 days so it was like working for six months somewhere else.

One time we were waiting as the hook was to be swung. The hook is on the bottom of the blocks that have to be swung over to catch a loop which is attached to the swivel. The driller brought the blocks up fast enough that he swung that loop right over in front of us. If I had been outside the girts or the framework of the derrick, my head would have been taken off. You learned to stay out of the way and if there were any loud noises, you quickly got behind something big.

On the derricks I usually worked the motors until I worked with Dennis, a guy from Saskatchewan. Dennis wanted somebody he could count on and he set me up working derrick.

I sometimes worked as a swing driller if we were short-handed or somebody quit, or got fired. I was gone in the spring because I was in rodeos then. I could make three to four times as much money from the rodeos as I could in the mud mill business. And it was something that I liked to do. The dirt, the filth and the sloppy conditions - they were just part of it but you got paid for it. And I never had anybody not pay me. I was never fired. I suppose that was something that was more luck than good management but it never happened.

I was told to go over and wake the toolpush up one time. It was about a quarter to six in the morning. I knew the toolpusher and I didn't care for him anyway. I didn't know it, but the bed was on sawed off stumps and he had a woman with him. When I jerked the door open, and asked, in a loud tone, if anybody was alive in there, they both tried to come out of there at once. But they couldn't, because the bed fell in front of the door. It was a hell of a commotion. That was one of the most humorous things that ever happened.

We were running casing down by Hanna one time. And one fellow got hit in the back with the tongs, the pliers that tighten things up. And the tong hand said, "Oh, you got to look out, or you'll get another one of those." And the guy said, "What do you mean? That first one was just a 'weevil bite'." He didn't have any broken bones but he knew he'd been hit in the back for awhile but he didn't quit. A 'weevil bite' was getting hit in the back. If you got a finger pinched or lost a fingernail then that was a 'weevil bite'. Today, it's a 'major' accident. You have to go on 'light duty'. You can't do anything where you might hurt that finger. Before, they sewed it back on and you went to work.

In the winter of 1979 and 1980, regulations were coming in pretty strong. You had to have special blow-out prevention equipment on these rigs. One person on each rig had to have a metric blow-out prevention ticket. I had one, so my job was quite secure and I got away with some things that I shouldn't have, especially with how I expressed myself. It's nice to remember that a guy could do that.

On one rig the two cooks were younger gals and they entertained the roughnecks and the lower personnel on the crew level. It was in February and it was about 65o F above zero. One cook was entertaining a roughneck on top of the kitchen.

The rig water hauler was little and stubby and his belly stuck out. He had trouble holding onto the ladder as he climbed up. When he got up to the top to see if the water tank was flowing over, he saw these people's eyes looking up at him. This poor bugger almost fell over backwards off that ladder. And I'll never forget it because his eyes were rolled back in his head when he came down.

The next morning the lead cook was in the shower with the motor. The foreman went to use the bathroom and walked past this little episode. He didn't say anything. He just went to the bathroom, left and came back to the kitchen. The gal came back in after a while and the foreman said if they were going to entertain some of these personnel this way then they would have to handle all of them that way. After lunch, both cooks walked off the lease and we never saw them again.

In 1970 I worked for Peter Bawden in Innisfail. It was the first time that I remember that I got a travel allowance to get to work. We got four dollars a day. The guys would eat my lunch all the time. I was the only guy who was married on that crew so I lost my lunch every day. I had Linda make up my lunch with blue cheese. A couple of bites of that and I still had all my lunch. They weren't bad-headed people because they didn't throw it out just because they couldn't eat it. They left my lunch alone after that.

Drilling practices changed a lot over the years. The mud pumps are more sophisticated because there's more consistent pressure on them. The drill bits are much more efficient. If the bits are selected properly then you can cut your rig time in half or more.

If I could do it over: I would have probably got on with a service company quicker. Over the winter of 1982, I worked for 9 different outfits because things were slow. Our family was young then and I had to stay working. I got on with a mud company then and I was trained under a government program. I stayed with a major mud company, because I was pretty loyal to the people I worked with. If I had to relieve somebody, it was normally a trouble-shooting job to try to retain the account. I didn't care for that in the service business and when I was finished with the service business it was like quitting school. But it's the grounds for your experience to be a supervisor.

I'm still working in the oil business, but I'm not working on the rigs anymore. I've been a drilling foreman or well site supervisor for four years now.

Dave Garstad (1997)

Einar Garstad

Einar started roughnecking on a rig for Peter Bawden in 1953. He spent several years with Canbridge Drilling and then began working for Christensen Diamond Coring. In 1977, Einar began working as an Oilfield Consultant. His work has taken him to Europe, the Middle East and the United States. He and his wife, Margaret live in Edmonton.

I started in the oil patch on January 9, 1953 with Peter Bawden. I was 19 years old. Before I went into the oil patch, I worked for farmers. The fall before I started in the oilfields, my school buddy and I boarded the train in Veteran and went to Slave Lake to work in a lumber camp. We were there approximately four or five months until they shut down for Christmas. While I was at home for Christmas I landed this job with Peter Bawden. When the drilling in the Coronation area was finished, the rig was being moved to Rabbit Lake, at town 45 miles north of North Battleford, Saskatchewan. And that's where I started my oilfield career.

The money was big, a lot more than I had ever seen. Things were quite different because at that time I was the only green man that they had on the rig.

One night during my first or second day at work, it was 30o F below. There are components on the rig that are called the mouse hole and the rat hole. One of the men had me sit on a five gallon pail on the rig floor and then gave me a shovel handle to keep the rats out of the mouse hole. I sat there for an hour before I realized that this was a joke. I had just started and I didn't argue with the orders because I thought that I would be run off if I didn't obey.

Then there was another trick pulled on me. On that same hole that we were drilling, they sent me up with a five gallon pail of water, to what is called the water table up in the crown on top of the rig. I was struggling to hang onto the ladder because I was scared of falling down. I was about half way up the derrick, about forty or fifty feet off the floor and I was hanging desperately onto this ladder and pail. The handle of the pail came off, the pail fell down and the toolpusher got drenched with water as he was walking out of the doghouse. When I came down, I heard him lecturing those guys about pulling tricks. Because I was the first one in my family to work the rigs, I was able to clue in my brothers about tricks played on new men.

After these tricks were pulled on me, I learned quite quickly. The driller who I worked for was very good because he hardly said anything. But, the guys who I worked with were always a hollering and screaming at me. In those days, there was no such thing as drilling schools. We just got in there and learned. Peter Bawden ran a pretty safe operation. They believed in safety on the rigs.

We lived in a little hotel in Rabbit Lake. It was run by Ukrainian people. We ate Ukrainian food all the time. We'd have cabbage rolls every day for lunch and it was very good.

The rig was about ten to twelve miles from town. I never had a car but we would ride with the driller or the other ones would take turns driving and we would pay them so much a day. It was quite a big rig with a triple mast on it. We worked on the rig for about two weeks before finishing up on the well. We drilled three holes in this area.

We were sitting in the cafe having dinner just before we went to work. The toolpusher came in and said, "I have to talk to you for a minute." I thought for sure that I was going to be fired. He took me aside and said, "I really have to apologize for this because I have a telegram for you here and I think it's quite serious. It has been opened. The derrick man on my crew didn't know you so he had carried this telegram in his pocket for two days." The telegram was about my father passing away. The toolpush was quite sorry about this. He said, "You get your clothes together and I'll drive you into North Battleford so you can catch the train. I'll get you a train ticket home and a return ticket for you if you want to come back." So that was what we did.

When I got on the train in North Battleford, Alberta had a big snow storm. Everybody traveled by train if they didn't have a car. I remember my two sisters were married and they were trying to get home. They were stranded in Halkirk a couple of days and I was stranded in Lacombe for two days because they had stopped the trains from going east to Lacombe. We did finally get home and I got back to work. In those days, people were very good and helped you out and life went on.

When I got back to Rabbit Lake we worked until spring break-up and then the rig moved back to Coronation. We drilled one hole then we moved from Coronation to I think, Lougheed or something. In the meantime, the rig had shut down and I started with Canbridge Drilling. I worked for them for about twelve years as a roughneck, derrick man and driller. People didn't move around that much in those days so you stayed in one place for quite a while.

While I was working for Canbridge Drilling, I'll never forget the time I was working derrick in Czar. We were on a small rig and we were dismantling the rig for a move. I was working derrick and one of the roughnecks was up there with me. We were in the process of laying down the monkey board. You had to lay it down on those small rigs then. While we were doing this, the driller was controlling the rope that was going to lay it down. The rig motor ran out of fuel, we had the monkey board ready to go down and the driller couldn't hold it. The roughneck went underneath it and I jumped off down on a guide wire. I lost sight of him and when I got down, he was pinned in between the monkey board and the derrick. Right away we knew it was too late because he was squashed in there.

The rig shut down for a whole day over that. I'll never forget the driller, he was having an awful time. We couldn't even talk to him for the first six hours and we had to get this guy out from under the mess. We had jacks up there and we finally got him out. By that time, the police, the toolpusher and all were there. Work started again after two days. That was one of the worst accidents that I saw.

I was single when I started working for Canbridge We had lots of good times and bad times but I remember particularly one time when I was working in Fort St. John and they transferred my crew and I to Peace River. We met in Peace River. Some of us flew in but I ended up driving in with one of the truckers who was taking equipment in. It was a fourteen hour drive from Peace River to where the rig was, in the bush straight north up in Buffalo Head Hills.

The cooks were there already when we got to the rig. And this little blonde girl with big blue eyes was there. She was the second cook. We worked there all winter and I could never take my eyes off of her. By the time spring came around, we decided to get married. We will be celebrating our 37th anniversary this year. So that was one of the highlights. We still followed the rigs after we were married. We got married in the spring and ordered a 10 by 32 foot trailer. We waited for this trailer for almost three months. My wife stayed with her cousin in Edmonton. I stayed in hotels and worked in different areas in Three Hills. We finally got our trailer after a lot of dickering and bickering. We moved with the rigs. Sometimes there would be seven or eight trailers going with the rig when we moved. It was always a rat race to get on the road first because you would get the best parking place. My wife would take the car and I would take the truck and trailer. And Kevin, our son was very small and just a baby then. I can remember Margaret would always have to make a big playpen for Kevin in the back of the car when we moved from place to place.

Most memorable recollection: When things were slow, Canbridge always managed to get us on different rigs so we pretty well knew all the people who worked for Canbridge and got to know them quite well. So there were a lot of times that we would play cards. Times were a little rough so we didn't have that much money so we would do things together like play cards and go to the country dances. Of course, we used to like to drink quite a bit but we had lots of good times. We would go to dances and we would always hear somebody say, "Oh my God, there's the rig crew coming in here." But before long we were all friends so we had good times. We were parked in Wetaskiwin for quite awhile so we got to know quite a few people there. I remember our get togethers in there. On a Saturday night, we would send somebody to a hotel in Wetaskiwin to reserve a table so we could sit together. That was our highlight of the entertainment. There was usually lively entertainment. We used to have some good times with this.

In those days, we didn't have as many conveniences on the rigs as we have today. Everything was done by hand more or less. Today, they have machines for almost anything. The drilling practices on the rigs are a lot safer today than they were then. We were a lot more careful then than they are now. I often wonder why we didn't have a lot more accidents because there was a lot of drinking in those days. Lots of times people didn't even wear their hard hats if they could get away with it. They would slide down hoses and drill pipes. Now those things aren't allowed. Everything on the rigs now is computerized. Now it's a lot shorter. Nowadays, the drilling is speeded up so much through these technical practices. It takes you not even a third of the time to drill a.well now as it did 20 or 30 years ago. The length of drilling time used to take three weeks.

I left the rigs in 1976. I had just spent three years in Rainbow Lake and then I had a chance to go to work for a service company. I started with Christensen Diamond Coring Ltd. That company was later bought out by Baker Hughes.

I was away from home a lot. We used to spend weeks in the Arctic on some jobs. We couldn't leave until the job was completed. Through working with Christensen I was fortunate enough to travel overseas and see a lot of country. I was in Norway, Germany, Holland, Scotland, and the Middle East. I particularly remember some experiences in the Middle East. In these countries, they seemed to have quite a bit of respect for Canadians. I was very proud to be a Canadian.

The worst place that I have ever been was in Libya. I was there in 1990 for eight weeks, and I was happy to leave. I got out just before the Desert Storm war broke out in Iraq.

Since 1977, I have been consulting in the oil industry. Over the 20 years, my work has taken me throughout Canada, different parts of Europe and the United States.

Of all the places where I have been, Libya is the one place that I remember the most. I thought I had seen poverty before, it was really something else going through those desert towns over there.

If I could do it over: I wouldn't change a thing, I've enjoyed my years in the oil patch but if I could do it over, I would have started drinking soda water sooner. After being in the oil patch for 44 years, some people ask me, "What are you doing here?" I tell them that I'm not thinking of retiring. I enjoy working in the oilfield, it's been my life since I started working. I've tried to get out of it a couple of times but I've always come back to the industry. That's where I'll stay until I decide to retire.

We still live in Edmonton and have lived here since 1967. Margaret and I are still working. Our son, Kevin is with the Edmonton Police Service. He and his wife, Alanna have two little girls - Alyssa and Taylor.

Einar Garstad (1997)

Howard Garstad

Howard started working on the rigs at age sixteen. He began roughnecking and continued working his way up the ladder. In 1968 he went overseas to begin what was an eighteen year span of working in many countries including Libya, Iran, Africa, Russia and Egypt. He is currently working in Alberta contracting his services as Drilling Completion Workover Supervisor. He lives at Wildwood.

In the summer of 1961, I got a chance to go to work on a Cambridge rig in the Cessford area. You bet I remember why I wanted to work on the rigs. Growing up on an Alberta farm, I wanted more. Now I'd have money in my pocket and a car of my own. Four of my brothers were working on the rigs, making good wages, raising hell and having a good time and now it was my turn.

We boarded in private homes in the sixties. One of the ranch houses, in Manyberries, southern Alberta, had fifteen rooms. It was cash money these people hadn't seen before.

The food was great: big lunches and all for $90 per month. We worked for $1.84 per hour. This was at the time that people worked in grocery stores fifty hours a week for $85 per month. We thought we had the world by the ass on a down-hill pull.

There's no longer too much humor in the workforce. The oil patch has lost it's fun part. Before, we used to go to work and laugh like hell, work all day under mighty hard conditions.

One time up in Swan Hills, working in that blue mud, we were shoving planks under the mud. We didn't have matting in those days so we had to lay the planks. This toolpush was a bit of a hard headed jackass and he come over and told us, "Hey, I just don't like the way those planks are stacked on the Hi-Boy."

A big fellow working with me, just stood up and stared the push down and said to him, "Well if you don't like it mister, you just unload the son-of-a-bitches and load them the way you want." He stayed on the job too. He was bigger than the toolpush. In those days that kind of thing happened. It's not like it is now when you stand back and bark like a small dog.

One time a guy was working on the "swivel". He fell over backwards and his feet got caught up. He was hanging upside down screaming like a pig on a hook. This kid had a bad habit, his personal hygiene wasn't too good. One of the guys grabbed a scrub brush and announced, "I know who'll be doing the washing this time." Oh yes, we got him out of there. His foot was wedged under the bales. He was OK and we all went back to work.

I didn't spend too much time in the Canadian oilfields. Most of my time was spent on the international scale. I went overseas in 1968. The first posting was Libya. It was a base station and we worked out in the Sahara. We had housing in Tripoli in a place called Georgimpopoli. This was an American Sector. There were over 3,000 American military personnel there and we had access to the American PX.

King Idris ran the place and he allowed us to come and go as we wanted. It was a very beautiful place to live. It was a good life. You could get anything you wanted, really. I had a young family and they came along with me. We had several good years. Things didn't work out the way they were supposed to and that marriage ended in the early seventies. We went to the oilfields for two weeks and came out for one week. There was an American toolpush, driller, mechanic and a derrick man who was called an assistant driller, on each crew. Native people were hired as laborers. They did work such as tripping, roughnecking and stuff like that.

You really had to watch these guys because they had no concept of danger, no concept of weights. They could watch a ten inch drill-collar roll down the pipe-rack and stick their hand out to stop it. Things like that. A ten inch drill-collar weighs 340 pounds per foot.

I spent about eighteen years in and out of the Middle East. I worked in Northwest as well as South Africa, Madagascar, Nigeria, Ethiopia, Egypt and Sudan. I spent about two years in Russia, which was not nice. Norway. I was there to visit, I could read and write and speak the language, but was never sent to work there.

I've progressed up the ladder some. Been doing the same job for about 20 years. I have been a drilling completion workover person now since 1974. Knock on wood, I have only had a couple of minor accidents. A broken foot and a twisted up finger or two. Throughout the years, I've seen some bad accidents but have only been hurt twice myself.

I've worked on a Failing 500, Big National 1520, posted barges, off shore drilling platforms, and jack-up platforms. In the 36 years on the rigs, 28 have been on land.

The oilfields have changed about 180 degrees. It's not a happy-go-lucky situation. "It's not what you can do for yourself, it's what you can do for others." But, it's a good life. I like it. Right now it's good but that's gonna come down quiet too. Maybe two to three more years. We have to wait and see. It all depends on a lot of things. There's some people on top of the heap that control that. We have no say about it.

But, it's still the same style of operation, different configuration of tools, different approaches. Basically there's one thing that rings the bell and that's common sense. I say, don't go into something you don't have positive knowledge about. I can say that from a supervisor's point of view. If you're responsible for the equipment and people, you better know what the hell you're doing because if something happens, an inquiry can be brought back to three years. Some rotten, sorry son-of-a-bitch can come up with something that can ruin someone's life that way.

I've got a few years left to work. They're looking for people to work in Sudan, rotating 28 days in, 28 days out. I'd like to go because I can come home on my time off and do what I want to do on my farm, and spend some time with my family. I can go back to work and maintain the standard of living that I like.

I think the International Rotation System is superior because when you are at home, your time is your own until you get back on the plane. Here you're beat on from both ends. You dare not leave the phone because you can't miss a call. It might be a job. The damn telephone line is your life line, good thing we've got it. And now we have COMPUTERS.

Howard Garstad (1996)

Mark Garstad

Mark worked approximately 30 years in the oil patch. Most of the years, he worked in the winter months and rodeoed in the spring, summer and fall. He and his wife, Faye live on a farm near Ryley.

I was 21 years old when I started in the oil patch. I worked for Canbridge Rig #10 at Bittern Lake. It was a small triple rig. I was there for a couple of weeks and then we moved to Rig #13 out by Gainford.

By the time when I finally got around the rigs, living conditions weren't too bad. When it was time to move the rig, some guys got hurt because of the rush and equipment breaking. I was fortunate that didn't happen to me.

Shortly after I began working, I lit a flare pit that should have burnt up everything around it including myself. The reason that didn't happen was probably because there had been two or three inches of snow the night before. I was working on a service rig and the lease was saturated with oil condensate. The flare pit had a whole bunch of paper and rags and garbage in it that I figured needed to be burnt.

At that particular time of the morning I didn't think it was going to hurt anything. There was no wind. I put a pair of mud and crude oil soaked gloves up on a clump of snow, struck a match, and threw it in that flare pit. It blew me straight back about 20 feet and I hit the ground running backwards. I didn't fall down and never lit on fire. But it was so damn hot that I couldn't go near those gloves. I just watched them smoke for a while. Vapor began to come off of them and they lit up like a torch and burnt. That fire was probably 200 feet high and pretty damn warm.

There were two conservation board vehicles parked about 75 feet from the flare pit and they were locked and the people with the keys were gone so we just had to hope that they didn't ignite or explode. The paint faded on both sides on both vehicles on the side closest to the flare pit, but they didn't light up.

I didn't get any walking papers because there wasn't any substantial amount of damage done. I never lit another flare pit on a service rig. The main thing is I didn't get burnt up for it. That could have happened pretty easy because I didn't ask a question. If I had asked the driller I was working for if he wanted that flare pit burnt, he would have told me not to do it and why. The driller was from Nova Scotia, a pretty decent joker. Among the many quotes in the Bible, one is, "Blessed are the merciful for they shall receive mercy."

It was in the 1960's that I started going on camp jobs. The longest that I was on a camp job with no break was 94 days. I was in there for 94 days, with no days off, because I didn't want to go to town and spend my money. We were to work three weeks and get a week off. But I used to work for a crew that was short handed during the fourth week. That was in the winter of 1965 and 1966. I wasn't married then. I wouldn't stay over six weeks after I got married.

Once I got up there, they figured on me being in there from the time I went in until they decided to leave operations in April. It was January when I hired on. Three weeks went by and nothing was mentioned about a week off. So I informed them that I was giving them three more weeks then I was going home for probably two weeks. But I was ignored. So I informed the toolpush that I would like to have him book me a flight out of Rainbow Lake on such and such a day. He told me that there were no seats on the plane.

I was lucky when those six weeks were up. We had just cemented surface pipe and the cementers were going through Rainbow Lake either on their way out or to the next job. At midnight, or at two in the morning, when they were ready to leave, I was too. I took about three tamarack or fir logs and cut them the right size to jam the cook's door shut, the pusher's door shut and the camp attendant's door shut so nobody could get out. Then I got in the cementer's truck and went to Rainbow Lake. It was a good three or four hour drive to town. We got into town about 7:30 or 8 o'clock. And I knew that the plane came and went about 10 or 10:30.

There had been no arrangements made so I went to the operator's office. The fellow running things phoned Edmonton to see if there had been any arrangements for Garstad to get on this plane. The personnel man was sitting in his office and asked, "Well, what's the matter? Is he sick? Is he hurt? What's wrong?" The answer came back, "No, I think the guy has got it real bad. He's going home to his wife whether you like it or not.

Anyway, the plane was full when it arrived. It didn't look like I was going to get on the plane. They were going to take something like $175 or $225 a day out of my wages while waiting a week for the plane to come back. I said, "That's all right. I'll just sit here and wait." But as luck would have it, one company's drilling crew had decided not to go out that week. So there were six empty seats on that plane and I got one of them. I went into the office and was told they didn't need me anymore because I had broken my contract. I said, "Not my contract, yours."

So I went to work for Westburn at Fort Assiniboine and finished the winter there. I was offered drilling positions several times and didn't accept them because I rodeoed for six or seven months during the summer and worked on the rigs in the winter time. I finally did accept a drilling position at a place called Bonanza with Nugget Drilling in the winter of 1978 and 1979.

In 1980, when the Liberals swept in to power with a full majority government, the drilling industry died when the Energy Policy trick was played on western Canada. There were significant changes in our household income. There had been some rewarding experiences since I left the drilling industry.

In 1982 and the winter of 1983, I borrowed $2,200 from the Alberta government to get myself certified for the drilling industry. I obtained the five certificates that I was after which included certificates for H2S, St. John's Industrial First Aid, Oilfield Boilers, and the First and Second Line Well Control. I was well papered but I didn't get any work with those papers.

I once was fired on New Year's eve so I wouldn't get double time for New Year's day under the pretense that I was at fault for something someone else had done. But as everyone knows, the drilling industry is a fast money field. You run into the best and the worst types of people there are. There's a lot of the bad and ugly but the good ones are worth being around. Virtue has it's own reward.

I attended a wedding of one of my sister's grandchildren in April 1997 and chanced to be re-acquainted with a couple who were single when they had last seen me. All three of us had worked together on an Imperial Oil operation. If I remember right, it was rig #49 of Brinkerhoff's at Tuktoyaktuk in the Northwest Territories. At the time they worked with me in 1974, Ron was a roughneck and Barbara was a dishwasher. Now that couple have three half grown children and they look like a happy family to me. It was very flattered that they should come up and ask me if I remembered them because I have to be truthful to say that I couldn't have placed them if I had tried. After all, 20 years does a lot to people. But it feels good to think that virtue has its reward. It took me a long time to do it but once I did it, I stuck to my commitment with my wife. We've been together for 27 years and these drilling rigs were hard on our relationship because I was away from home so much. But we got by just like everybody else who tries hard.

If I could do it over: Well, I think the things a guy remembers most is when you come closest to your appointment with destiny. One night I was working derrick. It was 30° F below and the wind was blowing hard.

We were sitting on a drill stem test and had just pulled a failed test. We were going to run another and the driller was upset.

He ran the blocks up empty at high speed. The derrick was full of pipe and the blocks hit the monkey board which hit the back of the railing. The collar I had ready fell across the derrick when I had to get out of the way.

I got down to the rig floor to find out what was going on. There was nothing pulling line over. It was just the wind howling that pushed the blocks into the monkey board. The lines were pushing on the pad that flips back so you can make corrections.

I told the driller, "If you put this bugger into low gear, I'll keep working. If you let it out of low gear, I'm comin' back down and it won't be safe for you to be around."

We ran in the hole in low gear with about 80 stands because it was a double rig.

If I could do my oil patch years over I would have probably drilled for a couple of years in the mid-1970s. The fact that I didn't have two years drilling experience was what stopped me from taking advantage of the foreign field when they were hiring people for the Middle East and the Far East. I missed out on that.

Mark Garstad (1997)

Raymond (Ray) Garstad

Ray began working on the rigs at age 16 near Jenner for Canbridge Drilling. Set up as driller at age nineteen, he worked eight years with drilling contractors and nine years with a service company doing drill stem testing and coring. Together with his partner, he operates a real estate company in Nisku. Ray and his wife Shirley live in Leduc.

Well, in 1954 I finished grade nine and I was 15 years old. The first winter I was working out, I worked on a farm. Then in the spring, through the assistance of my brother Einar, I got a job on a rig with Canbridge Drilling down by Jenner, north of Brooks.

I often wonder how I could have done that without some help from big brother because it was an extremely difficult transition. When you're a 16 year old kid you don't know bugger-all, and my biggest problem was not the work so much, I was able to learn that, but to try to keep up to the big boys who were 19 or 20 years old.

I worked steady graveyards. This was quite a task because I was so damn tired every night - I died a 1,000 deaths I think. But I had lots of fun and I don't think I could report anything earth shattering, except that I now had gained some ability to generate some cash. This was pretty exciting for me because I'd never had any.

I think that if it wasn't the first pay cheque, then it was the certainly the second, that I went and bought a car. I paid four hundred bucks for this car - it was a 1947 Ford. I financed as much as the bank would give me and away I went.

That started me on the way and for many years it was an interesting life. I never traveled overseas but I worked the western provinces in Canada. Along the way I saw some pretty interesting things. I met and worked with a lot of different people and it was certainly a different lifestyle.

One way that the single people could save a little money was to get room and board from some house in town or farm. I remember one in Buffalo, a small place 60 miles northeast of Brooks. There was one place in town that provided room and board. We slept in an abandoned house next to the main house, where we ate our meals. There were two crews I think, staying in this place. The damn house didn't have any windows in it. Most of the windows had been, and still were, broken.

I remember it was in the fall, it started snowing and we were sleeping in this abandoned house. We didn't have those big sleeping bags at that time. When one crew was working the crew that was home would take all of the blankets in the house and pile them on. Sometimes we would get up to go to work, and there would be a foot of snow in the damn place. Snow on the floor and on the beds. I guess we didn't have enough brains to go get some boards to cover the windows up. I remember one place, this little gal used to take a can of Prem and put it through the meat grinder twice to make it go further on the sandwiches. We paid $90 a month, which was quite a lot in those days.

My monthly earnings were probably around $350 to $400 a month when I was roughnecking and I would work seven days a week. Before I left to work on the rigs, I was getting $3 a day, $90 a month and room and board, working for a farmer.

It was a change in lifestyle, all right. You couldn't make that much money anywhere but the drilling rigs. Even the railroad didn't pay nearly as much as that and although the hourly wage was only $1.35 an hour, the roughnecks were in tall grass, getting money to buy booze, gas and a lot of other things.

I remember one time when we were down at Alliance, a guy was killed. It was pretty sad. The derrick hand went up to throw one stand in and didn't put his belt on. It was carelessness on his part but he didn't get a chance to repeat it, because when he fell he hit the top of the swivel bale, and that was it for him. That was probably the fault of more than just one person. Someone should have noticed that he didn't have his belt on.

When things like that happened, they would shut the rig down. In this case, it was shut down for about six hours. An investigation was done by someone from Edmonton but it was short-lived. It was determined that it was a high-risk industry. Generally speaking there weren't that many accidents considering the activity around the work place.

I worked down in southern Saskatchewan, actually all through Saskatchewan. We drilled some of the first potash wells around Saskatoon. They were drilling the wells to try and determine how much actual production they could expect in the mines. We worked there during the summer, and in winter we would wildcat through northern Saskatchewan. I did that for a couple of years, and then in 1957 I came over into Alberta. I used to work in the prairies in the summer and go north in the winter. You could make more money if you could get into camp jobs.

In sharing some of the recollections, I guess it was easier for me because I was single then. All I had was a damn car and a suitcase. But I often think about the married people and the life that some of those women lived. Most of the people that were moving around lived in trailers and they had small kids that weren't going to school yet.

Sometimes we would move every two or three weeks. They would just pick up and move with the rigs. These women would have to pack up and unpack and they would be running into all kinds of problems, some of which were just unbelievable! We, the single guys would be in the bar drinking and the married guys would be trying to park those trailers and fix their equipment and keep their women from chewing their heads off. It was something else!

I remember one guy in particular. He had a small half-ton truck and a 10 foot by 45 foot trailer. That summer we probably moved every two or three weeks. If we had to cross a river or go up hills, this poor guy would have to get a farmer to put a tractor on the trailer, hold it back going down the hill, and then haul it up on the other side. There wasn't enough power in his truck to make it work. Every time the guy parked his outfit, he would have to fix his truck. After every move Al would be under there putting a new clutch plate in his truck. I used to think, "How in the hell could a person tolerate that much aggravation?" But that's the way it was, quite a few people did that.

Some of those winters up north were quite memorable. I recall we drilled a couple of wells north of Green Lake, which is north of Meadow Lake, Saskatchewan. We used to travel with taxis because we were about 120 miles back in from town. We worked seven days a week, 12 hours on and 24 hours off. We had these taxi cabs driving us back and forth. Nobody had money at the end of the month because we spent it all.

I remember this one guy who drove taxi. They weren't really taxis, they were ordinary cars, owned and driven by people from town. One guy had a 1952 Chev and a heater that didn't work. It was like 50° F or 60° F below and he was dressed with mukluks and everything else. We of course didn't have warm clothes because we spent all of our money on booze.

We would virtually freeze to death traveling back and forth in this damn car. There were times when it would break down and then we would get another taxi. One guy had a much newer car, only a year old, and we used to get by without too much pain there. I remember some of the hardships that went with that experience were bloody unreal. It used to take three and one half hours to drive it one way.

When we lived in Meadow Lake, we stayed in motels. It was trying to say the least because it was very uncomfortable for the most part. The town was quite happy when we left, I think. In fact, during our break-up party we were asked to leave, and we were told that they were very pleased we were leaving town at that time.

We moved from northern Saskatchewan and went into Cynthia, out by Drayton Valley. I was single and didn't have a big problem but one of the married couples was pulling a trailer. I remember when we got to the river hill near Drayton Valley it was glare ice. He spun out and couldn't hold the vehicle from going back. We thought they were going to go in the river but the wheels caught onto some stuff, and held. We had to hook three trucks on the front of his car but we got them up over the hill.

By the time we got to Cynthia with that entourage, the frame of the car was broken right above the back wheels. There was too much weight from the trailer. That and the rough road just ruined his car. That's the kind of stuff that was happening and I'm sure that wouldn't happen today. Another incident happened in 1959 when I was working for Cambridge, up in the bush near Fort St. John.

Thinking back on some of the parties we used to have up there and some of the things we got away with, it's pretty amazing actually. One night I got in a little tussle in the bar. Somebody threw a beer bottle or glass and it hit me on the side of the head. If I hadn't had my friend, I probably would have died there.

I was bleeding profusely. I guess they picked me up and took me to a doctor. He sewed that damn cut up without any anesthetic or nothing. He was very irritated since it was two o'clock in the morning. He did fix me up though. I lost quite a bit of blood but went to work the next day. The first few days I was pretty weak, but that's the way things went.

I worked for eight years on the rigs, spent the first three roughnecking, working derrick and then started drilling.

There were good times and also some dangerous times. I remember once, I was pulling the packer out of the ground and miscalculated the height where the traveling blocks were and ran through the crown, with Cliff Johnson up in the derrick. Everything came flying down and the men bailed off into the shale pile or wherever they could go.

I went out of the doghouse, running as fast as I could run, thinking I'd come back to pick up the pieces later. All of us scattered like chickens in a high wind. All except Cliff, who couldn't go anywhere from the monkey board. He just crouched in the corner up there.

The block came past him and he wasn't hurt. Nobody got hurt, but it took us about eight hours to get things re-strung and sorted out. That was a situation where I was pretty scared.

In 1963, I went to work for a testing and coring company. I worked with them until 1972. The prairies were particularly bad in the winter time, because of the blizzards that could strike at any time. I remember one time down by Shaunavon, Saskatchewan, I was driving a testing truck. The toolpush and I were in town one afternoon and a blizzard came up. We decided to go back to the rig. I didn't really want to go, but the toolpusher wanted to get back and I said "Well, you're not going by yourself so we'll take my truck. It's bigger and we'll have a better chance to make it back to the rig."

We were only about three-quarters of a mile from the rig when we went off the road. You couldn't see two feet in front of you but the pusher said "I know where the rig is, let's go." I wanted to stay with the truck but he said, "No, I'm going to go." So I told him, "You're not going alone." We took the sleeping bag out of the truck and threw it over our backs and we walked. We couldn't see a damn thing.

We didn't see the lights of the rig until we were probably 15 to 20 feet away. It was damn fortunate that we found the rig. If we hadn't, we would have died on the prairie that night. There were lots of things like that, but then, nobody really thought much of it then.

There were some interesting times in those years. I guess one of the highlights would be when I tested the discovery well in Rainbow Lake. I think that was in 1966. That was, of course, the well that started the Rainbow Lake boom and Zama Lake. I spent three years up there, living in Grande Prairie, driving lots of miles and I spent lots of cold nights on the rigs.

One time in particular, I was going up onto the Horn Plateau from Indian Cabins, north of High Level. I had some coring bits on and other things I needed to go in to start a job. We were running late, somebody had forgotten to order the equipment.

We were flying in and left Indian Cabins about five o'clock at night and it was 55° F below zero. It was stone dark and we had Chevron's twin otter. There was two pilots, myself and the geologist in this plane. We started flying north and I asked the pilot, "How long is it going to take us to get to the rig?" He said "Oh, an hour and a half to an hour and three quarters."

We were flying due north and it was pitch black. There wasn't a light to be seen. Me and this geologist were sitting in the back end of this airplane. For some reason, they couldn't run the heaters and radios at the same time, so they shut the heaters off in order to communicate on the radios. They got their maps or strings and stuff out and they were drawing arcs on the maps and checking things. After about two hours of watching this, I started to wonder about these pilots because they were acting pretty damn strange. It seemed we were going straight north, but then the geologist said, "Well, I don't know what's going on, but I hate to guess what the hell we're getting into here."

We'd been flying for three hours and I was now thinking, "God damn. This is it, we've had it." We couldn't see any lights anywhere and the pilots were still checking things, turning their radios on and then they would shut them off. They were still drawing arcs on their maps. I remember saying to the geologist, "If this damn thing goes down, and even if we survive going down, it won't be very damn long before we freeze to death."

Neither me or the geologist said anything to those pilots. We just kept riding in the back there. They made the approach to the runway, and one of the pilots hollered, "Get the hell out of here, there's trees to the right." We just bent over and peeled out of there.

We buzzed the rig, "We're going to land on the strip, we're coming in." By that time the toolpusher had come and was shining his lights on the airstrip. We landed but I would never want to re-live that experience. That was probably one of the most scary damn things I was involved in.

There were probably hundreds of situations which were fairly close. We used to do some really stupid things, but we got past all of them, obviously, because we're still here.

From a humanitarian standpoint, I know that things were pretty tense for the wives of some of these guys on the rigs. I remember when we lived in Grande Prairie, we had kids who were really small, babies actually, and I would be gone for sometimes weeks on end.

I guess the longest I was gone was probably a month. It was very hard for these young girls. The older women who lived in the trailer courts would be sort of 'den mothers' to these young girls with the small babies. That, and the Oil Wives Fraternity helped these young girls to maintain their sanity.

That's how they survived I guess. They sure didn't complain very much anyway. The damn stoves used to go out and somebody would always come and fix them. In cold weather, it doesn't take very long for a trailer to cool down. I don't know how they actually tolerated that, but I guess most of them didn't have a hell of a lot of choice.

Some of the working conditions that might be worthy of mention are the camps that we had back in the 50's and 60's. The camps were of very questionable quality compared to what they have these days. I remember when I first went out, we were on one of Canbridge's rigs up north of Fort St. John, B.C. The camps we had consisted of steel shacks, eight feet by twenty and there were five people in those son-of-guns. There were three double army bunks made out of steel. The shack was poorly insulated and heated with a diesel stove. The top bunks would be so hot you couldn't stand it and the bottom bunks would be close enough to the ground so you would be damn cold by morning.

My God, I remember if you put your socks on the floor or up against the wall they would be frozen there when you got up and you'd have to pry the damn things off there before you could get them on.

Now, of course, the conditions have greatly improved but that was the kind of conditions that existed then. Some of the trailers that the married people lived in were very small and were certainly far from the comforts of the mobile homes of today.

Ray Garstad (1997)

Robert (Bob) Gorham

Bob and his wife, Marjorie now live in Bruderheim. He worked in the oil industry for a total of approximately 30 years. Beginning as a roughneck, he worked all positions. Bob was a driller for six years and pushed tools for 15 years. His work has taken him from Fairview to England, the Arctic Islands, the Middle East and West Texas.

When I started in the oil patch in 1950, I was 24 years old. I started working for Burgrim Exploration and Drilling, up on the Peace River country. It was a double, truck mounted drilling rig.

We were drilling sand formation tests and drilling the tops of the Peace River sands which was running from 1,100 to 1,600 feet in the Fairview area. We did that for four months then we went across the river towards Spirit River to drill a 2,600 foot exploratory hole for Hudson Bay Oil. There was no bridge across the Peace River at that time so they had to go all the way down to triangle, back through Valleyview and into Grande Prairie.

The truck was an old, chain driven English truck. The top speed was about 25 miles an hour so it took three days to drive that thing to the drilling site. We went back and forth, over the ferry from Fairview every day.

On the average, we left at quarter to seven in the morning and usually arrived home at seven in the evening.

We just done the one hole there then we brought the rig back across. But they took it across the ferry at that time in two pieces.

We drilled a hole on top of the Peace River banks on the Fairview side. Neither one of them were wells, probably today they would have been gas wells but in those days, the drilling techniques were so poor and you had to 'mud off' in little stands and then you couldn't get anything out of it.

In 1952, I moved over to Trinity Drilling. The company has bought a big new 80B National, a high drilling rig. Everything in it was brand new. I mean there wasn't even an old piece of pipe. We put it all together. We had to put all the air lines. We worked on it for almost two months in Fort St. John to get the thing ready to take out to the rig site.

This was the old folks home of the oilfields! You built a boiler house out of lumber. You built all your buildings out of lumber. The boiler house was 60 by 80 feet. It had all the change rooms, showers and the whole bit in We worked 12 hours a day for two weeks and you got paid for eight hours. Then you went home for a week and your name still went into the book for eight hours a day for the week. The other crews did the same. It was different. I worked for them until 1954.

Sometimes it was a month here and a month there on relief work. Then we worked at Cecil Lake which is 30 miles east of Fort St. John, east of the Beatton River coulee.

The derrick hands used the safety buggy off the derrick to go down with instead of going down the ladder. The brake was getting worn out. We talked the driller into going up and riding this buggy down. He was heavier than the rest of us so he went down faster and wound in the mud tank. He came down quicker than he could stop it. He sure wasn't very happy about that.

There was about 40 miles of bull dozed trail and you could go through it but it wasn't a road. That was a road from Hines Creek right through to Fort St. John. There was a gravel road put through in 1954 or 1955.

In June of 1954, I went to Drayton Valley. I worked Swan Hills too, but Swan Hills was never like Drayton Valley. The first guy I ran into was a guy that wasn't well liked anywhere. I asked him if they needed help. He said, "Get your cover-alls." I was just getting ready to run the production casing and I walked up there and I stood in the doorway of the door. I wasn't due then for about 20 minutes and this guy came in and asked, "Are you going to work?" I said, "No." He said, "Why." I said, "I couldn't work here with you guys for a half an hour." I quit like that. They were hollering steady at the men. The men were just treated like pieces of dirt.

I went back into Violet Grove and there was a Cascade company pickup there and a guy was using the phone. When he got off the phone I asked him if he needed any help and he said, "We sure do. Have you got experience?" I said, "Yeah, a few years." He said, "We want you." I said, "Well, when?" This was about two o'clock in the afternoon. He said, "Now, if you can go on the four o'clock shift. I don't know if he needs men or not but we'll put you on lease until there's an opening." I said, "Well, OK."

When I went out there, the driller was short of men so I started roughnecking. Actually I worked motors for Cascade. One time we started to pull out of the hole and the guy who was working derrick couldn't pull the pipe back. So the driller asked me, "Did you ever work derrick?" I said, "Oh yeah." So that's when I went up the derrick and that's where I stayed until 1965. Altogether, I worked for Cascade from 1954 until 1965.

We moved to Swan Hills in 1959. We moved on to the lease with a 10 foot by 45 foot trailer. I was pushing with an old National 50 rig. It was big enough to drill a 7,000 foot hole and we were drilling a 9,000 foot hole. It was quite a challenge. We drilled three holes that winter.

That was the second year of the activity in Swan Hills. There was a lot of snow on the ground and we were about twelve miles north of where the town is now. There were deeper holes in Swan Hills because we were quite high. That poor little rig was sure working. On the second hole, we went down a hill about 120 feet so it was a little bit better. I worked on that rig that winter and the next summer. After that, I worked in the Edmonton yard.

One time we took a new pickup truck from Edmonton to Swan Hills. We got to Fort Assiniboine at ten o'clock Sunday morning, it was four o'clock Wednesday afternoon when we reached the terminal which was 50 miles away. We had a power winch but there was to much water to run the motor. We'd take the hand winch and tie it to a tree to pull ourselves through or we would drive ten crow bars into the muskeg, weave a line through them and then pull the vehicle up. One day I think we made 1,700 feet in 12 hours.

We were ready to go up to the tower and there was no way. We were the second of eight vehicles. We walked up to the terminal to get a cat but when we got up there, and the cat skinners had all quit, so I took a TD International Cat and I became a cat skinner. It was seven o'clock at night when we got everybody up. From the terminal on, the roads were gravel and we just drove down to the rig. By this time, we had no brakes on the pickup. That was probably the worst trip that I ever made in my life.

In the fall of 1960, Cascade built the first diesel-electric rig in Canada. They moved the rig to Moose Mountain which is on the north west corner of Swan Hills. I dug two holes for them. After that I looked after that rig during the time I was at Swan Hills. I stayed in Swan Hills from 1959 to 1963.

In the summer of 1963, I went to England. Imperial Oil was building a diesel-electric rig. Rumours filtered down through that Esso was drilling some wells in England. I applied for a job over there as driller and I got it. Marjorie and the kids came over by ship. We lived in Balcolme, England. The rig was out of Haywards Heathe.

We had flown from Edmonton to Amsterdam and transferred into another plane. We got about halfway down the runway and the take-off was aborted. We sat on the ground for 5 1/2 hours before we got another airplane. We finally landed in London. We had been on the road for more than 24 hours. I went to work that afternoon. That was a little tough. The English driller left so the toolpush, who was an American, told me what to do and left. He wanted to cut that cord. In the log books, they were down about 1,900 feet and it had taken them 16 hours to make a round trip to change a bit. This sounds impossible but that's the way it was.

We just started getting ready to pull out of the hole and this young fellow came up and wanted a job. It turned out that he was Canadian and had worked for Redwell. He had lived behind our trailer in his house. I hired him and he started working derrick. About three days later, another young lad came up who wanted a job. He was Canadian and had worked for General Petroleums. He was a good hand, and I put him working motors. Then I had a crew. It was a good crew. The guy working motors was probably the best hand in all of England.

When we were drilling on that hole, the formation kept falling back in. We were supposed to go down 12,000 feet on the core but we got down to about 2,300 feet and we got a pretty good little gas well. It produced three quarter million cubic feet of gas a day.

We went down through a 20 foot layer of sand. We hit shale as soon as we got out of the sand. Every time we drilled, the hole would fold and fall back in. By the time we got to 8,000 feet, we got into some limestone. We were having lots of trouble keeping the hole straight and keeping it from slumping in. It was standing almost vertical. We went down another 1,000 feet and then they just abandoned it. We couldn't go to the next hole because they weren't sure of their geology. They told us to shut it down and finish up. Everybody packed up to leave and we got paid for an extra month. We were back home in St. Albert on November 20, 1963, two days before J.F. Kennedy was assassinated.

In the winter, I went to work for Cascade as a driller. I was working east of Valleyview at Goose River on Cascade #17. We lived on a farm after we got back from England. I worked for Cascade for two years that time and I wound up pushing tools for them.

When that rig finished up for the winter, I went up to Slave Lake and moved a rig, that came in by train. We moved it in by Nodwell down into the swamps. They had a bit of a camp set up at Mistehao Lake. I was doing the loading of cars and trucks.

I went to work for Mustang Drilling in the fall of 1964. It was a new company, just starting up with three little double rigs. I worked for Arrow Drilling south and east of Slave Lake. I stayed 'til spring.

Al Mundt had some little 2,500 foot Failing rigs. I rigged those rigs up. Lloydminster was the first hole. We drilled 42 holes and two workovers in 51 days. The fastest hole we drilled was done in 16 hours. We went down about 1,900 feet and we drilled them with one bit.

About that time, I left the rigs and my family and I went to British Columbia doing drywall work and the service station work. After a couple of years, we came back to Alberta and I went to work for Gustavson drilling. We stayed in a little rooming house in Stettler and worked out of Foremost, about five miles south and west of the town.

We were on short change, changing from daylight to graveyard shifts. In those days, we had eight hours off between shifts. We got off shift and it started storming just as we were about to leave the rig. The relieving crew made it into the rig and the other crew got away except the derrick man who couldn't get his car started. By the time he got his car started, he couldn't get off the lease. We didn't move anything for 93 hours. We had just drilled out, under the surface casing, in the hole and we were waiting for the logging truck. We had no camp. The toolpusher shack was all that was there.

The guy working derrick for me lived on the same quarter so he supplied the meals. He had a tractor with a dozer blade on it and we were taking water out of his dug-out so we could keep the rig running. We kept things going. We were paid well for all this.

A short time later, we got snowed in again for 72 hours. The rig was out of Castor by a Hutterite Colony. The Hutterites had gone in the ditch when we went out to work four o'clock New Years Eve. Our cat-skinner pulled them out with our D7 cat. The Hutterites made meals for us while we were stranded out there.

I went out to Whitecourt, and we were 'sposed' to work eight hour days there for 115 days, 14 hours a day. That's what I got paid for. I had two 30 hour sessions out there without any relief. The toolpush was there but wouldn't relieve me.

In 1970, I went to work in the Arctic Islands for Adeco Drilling. When I hired on with them, four pushes were flown to Texas for two months. We worked with a guy who worked opposition to Red Adair.

I worked in the Arctic from 1970 to 1975. In November 1974, I flew into Resolute Bay with nine men. The next day we charted a twin otter and flew out to the location. We landed on location with this twin otter. They were 'sposed' to have a tent at the end of the airstrip and fuel there. Well, the tent was set up a mile and a half from the airstrip. There was so much snow that we couldn't taxi the aircraft up to it. The rig had been shut down since March 1973, so there was nothing much good there. They had a little propane cook stove and a diesel heater. We had to pack all that stuff from the airstrip so we took two guys and myself. They helped make the trip, got the fires going and everything. The pilot and co-pilot made another trip up and we got stuff set around so we could live. I wanted to get another load and they wouldn't leave. The wolves were howling and the men wouldn't go down there. I went down and got the rest of the load myself. I took a scoop shovel and a piece of rope and tied this ten gallon fuel barrel on there and brought it in.

The wolves didn't scare me any. They were about the size of a good size pig. I wasn't scared of those wolves. The plane was supposed to fly back the next day. There was a D7 cat and we had to get it going to clear the snow for a landing strip. We went out to start the cat and had a small light plant with us. We took rolls of 40 foot wide polythene, thawed it out and built a tent over the cat and then put a heater under the tent. It took 32 hours to thaw the cat out. We plowed the airstrip and made it 30 feet wide. We were just finished when the plane came.

I went into Resolute Bay and got some more men, got the plant going and started up again. We finished the first of February. It was 70° F below zero the week before we left the Arctic. I had a bad bout of pneumonia and I came out of the Arctic in 1975 and then I went ot the Middle East.

When I came out of the Middle East, I went to work for a Calgary firm on November 14, 1975 as a consulting engineer. We were out at Edson on a Gustavson rig. I looked after that rig and I was building a location out at Obed. I worked for them 'til I quit in 1981.

If I could do it over: It was good money, good pay but the living conditions were very hard on family life. We weathered it though. We've been married for 48 years. Marjorie probably deserves a medal.

Robert (Bob) Gorham (1997)

Richard (Dick) Hazen

Dick's career in the oil patch began many years ago, At age 17, he quit school to go roughnecking on a steam drilling rig near Turner Valley. He worked for Young's Drilling around Leduc in 1947 and then went farming for 11 years. In 1968 he returned to the oilfields again in a supervisory capacity. In 1974, he and his friend, Keith Babb formed Hazen and Babb Drilling Consultants Ltd. They both planned their retirement and did so in 1990. Dick and his wife, Jennifer live in Edmonton.

It all started in the fall of 1942. My father had a stationary steam engine engineer ticket. With his steam engineer's ticket, he was able to fire boilers on the steam drilling rigs in Turner Valley. Consequently, we left the farm in Daysland. We moved to Millarville close to my father's work.

I finished grade ten in the Daysland area and my mother arranged for me to attend the Sheep Creek School, which was northwest of Millarville. The next day I conveniently left home looking for work. I traveled 30 miles to the south end of Turner Valley and found a job roughnecking on a steam driller rig. I was 17 at that time.

When I reported back home, needless to say my mother was rather upset. However, I made the decision to continue working rather than go to school. I started with the Newell and Chandler Drilling Company in November 1943. I continued to work on the drilling rigs in the Turner Valley area.

There was a slack time in 1946 when it was impossible to get a job roughnecking because it was the first 'bust cycle' in the oil industry. It was very hard for people to get a job because the boys who were coming home from overseas. They had worked for these various contractors prior to joining the service. They were rightfully given back their jobs when they returned. Consequently, there wasn't room for us younger fellows and we were left unemployed.

I went back to the Daysland area and I worked on the farm for my uncles. I went to the Valentine's Dance in Daysland on February 14, 1947 and I had heard about the Leduc discovery which had happened the day before. I told my future wife, while we were dancing, that I had found a job in a career that I would prefer, and that I would probably ask her to marry me and come with me to the oil patch. There was no answer at the time, however, love did carry on.

In the fall of 1948, I was set up as a driller and I was one of the youngest drillers around at that time. On my first shift as a driller, I followed a driller who spoke with a Swedish accent. He was working afternoon tower. When I relieved him at midnight, he said, "Kid, you're only gonna have to learn to write one thing on the tower book and that will be 'twip'." He couldn't pronounce the letter R, but he meant that I would be 'yo yoing' the pipe in and out of the hole and not on bottom drilling.

During a rig move from one location to the other, we got married on January 2, 1948. I was steadily employed from that point on until the spring of 1957.

I was working for Young Drilling Company when Leduc first started. I wound up working for Gene Young on Young Drilling rig #1. We drilled Imperial 8, that was our first well. Our second well was Imperial #16 and from there we moved to Imperial #26, which was on the same LSD as Imperial #1, the discovery well. When Imperial drilled #1, they found oil in the D2 zone and completed this wildcat well as a commercial producer at that depth.

Imperial drilled #2 and #3 and found them unproductive in the D2 zone. Geologically the decision was made to deepen both wells in search of another zone. After penetrating roughly 150 feet of shale below the base of the D2 zone, the D3 zone was discovered, which turned out to be a very prolific producing zone in the Leduc field. So, in essence Young Drilling Co. skidded from Imperial #16 to the same LSD to drill the twin Imperial #26 on the same location.

In the spring of 1957, I quit a drilling superintendent job to buy out my father's farm in the Rosalind area. We had four young children and we needed a place to stay put so we could send them to school. This seemed like the right thing to do. We successfully farmed for the next 11 years. In the spring 1968, our older children were attending university in Edmonton and it was decided then that it was best to sell the farm and that I would go back to the oilfields.

I was 42 years old when I returned in 1968. I went back in a supervisory capacity with a new consulting firm called V.H. Hunter and Associates. As you will recognize, he was the toolpusher on the original Leduc #1. I continued working there until Vern's retirement.

In 1974, I formed Hazen and Babb Drilling Consultants Ltd. with my friend and fellow toolpusher, Keith Babb. We had a very successful business for 17 years. We both planned our retirement and when we turned 65 in 1990, we both retired.

During the 17 years of operation, we were constantly at the mercy of the telephone. Many a 'down hole' problem were rectified at 3 am while sitting at the kitchen table, talking on the phone.

Having said this, there were times when I had to 'pinch hit' and be financier as well as marriage councillor to my employees.

If I could do it over: I would probably fall into the same pit-falls but I have no complaints. The oil industry has served me very well and I feel it an honor to have been able to participate in it to the best of my ability.

Dick Hazen (1997)

Clifford (Cliff) Johnson

Cliff has worked in the oil industry for 36 years. He started as a roughneck, progressed to toolpush and later was an oilfield consultant. He works part-time as an instructor of Well Control and Blowout Prevention at the Petroleum Industry Training Service (P.I.T.S.) in Edmonton. He and his wife live in Wetaskiwin.

I started working on the rigs for Beta Wells, March 07, 1956, at Redwater on a service rig. Dick Curber was the toolpush and Jake Corella was the driller. This was in the Redwater Field and we were working on these small rigs more or less doing odd jobs and pulling tubing.

I was 19 years old when I started on the rigs. We were working around Calmar When things got slow, there wasn't much use in staying around Buck Creek was going pretty strong then so I went to work for High Tower Drilling.

The thing I remember, out at Buck Creek, there wasn't much for accommodations. There were two restaurants in town Of course, with not much money and not knowing how long it would be until payday, we'd get a little short. I remember the first morning I was there, I went to the restaurant and it was full. You had to get in there early to get breakfast. The guy who owned the restaurant certainly was a trusting soul. He told everyone who came through the door, "Just come in, I'll give you the bill, you sign your name and the company you work for, and you can pay me later." You walked in, ate breakfast and walked out, just like that. That was pretty good, trusting a person they had never seen before.

High Tower had several rigs working in that area so they put up their own bunkhouses in town. All the men stayed in them but I didn't know that at the time. I was told to find an empty bunk and take it, which I did. I had just got to bed and someone said, "You got my bunk." He had taken his bedding off so someone else wouldn't take it, I guess I found another bed. Then it started to rain. Soon, the roof was leaking. There was water all over the place.

Buck Creek was in the Pembina Field, about 15 miles west of Breton. In those days it was a long way because the road conditions were really bad.

Later on in the fall of 1956, the rig I was with didn't have any work. I went to work for Ilrich Drilling, which isn't in business any more, up north of Slave Lake in the Wabasca area. Just a small rig. That was a cold winter.

On these small rigs, the length of time we drilled could be anywhere from three weeks to six months depending on how smooth the drilling went. Most times it was three weeks. It depended on the location. I was single then so it didn't really matter.

In those days, I stayed in hotels or motels and in private homes. Most winters, we were in camp jobs. The camps were nothing like they are today either. There was just a shack with beds in it, that was about all. There was no television, we had nothing for recreation. We did a lot of card playing.

I was in the oil patch close to 40 years. In 1958, I quit the rigs and went into construction, doing different jobs until 1961, so I was in the patch for 36 years in total.

I remember an incident that happened in Drayton Valley, in 1956 or '57. There was a brawl going on in the hotel. One of the rig hands was just coming in for a beer, just after work. As he was walking in the door, someone was throwing a guy out, by the seat of the pants. The fellow held the door open for them as they went out.

It turned out that the bartender was the one that was being thrown out of the hotel. The bartender recognized the rig hand, or remembered him from some other time, so the rig hand was one of the guys that were charged in the disturbance, even though he had nothing to do with it. He knew nothing about it. There was always a fight in Drayton Valley, so the rig hand thought he was doing someone a favor by opening the door.

I do remember one time and that was when Einar Garstad was drilling. I was on graveyards, we used to have to dump the mud tanks in those days.

It was three o'clock in the morning, they couldn't find me because I was asleep between the motors. They went around looking for me and one of the hands said he stuck a shovel in the tanks and figured someone had dropped a gunny sack in there. The men began to think that it might be me at the bottom of the tank, that I had fallen in and drowned. They began dumping the mud tank, trying to find me.

In the meantime I woke up, and I'm standing over the hand rails and watching these guys running around, searching for me. When they saw me standing over there they were all so darn mad at me they felt like throwing me in the tank.

One of the worst things that happened, I suppose, was the time when we were on our way to Whitecourt and rolled the trailer. Douglas wasn't quite two years old. It was so windy, the road was glare ice. The trailer caught the ice on the shoulder and it rolled. We had no place to stay but everyone was so cooperative, the toolpush was so helpful, they found us a place.

Everybody was helpful. A Haliburton truck, a tow truck, and a guy with a little winch truck came along that time. I can still remember, that same day I started out, I had stopped for gas and left my gloves at the service station so I didn't even have a pair of gloves. One of the truck drivers lent me a pair. When he left, he wouldn't take any money because he said, "You've had enough trouble for one day." When I got away from there, I even ended up with a pair of gloves.

If I could do it over: I would have saved a little more money, that's for sure.

Cliff Johnson (1997)

Richard (Dick) Johnson

Dick started in the oil patch in 1951, driving for Shirley Brothers Trucking in Edmonton. He worked as a roughneck for Brinkerhoff Drilling during the early fifties and also worked in the field for a seismic company. Dick then moved to a location in northern Alberta and began driving a water truck, supplying water to one of the major drilling rigs.

Edmonton was a booming oil city in the early 1950's. Since Leduc #1 ushered in its promise of wealth in 1947, the status of Edmonton and area changed dramatically. The coal mines, which were approximately 180 miles west of Edmonton, were in the process of closing down. Villages and towns with names such as Coal Valley, Sterco, Foothills, Mountain Park and Cadomin were being slowly abandoned into history.

There was not the great need for coal now that oil was used by the railroad to fuel their big diesel locomotive engines. Heating the home did not require the drudgery of packing coal into the house. Coal meant dirty, dusty ashes must be removed after shaking the grates down in the old coal and wood stove. Oil heating was the answer. Yes, a blessing it was, this black gold of the 1950's but not for all. Let's consider the coal miners — their livelihood was eliminated, and their jobs were disrupted to the point of no return. Some miners had worked for 30 or 40 years in the depths of the earth.

Many young men had quit school while in their early teens to work in or around the coal mines. Lay offs at the coal mines were devastating to most. With a limited education and no knowledge of other occupations, coal miners had to leave their secure surroundings.

It was a new world away from the mines. What to do? Some of the younger mine employees migrated to the gold mines in the Yellowknife area. But wait, if oil was to be the future energy commodity an opportunity in the oilfields should be a good possibility. It was. Men with ambition and an eye on progress took advantage of the numerous and varied employment categories presented with the advent of the oil discovery. Truck drivers, rig hands, cooks, camp attendants, seismic personnel, warehouse workers, geologist and heavy equipment operators were needed. The list goes on and on. There was also the service rigs, oilfield cementing companies, 'power tongs' and 'fishing' crews when a drill bit was inadvertently lost in a hole. And of course, pipe line construction. There was no end to the numerous oil related spin off opportunities in Alberta. Many businesses were established because of the blessings of the 'Black Gold' in Alberta.

Oh yes! The coal miners? A better life was now unraveling for them. No more dark, cold mines, where danger lurked in the depths of the earth. Dusty, frigid coal loading 'tipples' were now just an unpleasant memory. Oil had liberated the miners when many jobs and careers were realized where the pay and benefits were greater than they had ever known. Some miners joined all categories of railroading such as diesel locomotive engineers and brake men.

I personally experienced this transition into the oil patch when I was 17 years old. In the early 1950's, a few trucking companies were in the business of dismantling or tearing down large oil drilling rigs and transporting them to new locations for drilling. Many oil rigs were operated as 'camp jobs' where living quarters and all amenities were supplied.

When I hired on as a 'swamper' and part-time driver for one of the large trucking companies, the rig we were to move was temporarily stored on a farm south of Edmonton. The rig's destination was in the area of Maple Creek, Saskatchewan. Four trucks were scheduled to leave Edmonton in the morning with the main derrick, the substructure, the big diesel motors and many lengths of drill pipe. An extra large water tank was to be transported on a 'low boy' trailer. No one had really scouted our travel route south on old Highway #2 which ran through every little town imaginable. We also had to navigate our way into the city of Calgary and hopefully out the south end to continue on Highway #2.

It was a bright sunny Monday morning in March as we proceeded on what we hoped was a carefree journey south on Highway #2. All went very well through the towns and villages. Our convoy moved along without a hitch. It was late in the afternoon when we approached the beautiful city of Calgary which is nestled in the foothills of Alberta with the snow covered mountains in the western distance. Most of the snow in Calgary had gone with the warm spring chinook winds. The streets were quite dry in Calgary, just a trace of snow in shaded areas.

Most of the main routes through Calgary were conveniently strung with power lines to accommodate the transit trolleys This would definitely present a problem. The large water tank on the low boy was very high. Would it touch the overhead power lines? Should we take the chance? The power lines in the midst of the city may be lower where the copper lines may have stretched an inch or two from more use. We couldn't just sit here, it would be dark in an hour or so. Our convoy proceeded with the tank truck leading the way. I was thankful to be in the second truck with a load of drill pipe.

I estimated the large tank to be within about six inches from the trolley lines. Every time the low boy would hit a bump in the street, the tank would bounce up a few inches. "God! There it goes," I thought. "A 'fried' water tank, along with the truck and the driver." The tank truck driver insisted that his 'swamper' ride with us. As he said, "No use both of us gettin' killed." It was a scary hour or so before we were free of the power line danger. At the south end of Calgary was an older motel and all the trucks pulled in there. We congratulated the driver of the tank truck. He said he was OK but would never do that again.

One of the younger men from our happy caravan took a taxi to the nearest liquor store. He said it was to celebrate our adventure through the city. I had not acquired the taste for the stuff but helped them drink the 'mix'. They were sure a good bunch of fellows. After a late supper the night before and well deserved sleep we all got up to a light breakfast and an early start. No other problems were anticipated, we should be in Maple Creek, Saskatchewan in time for supper. Little did we know.

It was snowing lightly that Tuesday morning when we left Calgary. It was near the end of March, snow was expected. As we traveled south about 25 miles from Calgary, we encountered a large iron bridge that had iron girders criss-crossed on the top structure to lend support to the iron side beams. It was another problem for the tank truck. The tank was much too high. It would definitely not fit under the support beams of the bridge. The solution was actually quite simple, but very time consuming. With a winch line attached to the metal skid ramp on which the tank was mounted, we carefully pulled the tank off the rear of the low boy. The tank, which was on its skid ramp, was then slowly pulled across the bridge. This of course took up both the north and south portions of the travel lanes on the bridge. Yes, the traffic was stopped for quite some time both ways. I was sure that we would hear from irate, impatient drivers. That was not the case. Most of the drivers honked, smiled and waved. I noticed that some of them were taking pictures. I guess it was kind of comical in a way.

The big tank was then re-loaded onto the low boy. As our convoy angled its way east towards the Saskatchewan border, it was snowing very heavily. This was not the weather that we had hoped for. The wind was blowing in gusts estimated at 50 to 60 miles per hour. The tank on the low boy looked like an uncontrollable big sail on a lost ship on a foggy, rough sea. The wind finally won. The big low boy with the tank was blown sideways into the ditch with snow swirling around it. With winches from the other trucks and half frozen men out in the blizzard, we finally got the low boy back on the road.

At this point, the snow had drifted around and under all the trucks. With tingling cold hands and ears, we shoveled snow for hours. It was a losing battle. We just got one side shoveled out and the other side had blown in with snow. No other traffic was on that forsaken road in the bald prairies of Saskatchewan. We slept in the 'comfort' of our trucks that night.

The next day we were fortunate enough to follow a snow plow into Maple Creek. For three days we could not move a wheel. Even the Trans-Continental train was stranded. The entire crew was broke by now. We had to get money to eat. One of the older men, who was in charge of our expedition and had a company credit card, had convinced a garage owner to give us cash and consider it as the sale of a couple of truck tires. We ate very well that day.

The storm finally subsided after three days. The roads were plowed out on the fourth day. The rig move to the specified location was uneventful. This was up on a gently, sloping hill. All the snow had been blown off this high ground. That first clear night on the rig site, you could see the lights of seven small towns in the distance. The full moon and glittering stars looked like God's beacons illuminating his many wonders. It was beautiful in the eyes of a youngster from the coal mines.

Our return to Edmonton with the empty trucks on comparatively good roads with happy companions was an absolute pleasure. The trip was an experience to forever cherish. I experienced many adventurous aspects of the oil business, some as follows: drilling 'mud' delivery, roughneck, seismic crew member, water truck driver, office accounts, etc. I'm very grateful to have lived in the oil boom era and had the opportunity to participate in a venture that had such a positive effect on all the citizens of Alberta and is still a major factor in our economy.

Dick Johnson (1997)

Fernand (Fern) Juneau

Fern started working in the oil patch in 1952, as a roughneck on the rigs. He changed to trucking and spent four years hauling oilfield equipment. Fern was also involved with moving supplies with pack horses into base camps for seismic crews in the mid-fifties. He now owns High Level Hot Shot, Tank and Pump Rentals. He and his wife Agnes, have lived in High Level for twenty-two years.

I was doing some hay hauling and living at Pincher Creek when my wife and I moved to Edmonton in the fall of 1952.

I got a job with Jensen Oilfield Ditchers. I remember they bought a new truck. They flew me to Montreal in 1954. I picked up this yellow Mac truck and drove it back to Edmonton.

I worked for Shirley Brothers with that truck as well. I did the hauling for Northern Oilfield Ditchers but when it wasn't busy with them, I would haul for Shirley Brothers. I worked at that for about a year.

There were no days off. You just drove until you got tired and you went to sleep in the truck or wherever you could get a place to sleep. Some of those places weren't very good in those days. In Drayton Valley, Shirley Brothers had a little shack set up for the truckers to sleep in.

In 1954, I roughnecked for awhile in Lloydminster, for Paul Guthrie Development.

Just before I got married, my dad, my future brother-in-law Walt Marshall, his brother Bud and I went up to Fort Vermilion to look at land to homestead. We had a dream of ranching or farming.

My parents went up to Fort Vermilion. We made the decision to go up there, and in 1956 we moved there too. My brother Jake and I rented a meat market. I did the livestock buying, my brother did the butchering and my wife wrapped the meat. We used to ship meat to Yellowknife on the plane from Fort Vermilion once a week.

One day, we were at the airport shipping the meat. There we met some men from State Exploration, a company from Texas. They had come in from Texas to begin seismic work in the Fort Vermilion area, to do gravity and magnetometer testing. They wanted men, packhorses and all else that went with organizing this expedition.

My brother and I got the job. This work was 55 miles into the bush south of Fort Vermilion, towards Red Earth. There was no road in there in those days. We rode horseback and used pack horses to pack the equipment. We got things started, with several men and thirty-seven horses.

When we first got those horses, they weren't broke to pack or anything, so there was some real rodeo stuff going on in the camp in the mornings. One horse that I bought for my cook, Pat Lafluer, was a real spunky little horse. When they got the pack on her, she started bucking and there was pots and pans and groceries all over the place.

I hired six people (slashers) to cut lines about three feet wide, just wide enough for a horse and pack to go through. One of the engineers was talking about the party chief and commented, "I don't know where he gets it from. He's got no compass, no surveyors, no tools, but he's right on target every time."

We had two teams and two wagons. We'd go back and forth from Fort Vermilion to this base camp, hauling supplies. My late brother, Richard, and Hugh Flett drove the supply wagons.

One day, Richard was driving one of the teams. They hit a soft spot on the trail and the horses stopped pulling. They just balked and he couldn't get them going. Finally, he unhooked the team, tied them up, proceeded to unload the wagon.

He then took the wagon apart, moved away from the soft spot and put it back together. After that, he hooked up the team and away they went. When he got to camp he told me, "I'm not driving those horses again."

We stayed in tents and the kitchen was a lean to. The main party chief got up one morning, went to the mess tent and poured himself a coffee and nearly choked. The slashers had made strong tea. They didn't drink coffee.

We worked for the company for three months. Dick Mitchell was my head packer. We didn't make too much money, but we learned lots. We learned we should have had a contract.

After it froze up, we all came home and then we started using dogteams to move the supplies and instruments. Gid Garstad, my late brother-in-law, worked for them or me, with the seismic crew. Gid was a hell of a worker and he knew what to do and how to do it.

They were all hard workers. I had good help. It was a great experience - for us as well as the Americans. Some of them had never even been on a horse, but they learned. The horses just grazed. We had bells and hobbles on them at night.

In closing this part of the story, I'd like to give a special thanks to my brother, the late Richard Juneau. A special thanks to the rest, including the late Gid Garstad and the late Pat Lefluer.

That winter, in 1957, Jake and I got rid of the meat market and we moved to the homestead. We drove school buses to keep the food on the table. We let the oilfield boom years from 1956 to the early 1960's all go by. We were raising the kids and we didn't really want to leave home for long periods of time.

We still had the dream of farming, homesteading and ranching, and finally the government made money available to anyone who wished to improve their operations. One day we were talking and my dad said, "You know boys, I don't like this business of borrowing money. When the government tells you to do one thing, you should do the opposite."

We didn't listen, we borrowed the money. At the same time, money was made available to every Tom, Dick and Harry in south and central Alberta, as well as Saskatchewan. It seemed that everyone bought cattle.

We had a nice bunch of cattle but after awhile, the prices went down. Interest rates went up to the point where the profit from the cattle wasn't even paying the interest on the money borrowed. I finally had to take the bull by the horns and go to work in the winter time.

I was tanking for T & D Carriers, hauling crude oil out of Rainbow Lake. I worked thirteen or fourteen hours a day for two months straight and came home in the spring. Every cent that I made driving the tanker was put back into the farm. One day I said to my wife, "It don't make much sense. Here I work like hell, putting two months in one, and I'm just coming in and putting the money down on the payments for the farm. I'm going to sell those cows." I got rid of the cows, and in 1975 I went back into the oilfield industry.

I went to see the manager at Nowsco and I asked him, "Do you have a job for me George?" I knew George Adams from years ago, when we used to haul fuel on the Mackenzie Highway from Grimshaw to Hay River. He said, "You're not serious." I said, "Yeah, I need a job, call me if you need me. I'm at home."

It wasn't very long after that and the phone was ringing for me to go to work. I drove a truck for Nowsco for seven years. I was trucking bulk cement to oil wells.

I got a pickup truck and I began doing some hotshotting on the side. In those years, I was never satisfied with what I had, I wanted more. The hotshot business was turning out pretty good and I had to hire drivers and a dispatcher.

One day the managers changed at Nowsco and I was told that it was either Nowsco or the hotshot. "Well" I said, "I think it will have to be the hotshot."

About that time, through my brother-in-law, Ray, I met up with Don Miller from Zetta Oilfield Rentals. He put some equipment up there for me to rent on a commission basis. From then on, it worked into a pretty good business in the oilfield rentals. I still have pumps and tanks to rent. The oil patch has always been there for me. I should have stuck with it, straight through, but I didn't. Hindsight is better than foresight.

If I could do it over: I don't think I would change anything. God gave us the freedom of choice and, if we knew what would happen in the future then it might not always be so good. That's the way I feel.

Fern Juneau (1997)

Curt Kobza

Curt began working on the seismic rigs at age 15 with Century Geophysical. When he started on the big rigs, he roughnecked and worked his way up to driller within 18 months. In 1977, Curt went overseas. While his young family was based in Singapore, his work took him to New Zealand, Scotland, the Far East, the Middle East and Southeast Asia. He owns Triple K Oilfield Services, a company that provides water pumping and vacuum truck service. Curt's dream has come true. He now lives in a house where he can look out any window and see a thoroughbred race horse. The oil patch helped him realize his dream. Curt and his wife, Debbie live on a small farm north of Gibbons.

I started in the 1960's. I think I left home when I was 14 or 15 years old. It was 1967 when I got my first job working seismic for Century Geophysical. We were sitting in Pacific 66 at the time, in High Level. It was probably between midnight and one o'clock in the morning and this drunk guy came in. The only reason I think he was looking for a hand was because he was too drunk to drive out to work where his crew was. He walked up to our table, there's myself and four of my buddies from Fort Vermilion sitting there. He came up to the table and asked, "Any of you guys want a job here? If you do, stand up." I went to stand up and a couple of my buddies grabbed me by my shoulders and sat me back down and told me that he wanted to fight me. But I just stood back up anyway. He said, "I think you're big enough." Then he asked me, "How old are you?" I told him fifteen. He said, "Well, you're hired." He asked me if I had a driver's license and I told him no. He then asked me, "Well, can you drive?" I told him that I could. So we went to Zama Lake and up the Checeli. Checeli is northwest of Zama Lake.

I sent all my money home. I was working with this driller, Art Kitsman, who was from Berwyn and he was a great guy. We learned to play a lot of poker in camp. I won enough money that winter to pay for my socks and mitts and buy Art cigarettes. We had a lot of Englishmen working on that camp. A couple of times it got pretty hairy. We got into fights over poker games. I remember that there was this one time when they were throwing tomatoes at me. Art came in and the fight was over because he kind of watched out for me.

We worked up there until New Year's' Eve. We moved the camp from Zama Lake to Fort Nelson. We stayed up Fort Nelson until April 5th when we moved out to Calgary. I worked in the yard for Century for a couple of months in the spring and I got lonesome and went home. I hung around home for a couple of months and then I went to Pine Point.

I worked on the diamond drills up there for two or three years before I started on the oil rigs. I started in Pine Point with Sedco Drilling. They had come up there to do some water wells for Cominco Mines. I hired on with Sedco and came to Alberta with them. I never looked back after that. It was always the oil rigs after that. I worked my way up to be a driller for Sedco. Fritz Lazonte gave me my first drilling job. I drilled for them a while, then worked for High Tower Drilling and I also drilled for Loffland. When one rig shut down, we went to another rig. At that time, you could go to any drilling company and you had a job. It was that busy. Times were great.

In 1975, I went to work in the Arctic. We had some great times up there. I was working with a couple of guys from RockyLane - Serge Scholtz and Larry Jensen. We kind of used to bet who would sneak more whiskey up there. I remember one time when we ended up there with 22 bottles between the three of us. We got in 's—' up there for drinking but I guess we were a pretty good crew because they never did 'run us off'. Lots of guys were let go. There were some good guys up there and one of the guys, I'll never forget, was Wally Storchuk. He was an engineer for Esso. He had a 'mean bark' but he was a great guy. As far as I know Wally is still working in the oil patch somewhere. Carl Kennedy was another good guy who absolutely hated me for drinking and raising 's—' up in the Arctic, and I think I hated him just as much at the time. I met him again over in Malaysia.

After Deb and I got married, we went to Australia for Rictor Baud. It looked like a good deal but we nearly starved to death over there. We went broke. Fifteen Canadian drillers went over there and they all had relatives with money or something like that. They borrowed money to come home but we couldn't. We had to just keep going. But I never gave up.

When it didn't work out for me in Australia, I phoned a few drilling companies in Singapore. The first guy who I talked to over there was Hugh Stevens who was with Westburn here. I had worked for Hugh in Canada. He said to me, and this was on June 22nd, "Curt, I'll guarantee you a job on August 1." I told him, "Hugh I can't wait that long." I hung up the phone and I phoned Western Offshore Waterco Drilling. I talked to Luke Smith who was the rig manager there. He asked me what kind of rigs that I had worked on and I told him. He asked, "How soon can you get over here?" I said, "How soon can you send me a plane ticket?" He said, "I can get you a plane ticket as early as tomorrow afternoon." I said, "Well, if you can, then just let me know." I more or less told him that I wasn't leaving my family in Australia. I did have enough money to fly them to Singapore. We stayed with some friends in Singapore when we got over there.

That's where I ran into Carl Kennedy when I went to work for Waterco. He was the first man who I ran into on the floor. I just thought to myself, "Curt, you ain't going to be here long because we just hated each other in the Arctic." Well, he must have been glad to see me because he treated me good. He'd been over there a couple or three or four years already by that time. I was his pet on the rig and I probably learned more from him than I did from anybody.

While I was overseas, I worked in the Philippines, all over Asia, Bankok, all over China. I was just off the coast of Vietnam and India. I nearly starved to death in India. I went over there on a 'fishing' job that should have taken about a week and I was there for 39 days. I lost 43 pounds because the food was so terrible. I was working for TriState and I was told to take along a care package. I did but when I got there, I met up with a Haliburton crew who had been there a week and I gave it to them. I couldn't tell them not to eat it.

I have worked in Scotland, New Zealand, the Far East and the Middle East. When the war started between Iraq and Iran, I was in what they called the 'neutral zone'. We were drilling a hole for A.O.C. (Arabian Oil Company) which is owned by the Arabian Saudi government. We could see the fighters flying. They looked like they were five miles away but they were probably 20 or 30 miles away. Deb was in Singapore then, and that's about the time that our son Colin was born.

We left when they bombed the western rigs over there. We were there for just about a month and there was a sour gas well going about 13,000 feet. We were just about to drill into that when Leon Moore called up there and asked, "How's tower pushing it?" I was night push. Then he said, "You guys just plug that hole and McDermitt is on the way. And you get that rig to hell out of there." I tell you that we were a happy bunch of boys. We were a day and a half plugging that rig. By the time that McDermitt got there, we were ready to 'off load' that platform and head back to Singapore.

When I was pushing for Brinkerhoff, we were drilling for Conico in what is called the Natuna Islands, in south Indonesia. We were flying in an old 'albatross' plane. It was a great plane and we had a good pilot but I tell you when you get those storms over there, they're pretty hairy and scary. We were flying in a storm and we were lost for four hours flying up and through the mountains. We were supposed to land in a specific little bay and the pilot couldn't find his bearings. If there was a break in the cloud, these old mountains would just look like they were at the end of the wings of the airplane.

Another time, we were crew changing. We were flying in a DC-3. I was usually one of the first guys to get on the plane. We were flying out of this little airport, just outside of Singapore. I went to buckle my seat belt and the seat belt was torn off, so I moved up. I went to buckle my seat belt again and there was no buckle on the seat belt. One seat belt was tied on with hay wire. I got off that God damn plane. We were already taxiing out to the airstrip but I just kicked the door open. The pilot heard it and stopped. I just told him flat out that I wasn't flying anymore in this piece of junk. Well, I think that plane made two more crew changes out there. On the second one, the plane crashed and we lost nine 'hands' because of junk airplanes. There were 17 guys on that flight and nine of them got killed.

Life insurance was all that they got. The families were flown home and taken care of that way but the families didn't get any other compensation other than the life insurance.

When we went to Saudi Arabia in 1978, we went there with a good grocery supply, including bacon and ham. Some of the boys had nude porno pictures all over their rooms. Pornography is against the law in Saudi Arabia. One day the Coast Guards, who were Moslems, came in and ripped up all our porno magazines. They went into our deep freezers and threw out all of our bacon and ham. All of our pork went overboard.

I went to India on a 'fishing' job and when I was finished, I had to take the train, because the choppers weren't flying for some reason. I was give a train ticket, - 'first class'. It looked good on paper. I climbed into this 'first class' cabin and there were goats, chickens and pigs in there. That was my 18 hour train ride from Vidguwada to Madras, India. You haven't seen poverty until you've been to India. I've seen things over there that I don't think Mexico could hold a candle to. I've even seen dead little babies floating in a river. Their food is something else.

One of the best places we were in, was Louisiana. Debbie and the boys came down with me and we stayed a whole year. It was a great place to work and live.

We enjoyed it in Singapore. We were there for nine years. When we came home it was time to come home because I was tired of flying. The six years that I spent with TriState, I spent more time in the air than I did on the ground. I was one of their youngest 'fisherman' worldwide. They sent me to all the exotic places where all the old timers wouldn't go. I never turned down a job.

There was one stretch there that I was in five different countries. I left home November 15 and didn't get back home until sometime in March. I left Singapore to work in Holland then New Zealand. From New Zealand I was sent to Australia. I just flipped out on my boss and I was given a full month off with pay and my bonus.

Most memorable recollection: I always wanted to come back to Alberta and start my own business and I was one happy boy when I knew that I was coming home. During the nine years that I worked over there, even though we came home for vacations each year, it seemed like the weight was never off my shoulders. The weight left when I got on that plane for the final time and I knew that I was coming home to stay. There's nothing like Alberta, people can talk and say what they want and complain about our taxes but there's no place in the world like Alberta. There's nothing like Alberta beef. When we came home, it was to come home to Alberta, to enjoy

Alberta beef and to start a business in the oil patch. I couldn't believe how much things had progressed here in the nine years that I was away. It's unbelievable. When we came home in 1985, I was surprised that Red Earth country still had a lot of exploration opportunity.

If I could do it over: I wouldn't change a thing about the way my life went. No, nothing. Because this oil patch has been great to me. If I ever had to live again, I'd be in the 'oil patch'. It does change your life.

After picking roots and rocks as a kid and then to go to work on a rig and see a real pay cheque - that was something! It wasn't too long before I got my first car. I got my driver's license when I was 15 years old. I just lied about my age because at that time you didn't have to show your birth certificate. I walked in and took a driver's test and wrote the exam. My first vehicle was a 1966 Pontiac Parisiane. I bought that car in 1970. I paid cash for it.

Curt Kobza (1997)

Lewis (Lou) Kolodychuck

Lou has been retired for twenty years. He lives in Edmonton and has worked on the drilling rigs for most of his working days. Starting out as a roughneck, he worked his way up to become toolpush and had many good years in the oil patch.

I was originally from the Holden area. I was staying at my brother's place in Leduc and I tried to get a job on the rig all winter. One day someone didn't show up for work and I was there, so I got the job. That was in 1949 and I worked on the rigs until 1975.

Yeah, they tried to play some tricks on me, being a new man, but my brother had told me about some of them, such as the one about taking a pail of water up the derrick to pour it on the water table. Another one was to try to get the new guys to clean the spark plugs on the diesel motors.

Not many safety measures were adhered to in those days. It was hurry, hurry. When the toolpush said 'hurry', he didn't mean walk fast, he meant RUN.

When I started, things were really booming around Leduc, Camrose, Haylakes and the Joseph Lake Field near New Serepta.

Our rig was the second one in after Leduc #1. It was a Dominion Rig, owned by the Spencer Brothers. One of these brothers used to go out to the rig, wearing a pair of cover-alls. He would pose as a new man, saying he'd been hired at the office, that they had sent him out to work in the yard. He would work with the men and at the end of the day, he would invite them all for supper and then tell them who he was. Cody Spencer was a great guy!

I was in an accident in Fort St. John, B.C. I was helping to tighten the chains when the trucker jerked on one of the lines, it came open, got away on him and I was in the way for a direct hit. It tore up my mouth and bruised me up some. Spencer was more concerned than I was and called me three of four times from Calgary to tell me if I wasn't satisfied with the care, he would send a plane and bring me into the city. He really did look after his men.

Drayton Valley was a story in itself. There was nothing there and then all of a sudden there were about 10,000 people. No gravel or paved roads, no accommodation.

Some people were sleeping in culverts. When it rained, they had to move out of there. It rained a lot then. There were make-shift shacks or lean-to's in the bush. Most men slept in their cars, if they had cars. There was no extra pay to compensate any of this. The wages were $2.75 an hour on the big rigs. It was good pay, far above tradesman wages. I was 23 years old and had a farm. Farm workers got jobs because they were used to hard work and most of them were mechanically inclined.

Nothing was there, when it all started in Drayton Valley. There was just a small grocery store, a post office and a small restaurant. I was lucky we stayed at Violet Grove. The company supplied bunkhouses. A brother-in-law of mine had a trailer so we had a place to eat. Others bought food at the store. One man, a very thrifty Dutchman, used to buy a loaf of Honey Boy bread and margarine; that was his lunch. We nick-named him Honey Boy.

In order to get to work, we would leave in a wagon pulled by a tractor. Usually there was a wagon full of men going out to the work site. It rained and kept on raining. The tractor couldn't make it through the mud so a cat was brought in. When it became impossible for the cat to pull the wagon through the mud then the men took off their shoes and walked in. There were a few older guys that couldn't make the hills and had to stop, rest and turn back. They couldn't get back to work before it dried up.

Two granaries were pulled together and this was named Penny's Cafe. One part was the kitchen, the other the eating area. There were 300 people coming in for food every day, around the clock. I got food poisoning three times. As time went on, better cafe's were built. Some were owned by politicians. There was about twelve murders that I know of and not one of them was publicized, in the paper or on the radio. These things were hushed up. They did not want that kind of publicity.

There were no unions in the oilfields but I was never mistreated. When you did your work, they looked after you and treated you fair. Sometimes it was eight to ten years before you could get a drilling job. Later you might get a toolpush job. There was no seniority, it was the best man for the job.

A few people had mineral rights on their land if the land had been bought during a specific two year time period. Hudson Bay and Canadian Pacific Railway both held mineral rights. Some people became very wealthy.

I went to work overseas (Libya) in the early 60's. I worked mostly overseas after that but did pick up the odd job in Canada. On Off-Shore Drilling the oil workers were not in a union but the mechanics and electricians were unionized under the Maritimes Law.

Once, on one of these jobs a light bulb burned out over a guy's bunk and the electrician was asked to change it.

Three days went by with the electrician lounging in his bunk reading porno magazines. The guy got tired of waiting and put the bulb in himself. You know what hit the fan - you weren't supposed to do that. It wasn't your job!

There's always time lost and the cost of operations doubles when there's a union involved.

Red Earth, which is east of Peace River, was something! Red Earth was just a snake trail going through the bush. It was bad in the winter. Twenty miles of road to the sawmill, and from there, it was a 'bull dozed' road for about 100 miles.

One time I was driving out and halfway to the camp my wheels went down deep in the mud and I was stuck!! One of the coring outfits was coming out with a company car. He didn't care so much about the car because it wasn't his and he was coming through. I could do nothing with my car so I headed back to Peace River with the core hand, taking my 'gas reserve' with us. I always carried a 15 gallon barrel of gas in my trunk.

We were in that twenty five mile stretch of muskeg for about twenty hours. We used up the core hand's spare gas, plus the drum I had, but we made it to the saw mill, and then finally to Peace River.

They had to corduroy the road using wood blocks, one beside the other like a bridge, so we could get through the muskeg.

The second year we were able to go through on the road until about mid-March. The Commonwealth rig didn't make it out by that time. There were trucks stranded all along that road and they sat there all summer. This cost the oil companies a fortune. Since the rig was on the trucks, the trucking company got paid and the men collected pay all summer. Some of the other companies involved were General Petroleum, Shell Oil, Gulf Oil.

Some guys got lost because one road looked just like another one. One of the drivers had a load of gas, strayed off on one road and drove around for three days before he got back out. Luckily he had that gasoline with him. The men worked so hard, they were human gin poles!

Today they get a truck to move things. It was hard work and sweat in those days. Living conditions were pretty rough.

Lou Kolodychuck (1995)

Dale McBride

Dale worked 26 years in the oil patch. In 1946 he left the Navy and arrived back home in Bassano. He began working on a seismic crew for Sun Oil. One year later, he began working for Regent Drilling and worked for that company for 25 years. He was Field Superintendent for several years. He had the opportunity to be involved in the oil patch before Leduc #1, and has seen many changes throughout the years.

I started working in 1946 for Sun Oil in Bassano. The company came in from Beaumont, Texas, and I was able to get a job on their rig. We seismographed the countryside, which included Bassano, Strathmore and Brooks. The job lasted late into the fall, to November. They decided they would pack it up, as things were freezing up and they weren't used to the cold weather. We loaded everything on the freight cars. The boys who had come up from Texas drove some of the vehicles back. The rest went in their cars, and there was no more oilfields that year. That following winter, in February, the Leduc field was discovered.

In the Spring, Regent Drilling had moved up from Chincoulee to Bassano and three or four of us fellows from Bassano got a job on that little rig. I was one of the later ones on that rig. Walter Leskowski and Art worked on that rig. We finished up in June and loaded the rig on the railroad and sent it off to Leduc. The toolpusher had phoned Leskowski and myself and we hopped on the train and headed up to the new oilfield.

Harold Ross, the toolpusher, met us at the station at Leduc and drove us over to Calmar. Regent had a bunkhouse with pretty small rooms but there were three compartments in it and that was our quarters. We had a little wash pan and the showers were at a chicken processing plant across the road.

For meals we ate at the Shanty, the restaurant where all the young girls were doing the cooking and serving. My friend and I had had a couple of beers one night and were late coming to the Shanty. There was nobody around at night much, and I wasn't supposed to be in the kitchen, but I kind of snooped in there to see what the girls were doing. One of the girls was making toast about as fast as you can make toast with a toaster.

Every time the toast popped up she threw both pieces under the counter. I asked her, "What are you doing with all the toast?" She answered, "Well, I'm getting ready for all you guys in the morning."

Under the counter was this huge cardboard box, filled with toast! The toast didn't taste dry at all in the morning. We were always hungry and so it tasted like candy to us!

We jammed that place in the morning because we all had to be on the job at 8 am. My driller was Barney Babbs. He drove the crew truck and Mike Yaskiw also worked on our crew. Barney knew all the Turner Valley people there and he used to talk to Mr. Tosh and some of the older Turner Valley hands.

After a summer of working at Leduc we got an oil well on Spotzes farm at Leduc and spent most of the fall swabbing, working probably a month getting the well in production. Mr. Spotz threw an enormous party. All the people that were partners in the well were flown in from Calgary. C.C. Cross was there, along with all the big partners in the oil company. It was quite a success!

We moved our bunkhouse into Edmonton. We were at 104th Street, about four blocks south of Whyte Avenue. We spent the winter there behind the Calgary Trail Service Station and worked out in Leduc. Later, we ended up getting a new rig and our destination was Major, Saskatchewan. Pat Toner was one of our drillers. After that, we spent the summer in the Marwayne area. I was set up as a driller. The other drillers were Jim Davidson, Milton Vossler and Barney Babb.

We moved to the Redwater Field, then on to Egremont, Calling Lake and Athabasca. We were caught in the bush the following spring and left part of the rig in there. From there we came out to Edmonton and began drilling in the Whitemud area. We lived at the Commercial Hotel in the southside of Edmonton. This was 1949 and we pretty well drilled in the Leduc area and the Whitemud area all summer.

When we ended up at Rochester, Bob Davidson was the toolpush. We shut the rig down there at Christmas time. At that time, our company had bought Northern Development. The boys shut the rig down at Whitemud, pulled the drill pipe into the casing and just left it.

I was boarding at a place in west Edmonton when I got this phone call. Milton Vossler and I got together. I was to go up to Rochester and get the clothes and Milt was to round up some of his men and go out to this strange rig at Whitemud, run the pipe in the hole and get it back drilling again. It was about 30o F below zero. I came in around midnight in a snowstorm, and we got this little northern rig back running again.

We spent the rest of the time, well into February, on that rig. At that time Dick Olsen was the toolpush. He was leaving and I was set up as toolpush. Ross Anderson was one of the drillers, Carl Guthrie was his derrick man.

We were in places like Hardisty and Westlock, then we went south to Barons.

I was married in 1951. The church was booked, the bridesmaids were ready and my bride had her wedding dress. My field superintendent asked, "Well, who's gonna relieve you, Dale?" I answered, "I got a driller I can set up." I didn't think I wanted to put the wedding off. He was set up and I went away on a two week honeymoon.

After we came back, we were moved to Milk River Ridge. Just before Christmas, my wife and I went into Calgary and bought a little trailer. It was much better than that cold little room we had in town. We spent our first Christmas in that little trailer.

I can recall putting up a clothesline out there on the ridge. I thought I had done a really good job. I had put this clothesline up with the frost in the ground. What can you do on the prairie? A big chinook was blowing. The first wash, a white wash, was blowing in the wind. All of a sudden, down comes the clothesline into all this mud. Boy, I'll tell you what, there was some big tears around that place!

We moved again and drilled a hole in Lakeview, and from there we went to Ferintosh. We moved to Gwynne, then to Provost, Alliance, Youngstown, Halkirk, and Hanna. From there to Big Valley where we stayed for over one year. We lived on the leases and moved around to fourteen holes right around Big Valley. After that we moved to Czar and Rimbey.

In the fall we went in to the Simmonette, south of Grande Prairie. We finished that hole and moved on into Kaybob in 1953. The drilling site was situated 12 miles back of the present Fox Creek airstrip. There was nothing there, only a trail into the bush. We went in on the frost, in March. That's where we spent the summer. During the spring and summer the road was being built out to the south end of the Iosegon Hill. The Chevron-Standard road was finished in the fall and we were able to drive out of the bush on it.

In the meantime we supplied the rig by airplane and we had stockpiled fuel and whatever. There were five families at the lease. It was a real experience. In the summer of 1956, I relieved Jim Davidson at Christmas Tree Creek. This was Imperial Oil's first well in that area and that's where Carson Lake is. We were twenty miles straight north of Whitecourt and we were serviced by a helicopter out of Whitecourt. This was south of Swan Hills, in the Judy Creek Field. The pilot asked me if I wanted to check the airstrip out. So we got in the helicopter and looked at the airstrip just over by Judy Creek. During that time the forestry officer came along and said, "We have to have your helicopter and your men, to fight fire." So we left a few men at the rig and took the rest of the crew, flew them over, and they spent the day putting the fire out. Everything was OK. They got it out and we flew them back again.

We were at Virginia Hills in 1957. In 1958, we left the rig stacked at Whitecourt and moved to Pincher Creek in the Carbondale area. We drilled the rest of the summer, then on to Didsbury and back to Rimbey, in the Westerose area.

We moved to Rocky Mountain House in 1959. We had television, complete with antenna and rabbit ears. The reception wasn't always the best but we had TV. The next summer, in 1963, we were at Lodgepole, west of there. We moved to Fort Assiniboine and then on to Swan Hills in 1963, and during that year I was set up as Field Superintendent.

We acquired a yard in Swan Hills, and we could store pipe, etc. I moved my trailer onto that property and then in 1966, we moved from Swan Hills into Edmonton. I continued working as Field Superintendent until 1971.

I stopped working for Regent Drilling to go building houses. After the collapse of the housing in 1982, the only time that I went back and worked on the rigs was one winter with Homco International out of Nisku.

I went back in as a 'fisherman' for Homco in 1985. The rigs had been upgraded a lot. I don't know what was so noticeable except the rigs were better than when I had worked in 1971. In the early days there was more manual labor. There was more moving pipe by hand; today they're using cherry-pickers and things we didn't have in those days. When we dug ditches we used a shovel, now they use a bob-cat. Things like that.

If I could do it over: I guess it would be the safety factor of a lot of things we did. It's scary to think of the chances we took. Some of the things that I have done, I couldn't think of doing them now. I remember one time we were pulling a loaded pipe truck up the Simmonette hill with a cat. I decided that I would take a cat-line, a piece of rope or a chain and tie it onto the pipe truck. I was going to pull my truck and trailer up the hill behind that.

This darned old cat didn't have enough ice-lugs to hardly get up the hill by itself. Over the bank, on that turn on the hill, you could see nothing down there but the river running. When I think of that time!! And I had my wife's car tied on behind that yet. She and the little girl were in her car.

We did this in order to save cat time. Halfway up I began to realize the danger, but by then there was no turning back. I started thinking, 'if one of these chains breaks, I'll never be able to hold any of this load. It'll all slip over the bank'.

We lived in the 26 foot trailer for five years. We bought a forty footer and lived in that for the rest of the time we were out in the field. The trailer was getting a bit small so while we were living in Swan Hills, we decided to build a skid house beside the trailer.

The trailer was 8 feet by 40 feet and the skid house was 14 feet by 42 feet. These were connected and we then had a comfortable 880 square feet of living space. We lived in Swan Hills for four years without moving. We watched the new town grow and even took up curling and enjoyed several bonspiels during the time we lived there.

Dale McBride (1997)

Harry Nazarenko

Harry set up shop in 1947 in the Waldorf Hotel, next to the bar. Business was booming, Leduc had oil rigs all around the area and oil people just kept coming in. He remembers working in the bar some Saturday nights until it closed at 10 pm, then cutting hair until 3 am. Harry still works in his barber shop and doesn't want to retire just yet. He and his wife, Mary lives on a farm near Leduc.

I was a young barber when it all happened in Leduc. The Waldorf Hotel opened up July 1, 1947. I came there July 15, 1947. There was a little barber shop in the corner and Mary had the beauty shop right next door next to the bar. I was just a young fellow and they had a barber shop set up with a chair and everything. All I had to bring there were my tools and set up shop. There was a lot a activity when I came in. Men's haircuts were 35 cents and a shave was 'two bits' but then you could buy a meal for 35 or 50 cents. I remember when I finally got to a dollar haircut. Boy I thought that was really something. That was in 1953 or 1954. We were cutting hair for 35 cents, then 45 cents and then 55 cents up until then.

The hotel was the only place in town that had running water. It had it's own septic tank in front and a big cistern at the back. Water was hauled water in by trucks.

Leduc was still a farmer's town so it was a Saturday night town. During the week I wouldn't get too many customers. The oilmen came in during the week but the farmers came in on Saturdays. Everybody would be busy and they would wind up at the bar. After the bar closed at about 10 o'clock then I got my customers. I cut hair until 3 am many times on Saturday nights. I cut hair until I had no more customers. If I hadn't done that, I'd have missed out on the extra business. In those days, the farmers worked in their fields so they didn't come in during the week, like today.

There were over a hundred rigs here at one time. They came from all over. On the weekends, you couldn't buy a loaf of bread in Leduc because it was all sold out. They would have to drive in to Edmonton when the bread sold out. Draft beer would be sold out. There was nothing left but bottled beer on many Saturday nights when the oil rush came here between 1947 and 1949.

In 1950, things had changed. The business people were more organized and ordered more food and beverage. Farm boys came into Leduc at that time and even married men came in here to work. They didn't intend to stay because you know how oil is. You might be here today and gone tomorrow. But they stayed and the young guys hadn't really made big money 'til they got on the rigs. Some of those guys had big pay cheques. They didn't buy whiskey by the bottle, they bought it by the case. Some Americans came up and some Canadians came in from Turner Valley. The rigs are shut down now. Many companies sold out and are no longer around.

I remember working some Saturday nights. I'd close the barber shop quite early and then I would go work in the bar. I remember carrying a tray of twenties the whole night. There was no two glasses of beer like there is today, but you could set down as many as the tables would hold. The tables were about a yard wide and they were full of beer all the time. Six guys could sit around the table and these were usually guys in between shifts.

The rigs went 24 hours with 16 men to a rig. One shift would come off and the first place that they would hit was the bar.

We had some garages but they didn't have room to house all the vehicles when it was really cold in the winter time. The toolpushers would have their pickups running in front of the hotel. It was so cold. When they got out they got out in the morning, they wouldn't be able to drive the truck because the front wheels were all frozen up. They would pull the truck into the garage to thaw them out. The vehicles would sit in the garage for maybe an hour or so until the front wheels came loose and away they would go.

Vern Kerber used to build rigs. He still lives in Leduc. At that time they didn't have the rigs that you could fold over and move. The rigs were made of wood and metal and they were put together like a jig-saw puzzle. Imagine, putting together and tightening bolts on a rig like this in 20° F or 30° F below zero. Everyone was in a hurry. They brought this stuff in and they wanted this rig together by the next night. It took longer to drill the holes because they didn't have the proper equipment, to drill, but that changed as time went on. There was lots of drilling going on.

The oil companies made the roads here. When they came out here they had to make roads to get into the well sites. The oil companies got a bull dozer in there, pushed in a grade, put gravel on it and that was it. A lot of farmers around Devon are still using the roads that the oil companies built. Like around the river and around Devon there's a road allowance but it doesn't go any place. It just goes as far as the river. There's no bridge there, so it only serves the people who live right in that area. They call it the Imperial road.

When Leduc got running water, the wells couldn't produce enough water so they built a dam. That dam is just off of Highway #39 and that served the town well. When the airport was built, Leduc got its water from there.

There wasn't a traffic light or even blinking lights in Leduc. I remember Maple Creek, my home town and Leduc were about the same size. Maple Creek is still 2,000 people and Leduc now has a population of 16,000.

During that first year, I remember one time in the bar, this guy threw a full bottle beer bottle across the room and it stuck into the plasterboard wall. Some of the beer was still in the bottle. After that, the guy wasn't in the bar for quite a while. He was escorted out. Steve was a wrestler so he ran a good bar. He didn't have too much trouble in the hotel.

There was mixed drinking in Leduc when the oil patch came in. I used to serve beer on Saturday night. The beer was ten cents a glass and it was a bigger glass than now. I remember going to the bar with my buddy. He and I could sit there all Saturday night and have ten beers. It would cost us a dollar each. That was a lot of beer for that price.

I am still working and I don't want to retire as long as my health holds out. Recently, I received a plaque for 50 years of service from the Leduc Chamber of Commerce. Leduc has come a long ways and the city is gonna grow now and so is Nisku Industrial Park.

If I could do it over: No I don't think I'd change too much. Fifty years went by so quickly. It seems like a dream. Well I'd like to be young again.

Harry Nazarenko (1997)

Jack Roberts

Jack and his sons own Roberts Conductory Cable. He has been involved in the oil business since 1955. He lives on a farm west of Stony Plain.

I had intended on making a career working on the railroad. I was married at age nineteen. I fainted at the end of the ceremony! The wedding was at seven in the evening, I'd had nothing to eat all day and a few drinks of gin didn't assist me at all. After this fainting episode, I recovered quickly and went on to the reception.

I wasn't permitted to be a locomotive engineer, because I had told someone that I had fainted. I continued for another year confined to just being a fireman.

When an opportunity came, in 1955, I decided I'd try something different Everybody was getting involved in the oil business and I began working with Perforating Guns of Canada, which was a wire line company.

I was 21 years old at the time, married, with one child. I remember the starting wages were $225 a month. Because I was married, an exception in my case was made and I started at $250.

I put a lot of effort into the oil patch venture and, when the phone rang, I just went down to the shop without question, telling my wife, "Well, we'll see you when I get home." It could be one day or one week. There weren't regular days off at that time and, of course, no restrictions on hours worked, so I sometimes went from one rig to another without coming back home.

Invariably, if one of the crew forgot to take their overnight bag, it usually turned out he'd be gone for a week. We became superstitious and made sure we had a small bag with shaving gear with us at all times. We were pretty sure, that we would be going home sooner.

After one year I was promoted to an operator of a truck. After four years, I became manager for the Red Deer area. I went on to Calgary and subsequently became involved in the operations of Perforating Guns of Canada.

In 1968, the company was bought out by Dresser Industries and the name was changed to Dresser Atlas. By this time, I was splicing and spooling conductor cable and quite happy doing so. In 1977, there was a change in managers. The new manager and I didn't see-eye-to eye and I quit working there.

I owned a farm west of Edmonton. We had four quarters at that time. The farm was paid for. We had four children and our youngest was finishing the last year of high school. After I quit, Dresser approached me and asked me to work as an outside contractor. That was the beginning of my own business. It turned out to be a very good thing, because not only did Dresser need my services but I found that several other companies were working with wire line.

I was based out of Edmonton. From there I would do a week or two in Swan Hills and later in Rainbow Lake and various places around. I never had to move my family other than from to Red Deer, Calgary and back to Edmonton. So I always felt our family, were very fortunate that we could stay in one place.

There were much fewer paved roads networked throughout Alberta than we enjoy now. Basically, there was just a Calgary to Edmonton highway. Even the road west, towards Drayton Valley, was not paved all the way in 1956.

In the spring of 1957, they were trying to complete a well for Esso, before the thaw. This was a camp job and we were able to drive in with just a little assistance from a cat.

After being there four or five days, the weather really got mild and then it took us a whole day to get out because even the cat got stuck, attempting to pull our equipment out. We had to pick up a long cable in Kinuso and go back to where the cat was stuck. The cat skinner hooked this cable to some trees. We managed to get the cat out and then a different road had to be made to get our vehicles back out to the highway.

I can remember in this particular camp there was a bear hanging around. He wasn't really bothering anybody. The cook would leave food for the bear on the far side of the sump. Some new roughnecks came in and took a shot at it and wounded it.

The cook was pretty upset about this. He told the young roughneck, who had fired the shot, and wounded the bear, "You better go into the bush and try to locate the bear." The roughneck was afraid to go, but finally, a couple of the men went in. When they came back, they said they couldn't find the wounded bear.

The new roughnecks weren't very popular in that camp. You know, if you get on the wrong side of the cook, it's not a good deal.

Speaking of cooks, one recollection I have, back from the mid-sixties, is being up in the area west of High Level, a year or two after the discovery of the Rainbow Lake Field. We were working off a service rig and we were told, "You're not welcome over at the drilling rig and don't go over there expecting to be fed."

We didn't have a mobile phone, there was a work delay so I wanted to phone in to town. I went over to the rig, primarily to phone. The cook recognized me and wanted to know what I was doing there. I told her, "Well, I'm here just to phone. We didn't come over expecting to be fed." "Oh" she said, "I got room for a good dishwasher." One year before, in a camp south of Grande Prairie, the bull cook had run off with the water hauler and the cook had been left on her own.

We were there for eight days. There were times when there wasn't anything for us to do on the well, so I used to do the dishes. It sure did pay off. She made a place at the table and not only fed me but the two guys that were with me as well.

I didn't have many dangerous experiences other than icy roads. Especially around Swan Hills they were bad. There were times if you didn't have chains on your truck and your truck started to spin, you went backwards pretty fast. I was fortunate that I wasn't involved in any serious accidents. Went off the road quite a few times, but no actual damage was done to the vehicle.

We were doing a project in Swan Hills. We had fifteen wells to do for Amoco. A senior engineer was supervising and, during the summer, there were two young engineers out of university. There was no real danger if anybody had thought about it.

We were working on water injection wells. My crew of two thought they had closed the master valve. Actually they had, but there was a flow line injecting water into the well at about 1,100 pounds per square inch. When the hammer took the top off the Christmas tree, it exploded up in the air. My two helpers ran in different directions through the swamp.

I was off to the side, getting ready to get the equipment to run in the well. One of the engineers got his camera out, thinking that it might catch fire but, since we were working with water, there wasn't really any concern. There was no rig, just a wellhead. I found which valve was open and closed it. After all that panic, the crew called me 'Cool Hand Luke'.

Later, during my career, I went to the east coast and did splice line down there on the off-shore rigs. I always had a good feeling about being on an off-shore platform. It wasn't really something you worried about until the Ocean Ranger went down, with the loss of many lives.

After that there was more concern about safety. It was a sobering thing when all those men perished. In the book, "Ocean Ranger", there was something written about the last man to leave the rig before it capsized. His name was Garry Wall. Garry lived in St. John's. There had been a fire, mostly smoke damage to the apartment, Friday evening. His wife phoned out to the rig on Saturday morning to inform Garry about the fire. There were no helicopters going out so Garry was going to wait until Monday, which would be their normal change-out.

After lunch, word come over the radio room that a helicopter had come out to one of the nearby rigs and was about eight miles away. They agreed to stop by and pick Garry up. When the helicopter arrived, it was very windy. It took three attempts before it got on the landing pad and Garry was able to climb aboard and head back to St. John's.

Six or seven hours later the hurricane was in full force and by midnight the rig capsized. All who were on it perished.

Garry Wall was a lucky Newfoundlander. Two years before that, while working in Labrador, the crew was scheduled to leave in a small, four-seater plane. At the last minute, was bumped in favor of a geologist. The plane crashed in bad weather with no survivors.

Another time, Garry slept in and missed the chopper. The crew that were to go with him were reluctant to travel without him. Word of his lucky charm had circulated, but they did finally board the helicopter and go in to work.

In more recent years I went to Africa on an off-shore rig. I was there for a week splicing line. The day before that I was to leave, my travel bags were stolen. I lost my passport and about six hundred bucks. I got a temporary passport and made it home OK

I also went to China for two weeks. I did two lectures in Beijing and Chungking. These lectures were to give the Chinese some assistance in the technical side of splicing and spooling cable. I was able to take my wife with me. The trip was enjoyable and we got to see some of China.

The one thing that could have been different, was that Shirley got to stay in Beijing, in a nice hotel, and I had to stay with the Chinese people and eat their food and drink their beer. They served us two litres of beer at both the noon meal and the evening meal. Then there was a drink we had to drink. It was just like white lightning, or gasoline.

The Chinese love to make speeches and toast their visitors. You are expected knock back one of those little shot glasses full of liqueur after each toast. I can't remember the name of it, but it reminded me of when I was a kid and I used to siphon gasoline and then taste it all the next day.

There was a problem with a cable in Hawaii. They had phoned the manufacturer but a spare cable was not available. The university in Hawaii was given my name, so there again on short notice, my wife and I flew to Oahu, Hawaii and spliced a cable. A ship was going to Indonesia. It was leaving on Wednesday and the cable was to be on it. We arrived the Sunday night before. We spliced the cable on Monday and on Tuesday we spooled it onto the ship. After the ship left on Wednesday, Shirley and I toured the islands, including the big island, and the garden island. We had been to Hawaii before, but it's kind of nice to go again, especially when everything is paid for.

I'm just about ready to retire this year. I'm sixty-three. I will, later on this year, cease to be active in running Roberts Conductory Cable. However, I will probably be available for the odd little junket, should it come up.

I have been going to Alaska for the past 14 years to do work. They have the machinery up there and no one on staff to do the work, so I go up once a month or so. I go to Prudhoe Bay which is the north slope. Actually, I think it was sometime last year that Prudhoe Bay out produced all of Texas in oil production, more than two million barrels a day. Texas production is declining and Prudhoe Bay is still being drilled.

There have been lots of changes since I started in the business. I think the whole oil business has gotten much more sophisticated. When I started, wells would take fifteen days to drill. Now they can be done in three or four days. The seismic information is much more helpful.

When it comes to oilfield logging, the business that I'm in, technology is now quite sophisticated. Computers are very much in use both in tools down the hole and on the surface. The engineer running the survey, turns it on and the computer does the rest. The survey results can even be transmitted from the lease to anywhere via satellite transmission.

A lot more of the work is being done too by contractors as opposed to in-house salaried employees. The work is contracted out and only paid for as needed. Usually the pay is better.

I've really enjoyed the work, but it means there's an adjustment in your home life. Whenever I did get some time off we tried to do family things with our daughter and three sons.

One year in July I was two days late coming back from being on a long job. I didn't even get a chance to go home. My wife had loaded our trailer and met me at the shop as I came in. The kids were all jumping up and down in the station wagon and we just left on vacation from there. She said, "I've got your holiday clothes and when we stop for the night, you can get cleaned up then." We made a point of going on a two week holiday every year.

Quite often when we got back, the phone would be ringing as we pulled up to the house. I'd run in and answer the phone. There would usually be some sort of crisis and, because of my dedication to the company, I would leave and go to the shop and be headed out on a job that same day. My wife would have the pleasure of unloading the trailer and station wagon and then bathing the kids.

I played a bit of golf but didn't get too serious about it because when I was home, the family would go on a picnic, or go swimming, or to the zoo.

I was fortunate to have a wife that would keep the home fires burning while I was away. I'm enjoying life. This year we will be celebrating our forty-fourth anniversary.

Jack Roberts (1997)

James (Jim) Rutherford

Jim has worked a total of 44 years in the oil industry. On discharge from the R.C.A.F. in October 1945, he began working for Imperial Oil, spent eight years working seismic and slimhole drilling. From there, he transferred to construction and spent the rest of his career in various locations in Alberta, B.C., Manitoba, Saskatchewan, Ontario and the North West Territories. Jim and his wife, Dot, live in Edmonton.

I used to work in Turner Valley before 1940. My family moved to Turner Valley in 1929. My dad was working as a steam engineer on the steam rig and I worked in the summer months while going to school. I must have been around 17 or 18 years old or somewhere in there then. Then I started picking up drilling reports daily and samples and bringing them back to the office in Turner Valley, working in the lab and washing and sorting the samples. I decided to join up in the air force in 1940. When I joined up, I went to youth training in Medicine Hat for four months. I first joined the air force in Edmonton on October 4, 1941. I was 21 the same month. And then I was stationed several places in Canada and then I went overseas. I was overseas for three years and returned in September 1945.

In the meantime, I met my wife on the same station in Yorkshire.

She was on motor transport and I was a mechanic. We were on the same station and we married June 9, 1945. I came home in the fall and she came home in April 1946.

After my discharge, I joined Imperial Oil working seismic. I traveled around the country, starting out around Cochrane. Imperial Oil had its first winter seismic crew up in the foothills outside of Edson.

When I came out there was a road ban on. We bought our box which we called home. That 8 by 16 foot trailer. And then from there, our first job after road ban was to Provost.

We bought the trailer in Calgary and we had nothing much as far as household goods so we bought a set of dishes and a few things like towels and other housewares. I decided to jack the trailer up on a jack to check the undercarriage and everything. The trailer fell off the jack and broke all the new dishes. And then we packed everything in boxes. On the floor of the trailer was a patterned linoleum, and the roads of course in those days was terrible. It was mud. We were plowing mud and everything.

We broke the hitch off the trailer and we had to leave it in the ditch overnight. Somebody came and helped us to bring it in to Provost.

We got to Provost and got the trailer set up and started unpacking these boxes. The floor of the trailer was absolutely filthy because the mud had come up the wheel wells. After Dot scrubbed the floor and couldn't get the dirt off, she said, "I can't get the floor clean." When we looked at it, the boxes and the mud had worn the pattern off the linoleum. So that was our first experience with the trailer. We had a lot of little incidences like that during the years because we lived in them for eight years.

I went from seismic in 1950 to what they call slimhole drilling. I worked on slimhole drilling in Alberta and Saskatchewan until 1954. While I was with seismic, I was on the rigs and then on the shot truck - the explosive truck. And then I was transferred to slimhole drilling supervising that, we had two rigs drilling around the country.

They were truck mounted rigs and I think the rigs we had were 1,500 failing rigs.

In 1954, we wound up in Saskatchewan. And I was transferred to construction with Imperial Oil. I spent all my career with Imperial Oil. I started out with Royalite which is a subsidiary of Imperial Oil.

We were doing pipelining and production facilities - what we call batteries and testing facilities.

We went to Dawson Creek from Regina. We had lived in Regina for eight years. We bought our first house there.

While Dot was living in Regina, I was working in Virden, Manitoba and Estevan and all through there. I was out on Monday and back on Friday night and home for Saturdays. After eight years of that, we were transferred to Dawson Creek. And then we worked the Rainbow Lake country. In 1967 Rainbow Lake and Zama country started to get hot. I worked through there but Dot stayed in Dawson Creek.

I retired December 31, 1982. Then I worked out of the city for Imperial Oil as a resource person. I have worked a total of 44 years in the oil patch.

If I could do it over: I would change the living conditions for the women. The sanitary conditions were terrible. The women were having to use old toilets behind machine shops and garages because the trailers weren't equipped with any toilets or anything like that so we used outside plumbing all the time.

We have had many very rough times but we also had some good times. And we met some wonderful people who are still friends to this day.

I remember when Dot first came to Canada in 1946, I borrowed somebody's car to meet her at the train. While we were driving to Turner Valley, we got to the rock cliff between Black Diamond and Turner Valley. I kept asking Dot, "Can you smell the gas? Can you smell the gas?" She answered, "No, I can't smell any of the gas." She thought somebody had relieved themselves in the car and she was too polite to comment.

Jim Rutherford (1997)

Thomas (Tom) Smith

Tom is retired. He and his wife live in Edmonton. In the early days, he worked on a seismic crew (Slim Hole) in Wainwright. From there he went to Taber with Cantex Drilling in 1942, coming north to Leduc in 1948. Born and raised in Vermilion, he worked in various fields and pushed tools for 14 years for Cantex and Regent.

Once, in the spring of 1947, I was on crutches with a bad leg at the time. I got a phone call to go to work. I told him I couldn't go right then. There was such a shortage of experienced men at that time and the fellow asked, "Well, can you run the crew? Can you look after the drilling?" I answered, "Well, I could try it."

I was getting around a little, but not very good. He said to me, "That damn toolpush up here can make your trips for you." I decided to give it a try. We had to walk in a quarter mile from the road at Taber. I walked in on crutches, then put the crutches up on top of the boiler house and went back to drilling.

I should explain here that in those days, the toolpush dressed up in a suit, rode around in a nice company vehicle. His assistant was called a 'Nipple-Chaser' (nothing to do with women). This guy was the one that did what most toolpushers did after Leduc #1.

When things started to boom in Alberta, they took that position away and the toolpush became a glorified roughneck which was the position of the 'Nipple-Chaser' in the old days.

Tom Smith (1997)

Patrick (Pat) Toner

Pat lives in Beaumont. He's been sometimes referred to as the "daddy of the oil patch", and probably is since he's been working on and around the rigs for 54 years. He's semi-retired, going out occasionally on 'fishing' jobs. His work has taken him as far as Africa, the Middle East, Peru and the South China Sea.

I started on the rig at Vermilion in March, 1943, as a roughneck for General Petroleum. I worked on a small drilling rig. We drilled down about an 1,800 foot hole in Vermilion. When we left there, we went to Brooks. We drilled down there around Brooks, Taber and Patricia for about three years. I met Smith in Taber.

By 1945, I was drilling. I would have been 17 or 18 years old. We grew up fast in those days.

In 1946, I went down to Windsor, Ontario, with Regent Drilling. We were down there all summer and drilled four salt wells. We came back and drilled a couple of holes at Lone Rock, Saskatchewan which is south of Lloydminster.

I think we were at Erskine, just out of Stettler, when they struck oil at Leduc. We worked on the Leduc field, mostly around Calmar. I was pushing for Regent then. There was more bull-work in the old days. Nowadays on the rigs they have around 20 drill collars. Those days we had one and then the rest was drill pipe. We started to use eight or nine in Leduc. I used about eight.

Then later that year, we went down into the mountains, back in from Fernie, British Columbia. We stayed in that camp about 17 months. It was pretty isolated. We went in there in the summer of 1951 and we came out in 1953. The closest town was across the United States border.

We built a hockey rink in there which, hopefully, got hockey teams started down there. I was single then so I stayed in a tent, winter and summer. It got a little frosty but it was OK. and we lived through it. Some of the married people had trailers and some cabins were built. A few of the single guys all stayed in the lodge that was there.

It took us three days to plow the roads out from the rig to Columbia Falls, Montana. There were three of us, the engineer, myself and the catskinner. On the way back, the engineer and I were drinking a little of the booze we had with us.

A moose appeared on the road and he wouldn't get off into the deep snow. I had a hatchet behind the back seat and I said, "I'm gonna get him." I threw the hatchet but missed the moose by about ten feet. I started crowdin' him with the pickup and he had his feet up on the hood. He was hunched over, but he didn't ruin my rad at all. We just had to wait 'til he got off the road.

We weren't allowed to take meat across the border. It was flown in but during spring breakup when the plane couldn't land, the food was dropped in. A bunch of us went to get it. We carried it to a swaying foot bridge. I took my belt off to tie the moose piece, that I had, to my back and my pants fell off halfway across the bridge. I had an awful time getting across there.

We used to go town once in awhile and I met this little woman in Columbia Falls, so then I got married when we left Fernie. When we moved out of Fernie, we drilled a hole at Winfield and then went on to Fort St. John, British Columbia. I was still working with Regent and I was 29 at that time. We lived on the lease.

In 1953, Brewster Drilling Equipment from Shreveport, Louisiana, was at that well with their equipment. The company did some promotional advertising of what was being used for Canada's deepest well. My picture was on the poster. See picture section. We were around the Fort St. John field for a long time, about five years.

I began working for Homco International in 1967 and I was stationed in High Level for about a year.

In 1975, I went to Borneo. I worked on an off-shore American rig patching casings. It was located about 20 miles from shore. I would stay out until I finished the job and then come back to shore. I was over there for one and a half months. It was quite an experience. The crews were made up of men from Canada, the United States and some native men. These men had painted their throats black and had signs painted to show which tribe they belonged to. There are wild men in Borneo!!

To get to Borneo, we'd have to fly to Singapore and then to Brunei, where the Shah lives. We had a very interesting time there. We used to throw dimes off the wharf and the little kids would dive for them, sometimes catching the coins before they hit the bottom. Fran came over for two weeks and on our way back to the States, we stopped at Singapore for five days and Tokyo for two days.

I worked in Johannesburg, South Africa, pushing tools for an American company. This was before the trouble with apartheid started over there.

I was sent to Peru while I worked for Homco. I was patching casing and worked out in the jungle for about a month. That was enough of that, but it was another experience.

In 1986, I was working with Drillrite on a 'fishing' job on the Ocean Ranger, off of Newfoundland. I came off that rig about a month before it blew over and went down. There were a lot of lives lost in that disaster and I knew most of the guys who were working on it.

Safety measures have really changed over the years. I remember when a toolpusher was fatally burned in a rig fire, in 1953.

We drilled a well at Mile 120 and we had a blowout one night. Before the rig was set up, a seismic crew had gone through and drilled a bunch of holes for testing. Six trailers were parked on the lease and they had to be moved. The steam lines ran over top of the seismic holes. As the holes began to thaw, gas began escaping. The pressure from the steam lines forced the gas up under the trailers. Everything was shut off to avoid an explosion. One of the guys had his trailer dug in for winter. He had to make about four trips around that trailer to get it out. His trailer was parked on top of one of those holes, and of course it started to blow underneath the trailer. The next day, all the trailers were all parked in Blueberry, a little town north of the rig location.

If I could do it over: I don't think I would change a thing. I don't think anybody would. This was our life. We did things a lot of people had never done before. I traveled all over the world, thanks to the oil patch, and I have a whole lot of good memories.

Pat Toner (1997)

Harvey Weegar

Harvey has been working in the oilfield industry for 43 years. He was 22 when he started driving a cat and scraper for Moon & Moon Construction. Harvey is foreman for Wales Construction and he and his wife Pat live in Clairmont.

The first job I was on, I got $1 an hour for driving this cat on cutline all winter for about six months. Then I came home to buy a brand new pickup. I went to the Chev garage and the guy there talked me into borrowing $500 and not to pay cash for the truck. I went down to the bank, borrowed $500, financed the truck and went back to the garage to pick it up.

The Chev garage was straight across from the York Hotel. I drove my truck one half a block, parked it and went to the bar. When I got up the next morning, I had no money, no friends left and not even enough money to buy a cup of coffee. I ended up going home with my pickup. My mother told me, "Moon phoned you and you're to go to work right away." I said, "You drive me down to Billy Moon's and then take the truck home and keep it until I get back - drive it or do whatever you want with it."

I didn't come back from Valleyview for three months and then I had made enough money to pay my truck off. I was working in the oil patch there covering up pipelines with the cat and scraping for the oil companies in a big plant site they had there.

Well, we were cutting seismic line on the Forestry Trunk Road, about 70 to 80 miles south of Goodwin. My brother Delmar and I came in for supper and the seismic guys around the jug lines were telling about a brown bear that was around there. He was kind of a mean one, they were always running him off the lines.

Just before supper I had to go outside to have a 's—-'. I went down the cutline about 100 to 200 feet. I was sitting there and all of a sudden I looked up and there was a bear between me and the cookhouse. I let a roar out of me and my brother came to the door just as I was passing the bear with my pants down.

Years ago, I was a stand-by cat operator with Duke Drilling. They paid a daily rate to the cat owner, plus an hourly rate for the operator on site.

It rained hard there a few times and when they were bringing the cement trucks in, I'd have to tow them all up the hills and then on to the rig. The trucks would have to be pulled back out and then another truck would have to be brought in. It depended on the number of trucks they had coming in, but sometimes, I'd work all night.

I was just supposed to look after the road into that rig for Duke Drilling. The roads weren't too bad, and some of the guys who were working there would go to town at night and not come back in time for their shift.

I would work on the rig for eight hours. Then on the next shift, there would be another guy who wouldn't show up so I would work another eight hours. Sometimes it was 24 hours a day, sometimes 16 hours. When the guys came back, they would pay me for the shifts that I worked for them. I never worked on the oil rigs very much after that. I never really cared for it because it seemed that it was all mud and water but it was fun just to be around there now and again just to work part-time.

The guys were all good to work with. It was lots of fun at times. They used to throw mud at you or get you to do something that was near impossible if you were green at the job. You got all of the dirty jobs if you were the new guy there.

Sometimes you would have to go wash all the floors off. If you didn't do it, they would turn the hose on you. There were different things like that.

At least I didn't get too muddy while driving the cat. I stayed right on the cat and didn't get off it. If the trucker wanted a pull, he had to get out and hook onto the cat to hook the cables up. Sometimes they'd sink right down to their knees in places.

I remember, I pulled the whole front end right out from under one truck as I was getting it out. We had to get another cat in to lift the rest out and finish the job. Another truck was brought out to bring the load in.

They'd get me to run the tongs when they were pulling the pipe out of the wells. And then one guy maybe wouldn't hang onto his end of it tight enough. And then you couldn't manage the other end and then the toolpush he would be roaring and hollering at you to get more done. "Get in there and do it." And then they would be all laughing at me because I was green at the job.

After the day's work was done, I would play a few tricks on them. When they brought the lunch out, I would go stash some away, just in case I needed a spare sandwich at night or on my next shift.

In those days the camps they had for the cat operators were wood heated. You had to get your own wood. I remember going into Grande Prairie one time and I was drinking with another guy. I thought of a plan, and said to this guy, "We got to leave about ten minutes before the bar closes because I seen two loads of wood out there on some pickups. Maybe we could just pick enough wood off them trucks to take back to camp with us." So we did! We slipped out and loaded up the wood and headed back to camp, thinking we wouldn't have to buck any when we got home, we had our wood in the back of our pickups. Percy Perry was the name of the guy we stole the wood from. I ended up marrying his daughter.

In 1957, I started worked for Archie Hackwell. I worked for him for about 16 years. I recall the one job down at Tupper Creek. We were cutting seismograph lines for the seismic crew to come in. A guy named Morris Dakota and I were working together and cutting line. The hills were pretty steep there in places. I was driving the D6 and Morris Dakota was driving the D7. We came to this one hill and we used to hook the winch lines together and I would go down the hill first. He would let me down with the winch line.

This one hill, he just threw the break off and let me go. Down the hill I went. When I got to the bottom the cat reared up and just about tipped over and knocked out a tree and then I was hung up at the bottom.

We got the cables unhooked and he went around and made a detour and come down the hill to the bottom and got my cat out of there. He and I had a 'pretty big' discussion at the bottom.

We went back to work. That night when we got back up, he said, "I'll take a short-cut back to camp. With the cat, I'll just go through the bush and plough a road out for us so we can travel a lot closer to camp." Because he knew the country, he had lived there all his life, I said, "OK." I took the truck and went all the way around. This took me about an hour and a half.

At two o'clock in the morning, he hadn't shown up so I drove back around to see if he had come out that way and he hadn't. I went back to camp, filled up some service bottles with coffee, made some lunch and went back to my cat. I headed into the bush to see if I could find him.

I finally found him, he had tracks everywhere on every cutline but all the wrong ones. We stopped and had coffee. I said to him. "Well, I never even went out to look for you last night, I just went to bed." I kind of lied to him a little bit. He said, "I didn't think you would even do that, but I thought you might be back in the morning." After some more discussion, he said, "The next time I want to take a short-cut, you just hook onto me and tow me down to the truck and then drive me back to camp."

The next summer there, we built leases and got them ready for the rigs to move in on. We spent a lot of time digging the cats out. Lots of times they would be down four or five feet. We'd hook a winch line on to them and pull them out.

The next year Archie put me as foreman to look after different jobs for him, and keep the operators working. I even had to do the cooking to start with because he couldn't afford to hire cooks.

On one job I was working 160 miles in from High Level, at Bistcho Lake. I drove in to High Level one day to buy groceries. I bought these on credit, put the order in and was going to pick them up in the morning. I phoned Archie Hackwell and he told me, "You just stay there. I'm coming up there right away. There's something wrong up there."

When Archie finally got up there we went down to the store. He asked me, "Why are you buying all this stuff? Like electric razors and stuff like this? Where's all the stuff going?" I asked, "What are you talking about?" I was getting quite upset over this. "Well" he said, "Your name is signed on all these papers at this store." I said, "Who else have you got working up here?" He said, "Oh, we have about three jobs going here." I said, "Well, let's go down to the store."

I asked the girl working there, "Am I Harvey Weegar?" She said, "Yeah, well you've been signing here." I asked, "Well, who's this guy who is signing my name to some of these sheets?" There was another guy, just standing back, who came over and said, "It was a big guy who signed your name Harvey Weegar to the bill yesterday." Archie looked at the bill and looked at the signature, handed it over to me and I said, "Well, that's not my signature but it is my name I guess."

Just then, it dawned on Archie who could be signing my name. There was no mention of names. He took me down to the bar and bought me all the booze that I could drink for the day.

Archie Hackwell had come up to fire me over this job. Good thing he found out it was this other guy who was buying electric razors and things and selling it in the bar for beer money.

There was only one hotel there at that time. There was a guy who was up there for a little while. One night he couldn't get into his room, so he had a pistol with him and he just took it out and shot the lock right off the door and walked on in.

Another time, I phoned Archie and told him that I needed two more cats. He told me, "God, I can't afford to buy any more cats." I told him, "Go down to Union Tractor and tell them that you will trade these two that I have up here off on two new ones, but that you can't bring them in until spring. Maybe they will go for that."

Archie went in and phoned his accountant and talked to him about it. The accountant said, "Boy, that sounds good. Go down and see what you can do." So Archie went down and two days later I had two brand new cats on the job.

The next spring Archie came in and paid off the two cats. He had enough money then to keep the two new ones and buy the two old ones back from Union Tractor. He really did well after that.

We prepared leases up by Fort Nelson. There was lots of muskeg and big timber up there, and lots of cold weather.

I met Herbie Wales when he come to work for Archie Hackwell. Then, later on, when he started Wales Contractors in 1979, I went to work for him as foreman. I'm still with them, we still do oilfield work. We build leases, not very much for seismic now, it's all oilfield work.

In 1993, one other incident happened when we were out at Fox Creek. We had turned off on the road going to Tony Creek. We had an operator down there who was told to go between the two pipelines, go down to wide turn-off, another road going to the left.

The road is only 20 meters wide but the guy missed it on the way by. He kept on going, made a couple of bends in the road. There were two pipelines there - one was an eight inch pipe and the other had a 16 inch pipe that goes all the way to Edmonton from Fort St. John.

He came down to a creek. The beavers had it all dammed up, but it looked like a road across it. The cat operator kept on going and down he went, through the ice on the creek, on top of the pipeline.

Another operator who had come along, hooked on to him to pull him back out. They wiggled back and forth, but couldn't move it out. The cat was on top of the Peace Pipeline, the main pipeline that carries the oil from Grande Prairie and Fort St. John all the way out to Edmonton.

The men phoned and said they had this cat stuck. When we got down there, there was about ten inches of the cat canopy sticking out of the water. Peace Pipe said later that the cat was sitting right on top of the pipeline with one track.

Peace Pipe said, "We've got to raise the cat straight up, off this pipeline. We can't move it or just pull it off of there. We have to lift it straight up."

We couldn't pull the cat out the way it went in, we had to get onto the other side of the beaver dam. We got a water truck in and a couple more cats and made snow fills, pumped water on top of the snow fills to freeze them down so we could get big trucks across.

About a day and half later we got over onto the other side. And once we got around there, we had to get matting brought in from a rig to set the big trucks on top to lift this cat up.

We had to get a 60 ton crane in from Edmonton and this had to come in on big trucks. We had to unload it at the road and then drive it in.

We got it in there and got it over onto the other side and backed in, got the lines onto the cat and hooked onto it. We had to make a fishhook deal to pull the cables around the winch of this cat. To get the dozer off, we got one side off by fishing around and getting the bolt out and the one arm off, then we just pulled it over to the side with the crane.

On the third day, they brought in this outfit from Red Deer that tested the line, listening on a monitor. Peace Pipe was really good about it, they didn't shut the line off. They kept it going as long as these monitors were on there. If they had shut it down it would have cost approximately one million dollars an hour, shut down time.

On the fourth day, we finally got all this hooked up. We laid the matting down and backed this big crane out there to pick the back end up. Then we had another big truck to hook onto the front of the cat to pull it out. Then we had two cats hooked onto this truck to hold it there while he was winching.

They were having safety meetings to make sure everything was going right, guys were on the monitors to check the line. They started lifting, and about 11 o'clock that morning, they finally got the cat out of there. The way it turned out, everything worked OK.

I guess my, Trevor would be around 20 or close to it. He was hired as a labor man to power saw and burn brush and stuff. I had two guys down there working, and when they started out that morning and I went over to this one guy and said to him, "I brought a new guy in here today. I want you to watch him and then tell me whether he works and whether he's any good and can run a saw or how he does things. If he's no good, you let me know right away and I'll run him right off the job. I'm not keeping people around here who can't work."

I went down to the other part of the job. When I came back, the fellow came running over and told me, "Boy, that guy is a good worker. He's really working. There's nothing wrong with him so far. He's really good." "Well", I said, "You just keep an eye on him all day. You make sure he works. I don't want no sluffing around. You make sure he works good."

That night, Trevor and one of the guys stopped in at our camp. Trevor came over and said, "Dad, how many hours can I put down for today?" "Oh", I answered, "It all depends on what you done. Did you do a pretty good job?" And he said, "Well, I think so." The guy with him came over and he said, "Christ, you never told me this was your son working here." I said, "Well, if he's no damn good then I don't want him around here."

If I could do it over: I wouldn't change a thing. I would do everything the same. Actually it's been a good life. There's some really good people out there. There's more safety rules to contend with now, but the people I work for are really good.

Harvey Weegar (1997)

Bill Weitzel

Bill was 20 years old when the wells at Leduc began producing. He recalls the days when he was trucking oil from the wells into the Imperial refinery in Edmonton. Bill began hauling water with a second truck and worked steadily in the oil patch until 1957. Bill and his wife live on a farm west of Spruce Grove.

It was winter about 1947 and we just got the tank on the one truck and the Atlantic #3 went wild; so we put a tank on the second truck. They were pumping the oil off the land into trucks then hauling it to the new tanks at the Imperial refinery in town. We had one truck working 24 hours a day for a straight year. After they were finished drilling Atlantic #3 around 1948, they had other wells in production. I tell you we did well. We bought a new truck and this truck ran 24 hours a day for a solid year. It was equipped with oil tanks and a two inch pump. And then we'd haul the oil to the refinery.

Anyway, we had a 50 barrel tank on the back because it was only a single axle truck.

In 1948, I was 20 years old. We had one truck hauling water for a drilling rig and the other truck was hauling the oil. The company we were working for was Commonwealth Drilling. Ronnie Minks was the toolpush and he was a great fellow. He was one guy on the rig who didn't drink after we had worked through the field at Leduc. For a while they started moving north of the river and we collected oil from several wells around the reserve area.

In 1950, we started north of the highway at a gas plant that was north of Winterburn. It was on Sammy Walker's place that we had a blow out there too. It just blew all over that quarter section that the company had to buy that land because there was so much oil on it. Sammy Walker, who owned that land, was quite a character. I was there when they came to talk to him and he said, "You bastards, you buggered it up, you buy it." The company bought it for probably double the land value was in those times.

We moved from there over to a well that lost circulation for six weeks. Ronnie Minks was still the toolpush and I hauled water there 24 hours a day. They just filled one pit and mixed 'er up and pumped 'er down and then they would fill the next pit and pump 'er down.

George and I would change off and then we discovered a big slough in the bush. I asked the toolpush if I could still get paid if I pumped the water directly up from the slough. He said, "Sure, why not." The slough was probably 20 feet deep so I set the truck half-way between the slough and the rig. I got a bunch of piping and hoses and pumped it directly into the rig. This gave me a break because I could sleep for awhile, get some food and come back to work again. What amazed me was that I was a young guy who had not seen anything in my life like this before.

Three Haliburton trucks actually did the pumping by the time that we actually got circulation back in the well. They had to get a little cat in to get the trucks out because the trucks were never moved and some of them were stuck. They got the little cat in on the night that there was circulation.

I don't know for sure because I wasn't actually involved in it but it was about midnight and the whole crew had been drinking. I am quite sure that they poured a bunch of water in the pit and never mixed the proper weight of mud to keep the pressure down. I was coming in with a load of water and saw all this mud flying around. Everyone was scrambling. There was gas and whatever coming back. They had lost circulation. The toolpush didn't think it was that serious so they immediately started to mix the mud up. They made really heavy mud and they pumped this down into the well and this all just disappeared. By then the engineers and men were all there and they mixed up this concoction of feathers, sawdust and sponges. A truck brought bails of feathers in. These big square bales of feathers weighted about 700 pounds. They brought in a whole truck load of feathers and a truck load of sawdust.

It took them a whole shift to mix this concoction and to pump it down. These feathers were compressed and when they were released, they were mixed in with the mud. The fellows were just covered with this mud run. You've probably heard the old story of being 'tarred and feathered'. That's what they looked like. When the Haliburton trucks started up you could hear these trucks screaming for miles. They'd be pumping all this stuff down and you could see there was nothing returning. It just kept going down. Finally it was quiet for a little while then all of a sudden you could hear gas coming back and they had some of these feathers coming out. This went on for days.

One day I asked Ronnie Minks, "Do you ever think you will get this thing plugged up?" He said, "You know Bill, I have been around the oilfield for 20 some years and I have never seen anything this bad. Usually you lose circulation for a day or two and then you are back in business. This thing has absolutely got me stumped. I haven't got a clue what we should be doing next." They had no other solutions in those days. Now they have the stuff that they pump down there and it expands and shuts everything off. But in those days, they didn't have this kind of stuff. Well they finally did get it shut off and in another three weeks they got it into production again. It was an experience that I will never forget.

We worked another year or so and then we went to Drayton Valley. Our truck was working on the discovery well. We were on the first well that was drilled there. Drayton Valley was the worst place that I saw. There were no roads after 'Campion corner' when we went there. The discovery well was west of Campion corner. The road was so bad that they winched truck loads of pipe all the way from Drayton Valley to Violet Grove. They had two cats - one would string out the line and the other would be pulling the truck out. They took the loads of pipe that way to Violet Grove for a distance of six or seven miles.

By that time, we were working on a rig which was west of Violet Grove and which was located on low ground. Although we were hired to haul water to the rig, we ended up pumping water away from the rig when it started to rain. After the well was completed, our truck sat on the lease for two months because we couldn't move. We were paid for all of the time that our truck was sitting there. There was no way that they could get the rig and everything out.

In 1952, I got married and my wife and I went from there over to Ferintosh. We lived in a little, old trailer. This 8 foot by 16 foot trailer had a little diesel heater in it. We hooked up to the power at the rig. The trailer is still standing and we use it now for a sheep shelter.

In those days, we lived on $25 or $30 a week.

From there we went to Tofield where we drilled one hole which turned out to be a dry hole. We went back to Drayton Valley again. By this time we had one child and we lived in the same trailer. We stayed there a year and a half. We switched from hauling water to hauling pipe and we worked for Miller Oilfield Hauling a few years.

We had two tank trucks working for a long time in Drayton Valley. One night it was so cold that we had to circulate the water back into the tank for about four hours. Then something happened, I looked in the tank and the water had frozen all the way around the tank. It was 50o F below zero. Al Bainley, our neighbor, and I came down to the river to load water. The driver had fallen asleep with the pump on. The water over flowed from the truck, covering everything in ice. Now it just looked like a iceberg. The driver is lucky we came down there, the truck was frozen in. You could hardly see the lights of the truck any more.

Most of these young guys were only 17 or 18 years old. In those early years, these young guys moved up fast if they watched their "p's and q's". One young guy who was 17 years old worked on the floor for maybe a month, then he moved up to derrick and he became a driller by the time he turned eighteen. Six weeks after that, he didn't have a job. That's how crazy these fellows were around the oil patch. One young fellow came to work drunk and fell from the steps and was lying there moaning and groaning. The toolpush saw that he had a broken leg and put him in a car and drove him to Wetaskiwin. One young fellow was told to check the oil in the drawworks. He'd been drinking and when he stuck his hand in there, he lost four fingers.

We worked in the oil patch from 1948 to 1950. My brother worked in it from 1948 to 1982. In 1960, Dad decided he was going to quit farming so we decided to take the farm back. It was not an easy life on the farm.

If I could do it over: I would change quite a bit. What I would do is go 'all out'. I'd have bought more trucks. The opportunities were there for anyone who were prepared to take a chance. We were kind of cautious. That's not a bad thing either.

Another thing for certain, my wife and I would have bought a bigger trailer. The one we had was pretty small.

Bill Weitzel (1997)

Maurice Wolfe

Maurice is retired. He and his wife live in Edmonton. He worked for Imperial Oil as a mechanic for 35 years. He moved to many locations but remembers especially the move to the Maritimes in 1958 for three years.

I started in the oil patch in Turner Valley in June 1942. I was 17 years of age. It changed my lifestyle a bit. I was raised on a farm in Manitoba. To start with, for about a year, I was digging ditches and that was the beginning of a 40 year career in the oil patch.

I worked on the 'Bull Gang' for a year, and then for about two to three years I went with the seismic crews, working mostly in Saskatchewan. The rigs were owned by Imperial Oil but worked under the name of Northwest. These weren't really seismic, where you drill a shallow hole and do blasting. It was really core drilling. We would set up, then go down and take cores at around 1,500 feet.

In 1945, I left the small rigs and went on to the big drilling rigs. By this time, I had taken a course in Heavy Duty Mechanics, and so began my job as mechanic on the rigs, for many years. Later on, I was given a Mechanics Service Truck and I traveled from rig to rig doing mechanical work and the supervising of it.

We worked six weeks on the job, two weeks out. That was difficult because our son was just a little wee fellow and he'd forget me by the time I would come home. We were working in Judy Creek, Dawson Creek and Fort Nelson.

Imperial Oil had a good safety record. There were many safety precautions taken to avoid serious accidents. One time though, we were drilling out there in Leduc. The engines took off because they were taking on the gas that was coming by. We thought some of the engines would fly apart, but they didn't.

The highlight of the service was a three year stint in the Maritimes. PEI, Cape Breton, New Brunswick. Our son was seven years old at the time. We have clippings and pictures of the trip down there. One reporter wrote that there were 78 people, 26 of them six years of age and under, and four dogs, on the four day train trip.

We were fortunate to find living accommodations at a dairy farm. We were very comfortable there. PEI was a great place to live. On days off we would go fishing or just sightseeing.

One of my other experiences with Imperial Oil was being involved with a man-made island in the Beaufort Sea. Issungnak, the island we were on, was off the shore-line about 15 miles from Tuktuyaktuk. We were in approximately 60 feet of water.

The first year we drilled on the island, the weather closed in too quickly. We couldn't get our own big rig on there in time so we hired a helicopter rig to do the work. They ran out of power before they could get down to the depth Imperial Oil wanted. The following spring, that rig was released.

That summer, we got our own rig back over there. There were two more wells drilled on that island. It was a two-story camp with everything supplied. They drilled on that particular island for three consecutive years.

You had to be careful of the polar bears. During the winter, it never did get to be daylight. Polar bears are white and blend in with the snow. There were 'Bear Monitors' walking around the island 24 hours a day with dogs and rifles. I guess one got in there somehow because there was one man killed by a polar bear.

The weather was very cold. This was right in the Beaufort Sea where the wind would blow right from God knows where. It was bad. But the rig was enclosed, and we stayed warm so the rig was never shut down."

After awhile, I went to work in the office in Edmonton, and from there I went to the newly opened office at Nisku in 1978. I retired in 1982.

Maurice Wolfe (1997)

Promotional advertising for Canada's deepest well, 1953.
Pat Toner on location, 400 miles N.W. of Edmonton AB. *Source: Pat Toner*

Shamrock Rig #1, Cessford AB, 1967.
Natural gas blow out. Water frozen - Winter frost. *Source: Doug Dunn*

Atlantic #3, 1 Mile East of Leduc #1.
Drilling contractors - General Petroleums. Source: Dick Hazen

Ideco drilling rig w/ British Petroleums, S. of Stoney Plain AB.
Joe Manning, Toolpush (60º F below zero for 5 weeks). *Source: Dorothy Manning*

Skid house, Camrose AB, 1948.
Maurice Wolfe and his family lived in this for five years. *Source: Maurice Wolfe*

Horse drawn shift wagon enroute to Leduc #2 - 1 1/2 miles S. of Leduc.
L. to R.: George Beattie, Paul Matvenko, Bill Wedderburn (Dowell), Fred Sowerby, Chubb Harley (sample catcher), Ralph Archibald, Lew Glendinning (driller).
Source: Ralph Archibald

Cat stuck pulling vehicles from lease to highway.
South of Kinuso AB, spring 1957. *Source: Jack Roberts*

Road into Kinuso AB, spring 1957. *Source: Jack Roberts*

Christmas morning, Swift Current SK, 1953.
Barry and Bev Smith in trailer home. *Source: Tom Smith*

Glider trailer, Flathead BC, 1951.
Tom and Betty Smith's home. *Source: Tom Smith*

8'x 16' Trailer, From Taber to Leduc, 1945 - 1949. Tom and Betty Smith's home. Source: Tom Smith

Trailers on lease, Mile 121, 1955. Pat and Fran Toner's home among these. Source: Pat Toner

Bud and Faye Osborne, May 1953. Leaving Ft. Saskatchewan for Ferintosh AB. Source: Faye Osborne

Christmas, North of Peers AB, 1955.
Olga and Sonja McBride. *Source: Dale McBride*

Christmas at the McBride's, Swan Hills AB, 1965.
Skid house and trailer connected (660 sq. ft. lvg space). *Source: Dale McBride*

Regent Rig #1, Big Valley AB, 1953.
L. to R.: Dale McBride (toolpush), Bob Gentles (roughneck),Henry Skypne (derrick man), Morgan Wolsey (driller). *Source: Dale McBride*

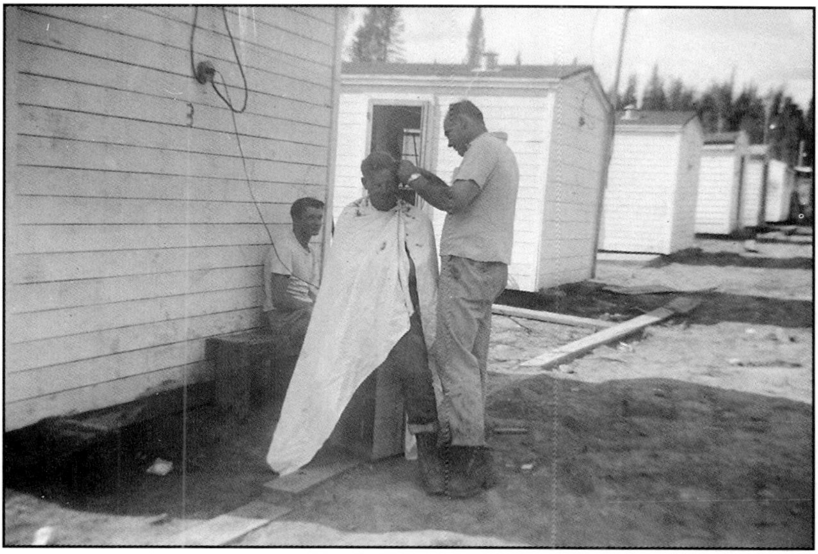

Kaybob Barber Shop, Fox Creek area, 1955.
John Domzey (barber), Dale McBride (customer). *Source: Dale McBride*

Wearing Dad's boots, Beaverlodge AB, 1956. Lynda Dreichel, 20 months old, in Dad's boots.
Source: Elsie Rosenau

Sonja McBride, 3 yrs. old, Kaybob AB, 1955.
Note: Bear paw print on door.
Source: Dale McBride

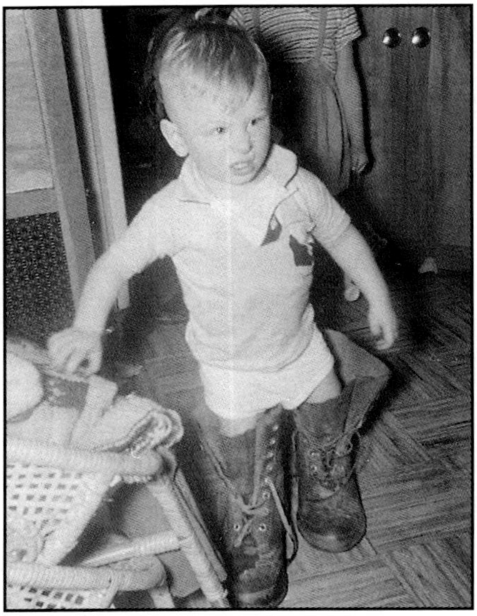

We're going to work', Grimshaw AB, 1958. John Dreichel, 21 months old, in Dad's boots.
Source: Elsie Rosenau

Drilling rig, Saskatchewan, 1996.
Source: Doug Dunn

Leduc #1 replica, 1996.
Source: Doug Dunn

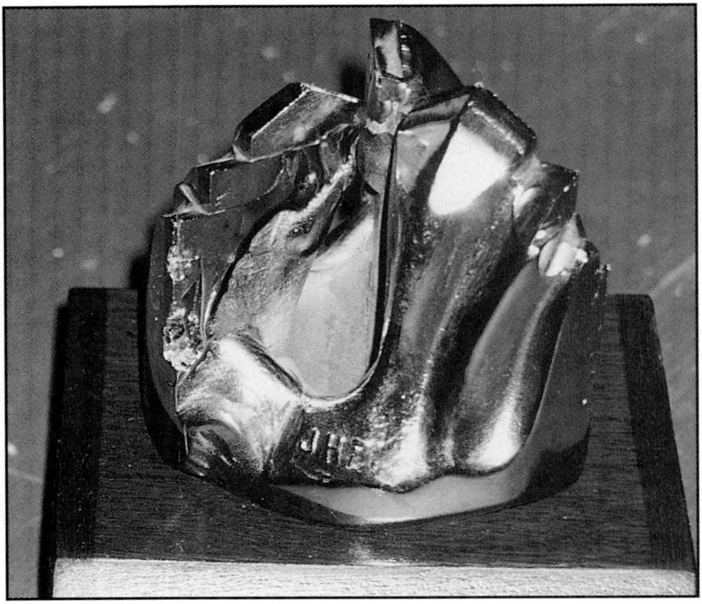

Drag bit (chromed). Source: Doug Dunn

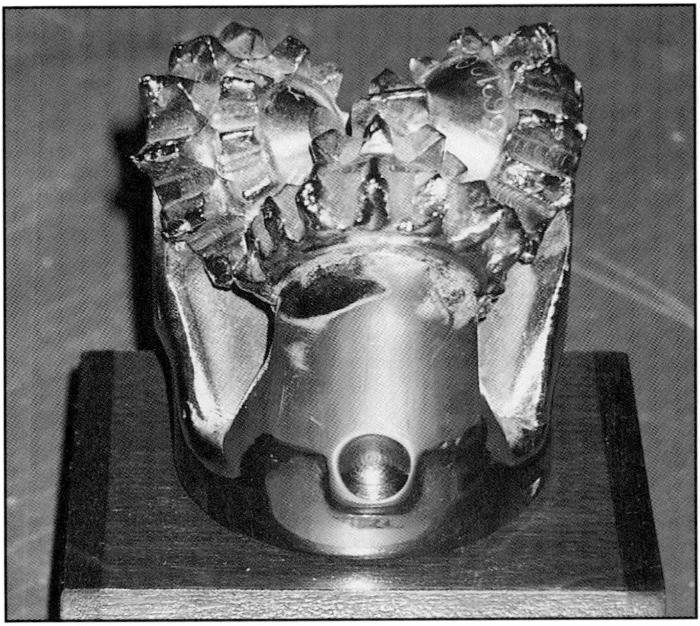

3 cone tooth bit (chromed). Source: Doug Dunn

Offshore drilling, South China Sea, 1975.
L. to R.: living quarters on barge, 14 wells under one platform.
Source: Pat Toner

Offshore drilling, South China Sea, 1975. 25 miles west of Borneo
Source: Pat Toner

(Top) 'Allis Chambers, Monarch' tractor used for ground work on Leduc #1 and other rigs in Leduc area in 1947. Bill Senior bought this tractor from a former Imperial Oil employee in 1983. He built a special shed for it and restored it to running order and its original orange color. Source: Bill Senior

(Right) "Home on the Lease", Pincher Creek AB, 1958. Artwork by Sonja McBride. Source: Dale McBride

THE TRAILER:
TODAY'S COVERED WAGON

Source: Birth of an Oil Town, 1965 Permission from Schlumberger

Source: Birth of an Oil Town, 1965 Permission from Schlumberger

THE WOMEN

DIAPERS

Source: Birth of an Oil Town, 1965 Permission from Schlumberger

NIGHT LIFE

THE MAC DONALDS AND THE JOHNSONS

Source: Birth of an Oil Town, 1965 Permission from Schlumberger

Source: Birth of an Oil Town 1965 Permission from Schlumberger

MUSIC

Source: Birth of an Oil Town, 1965 Permission from Schlumberger

Source: Birth of an Oil Town, 1965 Permission from Schlumberger

THE WOMEN

WOMEN AND CHILDREN FIRST! ....MOOSECREEK HAS NO NURSE BUT A BEAUTICIAN THERE IS!

Source: Birth of an Oil Town, 1965 Permission from Schlumberger

THE MEN

Source: Birth of an Oil Town, 1965 Permission from Schlumberger

Source: Birth of an Oil Town, 1965 Permission from Schlumberger

NIGHT LIFE

ON DUTY
AROUND THE CLOCK

Source: Birth of an Oil Town, 1965 Permission from Schlumberger

Source: Birth of an Oil Town, 1965 Permission from Schlumberger

The Women

who shared the
good times

and the other times

Jean Atkinson

Jean married a hockey player in Calgary the day after the hockey finals in 1940. Pete played with the Turner Valley Oilers against Calgary. She recalls the living conditions during the many times she moved around with her husband. Pete began working for Dowell Chemicals and in 1949 they moved to Edmonton, where he began working for McCullough Tool Company.

My parents moved to Millerville, in the foothills of the Rockies, to continue their ranching. We rode horseback three miles to Plainview school. Later, we moved further east to the Turner Valley-Black Diamond District.

My parents had a dairy farm. I was one of nine children and we were hard-working little devils. This was in the late twenties and early thirties, when the oil business was really coming into its own. As the oil people moved in, we kids would deliver milk to them on our way to Upper Turner Valley School.

This dairy business bloomed into a full blown 'slave' farm, where each of us milked cows twice a day, and washed bottles and cans before and after school.

In 1938 it was decided that there should be a hockey team in Turner Valley. It was known as the Turner Valley Oilers. The coach, Elmer Piper, was recruited from North Battleford, as were four former school boys and hockey players from there.

They came to play hockey and they started working in the oil patch digging ditches. It did get better workwise, when they began roughnecking. The wages for roughnecking at that time were $135 a month. The men had to drive to Calgary to practice hockey and to play their games, and still had to put in their eight hours of work each day.

With preparations for the war in Europe, many of our able-bodied men were recruited, including hockey players. There was an intermediate league started up by a Calgary Brewing Company, headed up by J.B.Cross. Some continued to play through 1942 and 1943. The oil patch too was moving on.

We were married March 20, 1940. I don't know how we did it, with buying groceries, paying the rent and everything else, but it was really something to be able to afford a car.

Then, my husband got a job with Dowell Chemicals. We were the first to leave and we were sent to Lloydminster in 1946. By then we had two little boys.

My husband went ahead to find accommodation for us, but it was like all these small towns, they didn't have extra housing. Some of the boys bought up army huts which had glazed windows, but they were all one big room. These were moved onto lots, divided into four or five rooms, no bathrooms, mind you, but glass was put in the windows.

We no more than even got settled there and Leduc came into its own. So he was moved to Leduc and it was hard to find a place to live. He got a room for a few months with some people who lived there while he looked for places for us.

In the meantime, I didn't have a car, only a sleigh to pull the kids downtown. We had lights but we didn't have water. So I melted snow for our wash water. I moved to Lloydminster in January and then we had to move to Leduc in March in 1947.

Pete got this old, old house, the only place he could find. It was a story and a half sort of thing and it wasn't on a foundation per se, but it had up and down floors and all that sort of thing. You know, so many young fellows came there or married and couldn't find housing either. They would come to our house to play cards in the evening or to visit when they weren't working.

Leduc became like a slave camp for these fellows. They were working day and night. My husband would come in off the rigs from cementing, testing, acidizing or whatever they were doing in the field. I would have a list of calls that had come in.

There had been a fire and Dowell's office, garage and two of their trucks had burned down, so our house was the only place, then, that had the company phone. These men worked very long hours and the boss, who lived in Calgary, didn't ever seem to realize how over-worked these fellows were.

The night and day working got to be too much for my husband so he went to work for Reed Roller Bit selling bits. That was a little easier, at least he had a company car. He visited the toolpushers who lived in shacks and trailers on the lease. They would order bits through him and he would run errands for a lot of the women who lived out there as well, because they didn't have cars.

I remember one woman who had three babies in four years and my husband would bring the diapers in for diaper service and then take them back out on his next trip. They were really good friends with my husband and the families all helped each other.

There were no paved roads around Leduc then. The only time there was a break when he was with Dowell was when the creeks were flooding. There were no bridges over them at all and they couldn't travel between Leduc and Devon. That was one time, in the spring, when they had a few days rest.

We moved to Edmonton in 1949 and bought a new house on 72nd Avenue. We were so happy to get a nice, new house after some of the places that we had lived in. My husband went to work for McCullough Tool Company, another service company. He was there until he retired in late 1970's. Jet Perforators hired him on, part-time, in his retiring years.

We had our fiftieth wedding anniversary in 1990 and our kids and family surprised us with an anniversary party when we went to Palm Springs. There were about 45 people from here who came down to celebrate with us.

It was in March and some of them were holidaying, but others came just to be with us. It was a real surprise and we were just flabbergasted by it all. It was wonderful!

If I could do it over: Probably not a darn thing, it was a very busy and interesting phase in my life. I remember being so homesick when we left the Rocky Mountains and moved to Lloydminster. It seemed that we were so busy all the time, a very active lifestyle.

Jean Atkinson (1997)

Hazel Augustine

Hazel is now retired and living in Edmonton. She recalls the difficulty of finding places to live in the late forties and early fifties. She moved with her husband and children back and forth across Canada, then into the United States, where she lived for 18 years before returning to Alberta in 1986.

We were married in 1948, and went out to Redwater in 1949. When we moved into Redwater, it was very small. It grew fast in one year. The town had doubled in population by 1950. There was a real shortage of water when we moved to Redwater. We almost had to beg for water from the neighbors. It got to the point with the water situation that a fellow decided he would make some money and began trucking it in from Edmonton and selling it.

My husband worked for William's Bros. at the time. We lived in a pre-fab shack and we managed to fix it up so it was a comfortable little place. There was a living room and kitchen. The other room was a bedroom. The length of the shack was in eight foot sections, and on skids, so it could be easily moved on a flat bed. It was ten or twelve feet wide and had a flat roof. This pre-fab shack had been used at one time for a bunkhouse for the single guys. We lived down there in the bush for awhile when Don had his own company. Later, when we got a spot in town we had it pulled up there. That's where I ran a Laundry and Dry-cleaning Agency and I also did sewing. A friend named Dorothy used to help me with the sewing.

Shortly after we moved to Redwater, Don started his own business and called it Don's Construction. He repaired wellheads, etc. on the pipelines. This lasted for a couple of years. Actually his ego got the better of him and he spent more time looking for more jobs than he did taking care of the one's he had, and the company went broke.

My first child was born in 1950. At that time, Don went back to pipeline construction. We were all over the country after that. When we were in Redwater, my husband worked close around home but after we moved away from there, he was away a lot of the time. Sometimes I'd go with him and other times there was no way I could travel with the children. He usually managed to be home for Christmas.

We moved to Raymore, Ontario where Don was Pipeline Superintendent. By that time we had three children. Raymore was where the men worked but we stayed at a place called Matheson. The housing situation was about as bad as Redwater.

We finally got a little tourist cabin. It was in a small complex with seven units. We were in one of the few that had hot and cold running water, and a shower. Oddly enough, the bathroom was bigger than the kitchen so the fridge was in the bathroom. There was one wringer washing machine for all the units. It sat on our front porch and when the neighbors needed to do laundry, they came to my place. This arrangement worked for everyone. We were all 'Oil Patch' and we were friends; we helped each other.

I remember a couple we met while there. The guy is still in business and living in Calgary. They had a little boy, 15 months old, and then twin girls were born. All they could get to live in was a unit that had only cold running water. The husband didn't want her to leave Edmonton until he had found a decent place to live.

The day he left for Ontario, she gave notice to vacate her apartment and then took the train and came to Matheson with her three small children. Those women certainly were not wimps. They did what they had to do, often in incredibly difficult situations. We helped her; she was busy with those babies.

The pipeline was going through Raymore and we lived there most of that summer. After that, we came back to Alberta. Don worked in Edmonton for a time and then went on a job in a sulfur plant in Fort MacLeod. The oldest girl was in school then but we went down there and stayed for quite awhile. We moved around so many times. I can't remember all the places we moved to.

The style of living that we lived was the way so many people lived. We thought it was normal in those days. Most people moved, picked up and left to go where the work was. The living conditions were pretty strenuous. You didn't ever have very much room but you had to take what you could get.

The working conditions for the men were a whole lot tougher than they are now. There was a bunkhouse for the single men on the pipeline, while they were working for Sparling & Davis. If you were married with a family, you had to find a place of your own.

We looked after a little kid, took him in to live with us while his mom was sick. In those days, you looked after the kids and helped each other through 'thick and thin'. Otherwise we wouldn't have been able to make it through the tough times. It's not the same these days. The camaraderie just doesn't seem to be there as much.

After Matheson, Don got laid off and received a good settlement. We went to visit my sister in Michigan. After that, we went to live in Toronto for six years. I gave up going with him then, because the kids were getting older and in high grades in school. He worked in the United States and Alberta - he was all over the place.

We were in the United States for two years on visas. I came back and arranged for papers so I could stay down there. I stayed in Michigan working in Food Services for 18 years. Don had a job down there but decided not to take out his papers. He did not want to go down there. We separated then. It was a tough life. He died here in Edmonton four years ago. By that time we'd gotten to tolerate each other again.

If I could do it over: I don't know if I'd do it again but I sure saw a lot of country and I met a lot of interesting people.

Hazel Augustine (1997)

Sheila Davidson

Sheila was a student at the University of Alberta in Edmonton when Leduc #1 blew in. She met and married Jim Davidson, a driller and toolpush, who eventually purchased S & T Drilling. Sheila has four daughter, two of whom live in Edmonton and two who live in Kelowna, B.C. She divides her time between the two cities, enjoying her eight grandchildren.

Jim and I spent eight years together in the oil patch. Most of those years were in bush camps in the Peace River and Swan Hills area of Alberta. Our home was an 8 foot by 28 foot 'Travelite' house trailer built in the United States. These trailers were built by people who had no idea of the challenge a Canadian winter would be for such a thinly insulated structure. We had to keep plenty of snow banked right up to the windows. The windows themselves were single panes which we covered with plastic held in place with masking tape. We didn't have clear plastic then; the best we could get was a translucent film which let in the light but was impossible to see through. The long winters could get pretty claustrophobic.

A diesel oil heater stood by the door; the kitchen had a propane gas stove and an electric refrigerator. It was actually pretty nice by the standards of the day. But cold! The bed clothes froze to the walls, and my scrub water would freeze on the floor. The storage area under the bed where I kept our suitcases collected so much frost that everything in it got ruined by moisture and mildew. You could call that first year a real learning experience for both of us. One of the things we learned was common to all of you who have lived in trailers: that always, on the coldest night of the year, the oil heater would get clogged up and quit. At the same time the cold would make the pressure inside the propane tanks drop so low that the cook stove too would quit.

Because Jim was a toolpush with Regent Drilling, he had to always be at the rig. For most of those year, we lived right on the lease just a stone's throw away from the drilling table. We had electricity once the light plant was set up and running but we never had running water. The cute little taps in my kitchen were never used. However, in the summertime we could let water out the drains. There was a shower (in which we put up storage shelves) but no toilet. Everyone used the outdoor 'biffy'.

The first thing my newly wed husband learned was how heavy wet laundry was, and how angry his bride could be when the clothes-line broke. I had finished my first wash and hung it on a wire Jim had strung from the bumper of his truck over the cab and across to the roof of the geologist's shack. As the wind came up, I noticed the line was slipping so I rushed out to the middle and lifted it over my head, calling to a passing crewman to please tell Jim I needed him. My arms were aching by the time Jim appeared at the doghouse door and sauntered down the steps. He started over toward me, then stopped and lifted his arms up in imitation of me doing my imitation of a clothes-line pole. Furious, I dropped it all into the dirt and flounced off into the trailer. He gathered up the wash and carried it into the trailer, and without saying a word, drove off to fill the water cans again and filled the wash boiler on the stove. Round two was a repeat of round one: again the line, strung up a bit differently this time, broke and fell into the dirt. The third line held. But after that, whenever we moved onto a new lease, as soon as the well was spudded, the welders would make me some magnificent steel pipe clothes-line poles, supported and braced like you wouldn't believe. I'm sure they are still standing out in the bush, to this day.

What I learned was not to ask questions about our water supply, like where did it come from, and what were those things floating around in it. "Vitamins", Jim would say, with a big grin, "and bits of protein." He hauled the water in two ten gallon milk cans, which also stood just inside the trailer door, opposite the heater. We'd get water wherever we found it, but mostly it was from the tank at the rig which was kept full by the water hauler. He usually got this from a nearby creek. We used bleach as a purifier; it seemed to be all right. Nobody ever got sick.

Laundry could be a problem. In the early days I had my own washing machine in the trailer. Later, in camp, my machine was put into the 'wash house', where some roughneck overloaded it and burnt out the motor. After that I would use whatever machine was available in the wash house. In order to keep out of the men's way I would get up around 4 am, slip over to the wash house, do our laundry and be finished and hanging it on the clothesline by 6 am, getting back inside just as Jim was waking up. That was my system and it worked well, except for one location in the Swan Hills. There the bears discovered how much fun they could have swinging on the line, batting and ripping the clothes. I'd grab the broom and run out yelling and waving, and because they were wild and had never seen such a sight before, they always ran off. I couldn't leave the clothes out too long because the bears usually would come back.

When I think back about those days, and that gypsy life, what I seem to remember most could be summed up in three words: mud, noise, men. The leases were cleared and leveled by bulldozer's; I'm sure there was gravel here and there, mainly under the rig substructure, but there wasn't much. Our sidewalks were single planks laid down on the mud. All of you who have lived in northern Alberta know how it can rain, and how deep and sticky the mud can be. When it wasn't muddy, it was really, really dusty! Yet my kids today have fond memories of playing on big piles of dirt, and of finding great hiding places in the mounds of stumps, roots and rocks. These same kids knew moose, deer and bears, but asked, "What are those?" at the sight of horses and cows.

Living by the rig meant getting used to noise. The big motors on the rig floor, the pump, the light plant, all kept up a steady roar day and night. Then there'd be a 'round trip' with the clanging and crashing sounds of the drill pipe being swung into place. A lull in the motors would change to a roar as they groaned to lift the drill stem, and be joined by the clattering and banging of slips and tongs. Add to that the continual traffic of cars and trucks of all sizes going back and forth with loads of water, mud, or drill pipe. I worried about bringing home our brand new first born baby, but I didn't have to. The motors just lulled her right off to sleep. "Just like a real roughneck." said Jim.

What terrified me the most was 'tearing out'. Giant trucks swarmed onto the lease and to me it looked like pandemonium. Everywhere you looked there were highboys, lowboys, things being winched up and dragged around, guys yelling and waving. I was sure one of these big pieces of machinery would come crashing through the trailer, but they never did, The kids and I stayed put inside while all these vehicles roared past. I'd be packing up and making sandwiches. When most of the trucks had left, Jim would come in and ask, "You're ready to go?" Then he would hook up the trailer and away we'd go. Years later, listening to Willie Nelson's "On the Road Again" I'd think of those days, rolling down the road to some new location, new town, new people. We were young, we were together and always anticipating where the next move might be. Those were happy times and life was just one big adventure.

Of course there were problems. Just getting in and out of camp was often a challenge — these were bush roads built with bulldozers in the winter when the ground was frozen. Rarely were there any straight stretches, these roads twisted and turned and travel on them was excruciatingly slow. It could take an hour to cover 30 miles. Once you reached camp and got set up, the water supply was no problem, but the food supply was. The camps were set up for men only. Families were not welcomed on the lease, but were allowed to pull in trailers and hook up to the electricity. We were warned to keep away from the cooks and their supplies, so we always had our own vehicles loaded with canned goods and non-perishables. The traffic flow around a rig being pretty steady, someone was always driving out to pick up the mail and would pick up fresh supplies. When we were really isolated the testers and the mud men and bit salesmen became my life-line. We women traveled together whenever we could, and did shopping for each other whenever it was needed. A trip into town about once a month was a really big occasion because we had very little social life other than coffee and card games. Still, I knew I was lucky to be at the rig as it was never lonely. Those wives who had to stay in town had a far rougher and lonelier time of it. They would see their husbands for the short interval of a 'long change' which was once every three weeks. The chance to see a movie or go to a dance would usually be during the spring break. When the frost came out of the ground the roads were banned to heavy traffic. The rigs would shut down and the crews were all laid off; those were our 'holidays'.

It was always very interesting to arrive in a new town. Usually we weren't the first oil people that the locals had seen — the seismic crews had come before us, roaring all over the place in their trucks, filling up the cafes and the bars, generally raising enough hell that, by the time we drilling people had arrived, folks would already be a little wary of us. Understandably so. In the late 40's and early 50's no small towns were equipped to cope with such a surge in the population. We crowded their stores, their restaurants and their hotels. There would be line ups at the bank and the post office, especially at Peace River in the winter of '52 when we had to spell each other off. To make things worse, not only were we strangers to the town folk, we were also pretty smelly because we reeked of diesel fuel. The smell was in our clothes, our hair and our belongings. My mom told me that whenever we'd get home for a visit, she just couldn't believe how badly we needed to be aired out. Well, if you lived in a trailer or a shack with a diesel oil heater, you would smell of the fumes. It couldn't have been healthy, but what choice did we have?

Whenever we arrived in a new town, Jim would put on some clean clothes and go introduce himself to the banker, the postmaster, the telephone operators and the bulk fuel dealer. We also became rather quickly acquainted with the local R.C.M.P. and the game warden. The sudden arrival of dozens of men all seeking some place to live, to sleep and eat, led in some places, to the springing up of shack town — virtually little slums as granaries, skid shacks, old abandoned houses, boxcars — you name it — were dragged into town and parked on the outskirts. Some of the locals were happy to become slum landlords. And the bar keepers prospered with the presence of so many men with little to do in their off hours but sit and drink. With the drinking came the inevitable fights and the social tension that it caused. Some towns quickly polarized into 'us' and 'them'. I wonder if there would be a Devon today, if Calmar and Leduc had been more accommodating?

The transient nature of the oil patch life meant that crews were always changing. A great variety of men came and went, so there had to be a few bad apples. But the nature of the work itself tended to weed them out; anyone who wouldn't pull his weight was soon gone. Those who stayed on to become the core of the crew were decent and honorable men. In our travels we met a lot of people who treated us very well, and we made many new friends, especially as some of the local farm boys started to work on the rigs. They made good hands, too, as farm boys were familiar with hard work outdoors, winter and summer, and they would stick around when the 'going got rough'.

Living at the rig as I did gave me a great opportunity to see what life was like for the men. I watched them horsing around, having paint fights and water fights and playing tricks on each other. 'Bailing out the rat hole' was a regular initiation rite for the new guy. But make no mistake about it, this was not fun and games. It was work that was heavy, dirty and always, always dangerous. I saw them covered with mud, coated with cement dust, smeared with paint and soaked with salt water. They sweated in the heat and shivered in the cold. They worked so hard and long at times that they could hardly stand because of weariness. Teamwork was vital — good crews worked together well and always looked out for each other. I will always have the greatest respect for those who worked on the rigs. They were my heroes.

Here is a definition of heroes from Thucydides: "They dared beyond their strength, hazarded beyond their judgment and in extremities were of excellent hope."

"Stork Race" in Peace River, '51 -'52: Our first camp in the winter of 1951 to 1952 was at Harmon Valley in the Peace river country. The camp was only 34 miles of bush road once you got past Joe Stuffco's farm but it took two hours to get from the rig to Peace River. It was quite close but it seemed a lot longer the night Doreen O'Hagan's baby was born. I'll never forget riding through that cold, dark, snowy night — comforting Doreen who was struggling with the spasms of labor and watching the sweat pour down Bill's face while driving us in with his pickup. Any skid on that icy, zigzag road would have put us in a big snow drift. We arrived at the Peace River Hospital around midnight. Bill dropped me off at the Victory Hotel and then returned to the hospital. There were no rooms at the hotel but luckily there was still one empty chair in the lobby. I curled up in it and fell sound asleep.

The next morning the lobby was jammed full of men. One or two men were still asleep on the floor but most of them were lined up waiting for the cafe to open for breakfast. I recognized Bruce Rome who grinned at me and yelled, "Jim throw you out?" He bought me breakfast and drove me back to the hospital. Bill was sound asleep in his truck and Doreen had a beautiful baby girl. I felt very honored that they named her Sheila.

"Bill and Mary" in Peace River, '51 - '52: Our first camp taught us that cooks can be very temperamental. We had a married couple who were okay except that he had a great weakness for Bol's Cherry Whiskey, he smuggled it into camp one way or another. One afternoon he got pretty loaded and went into the cook-house where his wife had just finished baking several pies. While telling his wife that the pies were no good, he tossed the pies into the slop pail. She picked up a big knife and chased him around the dining area until he ran out to their shack and locked the door which left her on outside. She served the men their supper and then, still finding herself locked out, came over to our place. When Jim Thomas came over, she sat on the couch with the two Jims drinking, telling us the story of her life, weeping, cursing and finally throwing up. At this point, the two men fled. I sat holding a dish pan under her chin and feeling very sorry for her. Just as I was thinking of putting her to bed, the men came back and told her that old Bill had unlocked the door at last. So she went back home.

We got the whole story of the fight from Gordon Benson (Skeezix), a young teenage roughneck, who happened to be in the dining room when it started. He dove under the table and hid when he saw her pick up that knife.

"The Train" in Peace River, '51 - '52: One winter morning I rode into Peace River with Jim as he did his usual morning chores of phoning in the rig report and picking up the mail. We stopped by the railroad station to pick up a piece of freight. The loading dray was parked against the loading platform, so Jim pulled his truck in as close as possible to the dray. He parked it between the dray and the railroad track and went into the office. Sitting there half asleep, I heard a train whistle. As I looked up, the train suddenly appeared around the bend quite close. I suddenly realized that the truck was parked very near the track. I slid over to the driver's side for a better look and yes, it was very close indeed. I slid back to the passenger side to climb out but the dray was so close that the door wouldn't open wide enough for me to get out. Another look on the driver's side showed me that I would have to step out onto the track and walk around the truck. By this time, the train was getting too close. I was too scared to try this route and "Besides," I said to myself, "Jim wouldn't leave his truck and me where we'd be in danger."

At that moment, Jim stepped out of the office, saw the train and gave me a horrified look. The train flashed by and then I remember seeing another horrified look on the engineer's face. The truck and I were both fine except for the rear view mirror on the driver's side. It was gone — clipped right off by the train.

Jim always liked to tease me by saying, "I was put in this world to take care of you." He was implying, "Seeing as how you're too dopey to take care of yourself." To which I would answer, "Just so long as we both think you know what you're doing!"

"A Cold Camp" in Reno, 1954: Someone will always ask you what was your worst time. My grandmother saved the letter I wrote her, so I will quote it directly.

Reno, Alta.
January 14, 1954

Dear Grandma:
We're in a bush camp about 26 miles east of Reno, a small town southeast of Peace River. This well will be around 6,800 feet deep, for Shell Oil, and we expect to be finished sometime in March.

We left Athabasca in the morning of the 28th at 11 o'clock. One of the drillers, Rusty Bennefeld, took his car and followed us on the first leg of our trip, Athabasca to Smith. It took us 6 hours to make only 50 miles. The roads were very bad — slippery and heavy with snow — we had to be pulled several times, once by the snow plow which was coming along behind us. We ate supper in Slave Lake that evening and kept going to High Prairie where we intended to stop for the night. But along came Bill O'Hagan, one of Jim's old drillers, to meet us. His trailer was in Donnelly, another 40 miles along, so we kept going and reached Donnelly by midnight. The roads were good from Slave Lake on.

Next morning we started out again and reached the camp by 2 o'clock that Tuesday afternoon. Jim had been told by Regent's office that the camp was in and the cooks were there and everybody was just raring to go to work. Well, we sure were in for a let down. The "camp" consisted of 6 shacks dumped down every which way on one corner of the lease. The lease itself was covered in snow about 3 ft. deep; the only sign of life was the catskinner's shack with a little wisp of smoke coming out of it. After some snow was cleared away, we pulled onto the lease, with the trucks loaded with the rig right behind us, and the cooks behind them, bringing in some supplies. There was no place to leave the food, so they left it in the trailers, and there was nothing

> they could do. The cook shack, having been dumped on its side, was a mess. The stove was all smashed to pieces inside (no firebox) and there was no coal or fuel of any kind to use anyway. So the cooks left and the truckers began unloading the rig, and I cleaned up the trailer and got supper for the men. Being the only woman in camp I was elected to cook. Trouble was, I had only dishes enough for six, so the men had to eat in 3 or 4 shifts, while I washed dishes. Had to melt snow to use for water as the men were all too busy to get any. They sure had their hands full trying to make those shacks livable — no light, no heat, no fuel, no bedding, 10 below. The first night the men had to be divided up to sleep in the trailers and the catman's shack. I've had two sleeping here right along.

What I didn't tell Grandma was that I was cooking for the 18 to 20 men with very little for food, just what we could find in the supplies left there. For three days the menu was the same: bacon, eggs and soda crackers for breakfast; T-bone steaks, tinned 'Scotch broth' soup and crackers for lunch; and the same for supper. No bread and no vegetables but thank heavens for the T-bones. Not being a good cook, I broiled them to death in my little gas oven. But the men never uttered a word of complaint. They took turns holding my eight month old baby, Shirley. They waited patiently 'til I put their dried out T-bones and crackers in front of them. When the cooks finally did show up, I was never so happy to see anyone in my life! I'm sure the men were happy to see them too.

That camp was memorable for the cold weather we had that winter. By mid January, the temperature had dropped to 54o F below zero. The men had to keep little torch cans of diesel fuel going under the lines at the rig. It was so cold that the diesel fuel itself was beginning to jell. I stayed in that camp for three months straight with no trips into town. Jim was afraid to put the baby and I into the broken down old company truck he was driving, for fear of a breakdown on the road in such bitter, cold temperatures.

One crew did have a problem on their way back into camp. They picked out one man to walk for help and piled their warmest clothes on him. But before he reached the camp, he was met by two cars from the rig. The crew members from the rig went looking for this crew that didn't arrive on time. The crew were plenty cold but OK and very glad to be rescued.

"Grizzly Bear" in Swan Hills, 1957: Jim came into the trailer about 9 pm saying, "I've got to get my gun. There's a big bear out in the garbage pit and we've been trying to scare it off, but it won't leave. Mrs. Kuhl (the cook) is having kittens about it, so I guess I'll have to shoot it." A few minutes later a single shot was fired, then Jim re-appeared saying, "I'm going to call Al Oeming. That was a grizzly bear I shot. I sure wouldn't have done it if I'd realized it was a grizzly. Downhill, in the dark, it looked like a great big black bear but it has grizzly claws."

By the time I walked out to see it, the guys had winched it out of the pit and up the bank. When they lifted it up, we could see that the bear was huge with great long curved claws about the length of my fingers. Next day some of the fellows skinned and buried the bear. Jim spoke on the radio to Al Oeming who asked him to please not shoot any more bears. Al would be in camp as soon as he could with a live bear trap. He wanted very much to capture a grizzly bear.

It was early May and we were stranded. The frost was out of the ground which resulted in the winter roads turning into mud and swamps. Our only means of transportation was by helicopter. However, two weeks later, a mud splattered but smiling Al Oeming stood in our trailer asking, "Do you have a vacuum cleaner I can use?" We watched Al as he meticulously cleaned all of his camera equipment. Then he was off with an eager crew of volunteer helpers from the rig who were going to help dig up the dead grizzly.

Having been in the ground for two weeks, the carcass was so 'high' that most of the volunteers 'cratered'; but Al waded right into the mess and carved the bear up. The skull was put to boil in an old bucket of water set over a fire which was built on the farthermost corner of the lease. Even at that distance, the wind would blow the stench our way.

Al came in with an assistant, a young Bible-quoting fellow who kept his little Book in his shirt pocket when it wasn't in his hand. When this lad discovered that the crews worked on Sunday and all through the holidays, he thought he'd fallen among some really wicked people and was ready to walk out of there. Of course this made the lad fair game and he became the day's entertainment for the crew. Frank, our cook's helper, told him that tying an Oxo cube in a little mesh bag and lifting it in and out of the boiling water would tenderize the meat on the bear's skull and would shorten the boiling time. So this lad followed Frank's instructions and sat beside that stinking bucket with a pole and a string, looking like Simple Simon, until his boss happened to step out and see him. Al soon put a stop to that!

Al reappeared at my door, smelling like the dead bear, asking for rubbing alcohol. I gave him a large bottle and he said, "Oh, that's just right." A few minutes later he brought it back. Floating in the alcohol was the bear's penis which he asked me to keep somewhere safe until he was ready to leave. In answer to my questioning, stupified look, Jim said, "He needs to keep it 'til he can examine it to figure out the bear's age."

Well, okay. A little later I looked at this object on my kitchen table and I was suddenly struck by a bright idea. Off to my neighbour's trailer I went, holding the bottle behind my back as I knocked on Jo's door. When she answered I asked, "Jo, how would you like to see a pickled pecker?" Jo's jaw dropped and she asked, "What did you say?" "You heard me right," I chortled while pulling out the bottle. She looked at the bottle's contents with wide, shocked eyes and totally NOT amused. Realizing that I had some explaining to do, I babbled, "It's the bear's" and on and on 'til she finally gave me a weak smile. She was too shocked to ask, "Where's the rest of the peck?"

Two smaller female grizzlies, both silver-tipped and very thin, hung around for a few days after the big male was shot and vanished before the trap was set up. The bear trap, which was put out in the middle of the garbage pit, caught a couple of black bears a week but no grizzlies. Releasing the trapped bears became the new entertainment. A crewman would climb onto the top of the culvert-shaped bear trap and lift up the gate. The bear would come charging out as hard as it could for about 60 feet then the bear would stop and look back before continuing on out of there.

Our dead grizzly bear was 7 1/2 feet tall and weighed around 800 pounds. The bear's estimated age was 40 years. Al said that it looked more like one of the last Great Plains grizzlies that preyed on the buffalo rather than a mountain bear. Jim always felt regret about that bear and he never shot another bear after that.

"Gerry Comeau: One day one of our senior drillers, Gerry Comeau, showed up at my door asking, "Sheila, would you do a favour for me?" I said, "Yes" and then found out that he wanted me to cut open his thumb. A steel splinter had gotten into it and the splinter had not festered but grown a hard lump instead. It was hurting to work with but he didn't want to take time off for a trip out to see a doctor. He felt that it was just a little splinter and that it wasn't very deep so would I take it out, please?

"Why me, Gerry? I'm not even a nurse." I said. And he replied, "But I want you to do it." So I gathered up disinfectant, tweezers and a razor blade. Giving myself no time to think about it, I sliced his thumb open with one stroke. He screamed and jumped but in that split second before the blood started to fill the cut, I caught sight of the piece of steel which was bigger than I'd thought it would be. In another second, I took it out with the tweezers, sloshed disinfectant all through and, holding his thumb as tightly as I could, taped it over. He was still praising me about it as I hurried him out the door, so I could lie down and fight back the nausea and dizziness that swept over me. He healed up beautifully but never again would I play doctor.

A Tribute to an Oil Wife: A friend summed it up best, speaking about his wife a couple of years after her death: "When we were first married, we didn't have a trailer. We lived in rented rooms, hotels, a garage and a skid shack. Some of those places were pretty grim but she would sew curtains, cut pictures out of magazines, make cushions and ornaments and spread them around. Werever we were, she made that place feel like a home. That's why I still live in our trailer and I haven't changed a thing since she died." What a better tribute could an oil wife wish for?

Sheila Davidson (1997)

Geraldine (Gerry) Dunn

Gerry lives on an acreage near Wabamun. She travels to the well site leases with her husband while he is consulting. Gerry is his girl-Friday which includes doing the secretarial work. She has traveled with Doug to Australia, Singapore, western Canada and the United States.

Yes, some of the experiences that I have had in the oil patch date back to 1957. This was the first experience that I had and it was my initiation into the patch. My husband went out to Sorrento Island, B.C. He was diamond drilling out there and it was quite an adventure. He had a trailer that the company supplied for him. He phoned and asked me to fly out.

This was my first flight. I flew from Edmonton to Calgary then boarded a plane from Calgary to Vancouver. We were just over the mountains and the engine caught fire on my side of the airplane. I was absolutely horrified. I thought, "Oh, my Lord. I lived in the mountains, I love the mountains but I don't want to end up in a plane on the side of a mountain."

We returned to Calgary. I was really scared. I phoned Doug on the Island and I said, "I'm sorry, the engine on the plane caught fire and we can't come right now so I will be late." We finally got another plane, transferred everything and arrived in Vancouver.

When I got there, I found out from Doug that I was going to catch a float plane on the ocean. I'd never done that before. And I figured, "Oh-oh, and I can't swim", but I went to this place and caught the float plane. The pilot said, "Don't worry Gerry, everything is going to be fine." When people tell me not to worry, then I start worrying. I got in the plane with my luggage. Taking off was really great because he had the pontoons on and we just went up in the air so nice and slick. I thought, "Oh, this is going to be all right."

There's a lot of ocean to look at when you are flying over the islands. When the pilot came down to land at Sorrento, he hit too hard and we just about went under the water but he brought it back up again. I was thinking, "This is crazy!"

My husband met me at the wharf and I said, "Don't ever ask me to do this again. Where's the rig?" He said, "Oh, we'll drive over to it." We stayed at the rig and I met all the fellows. They were very nice and everything turned around. I made friends with the cook at the camp and he asked me, "Gerry, have you ever had clams right out of the ocean?" I said, "No I haven't. Why?" He said, "Well, the tide is out right now and if you go out there with Doug and dig up some clams I will cook them for you. You will really enjoy them." So we grabbed a pail and shovel, and Doug and I took off in our rubber boots and went out to pick clams.

All of a sudden Doug picked me up and had me over his shoulder, and the pail and the shovel in one hand, and running like blue blazes. He was just heading for the shore. I shrieked, "What are you doing?" I was pounding on his back and I yelled, "Let me down." He said, "The tide is coming in." I said, "It is not." He said, "It is so, listen to the noise." He finally let me down on the shore and I said, "That wasn't the tide, the sea gulls were flying out." Well, that was another experience.

We went out to Australia in 1977 and lived there to 1979. It was really nice there. We lived in Surfers Paradise, which is Australia's gold coast. Doug was on a well out in the outback. He wanted me to get a ticket to come out and the plane from the rig was going to meet me at Adelaide. I got up to Adelaide and the plane ride over Australia was quite a different sight compared to Canada and the mountains. It was like a great flat pancake with a bunch of bubbles in it. And there were hundreds of different colours of green all across Australia. I found out later that there are hundreds of different types of eucalyptus trees. The koala bears eat them, it's their main food.

The reception I received at the rig when I got out there was unforgettable. The little town of Iniminka had a bar in a little hotel, and everyone went there if they wanted to visit. There were two 'campies' and they made up a bed for me and a bed for Doug and signs that said, 'his' and 'hers'. They had flowers in there for me, and I was really treated quite royally. That was the first time that I had been in the outback. I was shocked at how sharp the stones and rocks were because it was just like melted lava.

We were there on the tenth year and that is when it usually rains. When it rains in the outback, the ground is absolutely covered with yellow, pink and purple flowers. I was lucky enough to be there on the tenth year. It's got the good things and the bad things all mixed into it. Australia was a beautiful place and we really enjoyed it there. It's a lot like Canada.

The next memory that I recall was in 1980. We went to Grande Cache, where Doug was a consultant for Amarada. The rig was Westburne Drilling #4. We were in the bush with the bears and the wildlife, two miles from Muskeg Tower, on the Forestry Trunk Road. I met a real nice bunch of men there and they really treated me great. We had a good time! The rig was down away from the camp. You had to go up on a hill to get to the camp. The camp was really neat.

There was a young fellow from Newfoundland working on the rig as a roughneck. He used to come up for lunch and take it back to the men on the rig. One day, this young roughneck and I happened to be in the kitchen at the same time. I was talking to him and I asked, "How do you like it out here? Do you miss Newfoundland?" And he said, "No." We got talking and he said he had a very large family of twenty-one.

I said to him, "My goodness gracious. The two-twenty must have gone through every morning and your Mom and Dad probably woke up and didn't know what to do with themselves. What a size of a family." It took him awhile to catch on to that one. He was really a nice young fellow and he was a hard worker.

One day he came up for the lunch box. He was carrying it out from the kitchen at the camp and there was a sump right out by the door. His boots must have been slippery because he slipped on the iron step and down into the sump he went. I have never seen anybody get up so fast and into the bathroom under the shower with his clothes all off, in all my life. Of course, the lunch went into the sump when he went down, so the cooks had to make another lunch for the boys. He came out of the shower, put some clean clothes on, and took the box down to the rig. He didn't stop for lunch, he came back up and had another shower.

One day the doors were open and a brown cinnamon bear came in one end of the hallway and was just sniffing around. The cook finally saw him. Everybody began screaming and yelling. They jumped up on the tables. There was a lot of excitement for awhile. This was the bush and you had to expect things like this.

I've collected a lot of stickers over the years and I have about three or four albums of them. There are a lot of men, including truckers, who come up to see Doug in the trailer. I went up to one trucker and asked, "Do you have any stickers for your company?" He answered, "Yes, I do but no kissy, no sticky." I said, "Oh, OK." He didn't know who I was. I think he must have thought I worked at the camp or something. When the guy went to the other side of the truck, I snuck into the trailer so I'd be there when he came to get his bills signed.

I sat at the kitchen table, and when the trucker walked in the door, he looked at me and asked, "Can I get the uh?" I looked at Doug and the trucker asked, "Can I get this signed, Doug?" I said, "No, no, no, no sticky, no signy." I got lots of stickers after that.

Another time, in 1980, we were about 30 miles north of Hinton on Montgomery #43, when Mount St. Helen's volcano erupted. Doug was consulting and it rained all the time we were out at the rig that summer. It was absolutely horrible. It was like we were living in a bowl of mushroom soup.

The rig was down in the bottom and the camp was up the hill. We were sitting in a slough. The mud was up to the tracks on the tractor, you could just see the top of the tracks.

The D8 had to take everybody up and down and get the lunch box for the crews. So the skinner used to come and get Doug and I when we went up to camp. It was terrible. If one of the salesmen came, the cat had to bring him down, drop him off at the rig and take him back. Sometimes they had to come over and see the consultant. There was a walk along where the rig was. I sat at the window watching the men standing there looking down at this heavy mud and wondering where to step off!

Once I saw this one fellow step off and he went right down to his hips. I quickly ran and got my camera and took a picture of him. He was shaking his fist at me. Someone pulled him out. Things like that happened. When he stepped off the walk, I shouldn't have laughed but it was humorous. He came in later and told me, "Gerry, you took a picture. I'll get you for that." Those are the fun times and the hard times.

It rained all that summer up there. We were three months on that hole. When we came out, we were so glad to get out and we never wanted to see mud again. When I've been out with Doug to the rigs, I have met a lot of really nice service people and the fellows on the rig work so hard.

In 1993, we went to the Simmonette at Valleyview. The rig was 60 miles in the bush off of Highway 43, and that was one of the worst wells that Doug and I have ever been on. It was very hard on Doug. He was there for three months, and from the time he got there it rained, and they had to haul everything into that rig by cat. Nothing could drive through that mess.

I came in two weeks before they finished. I could only drive so far so the cat owner met me with a 4 by 4 and took me in. This was the first horizontal well Doug ever drilled in this country. It was all very interesting. They brought some machinery in there that I never ever dreamed that I would ever see.

We've gone out to a few other wells. We went to Saskatchewan and to Montana in 1996. That was more like a holiday than anything. Doug was doing a well down there for an outfit in Bridger, Montana. That little town had never had so much excitement as when they saw the oil rig lights go on, and stay on all night. We were right on top of a mountain and the rig could be seen right from Bridger. We were there for ten days and then came back to Alberta.

When we were down in Montana, we went to see the town of Red Lodge. This was an old mining town, started by people who came from overseas. It is the most beautiful, scenic spot that you would ever see. It was just a pleasure to be there to see it. We met a nice fellow down there and he said that if we ever come down for a holiday, he would drive us around and show us some more of the area. We'll be back.

I would like to say here that the oil patch is something completely different. You put up with a lot of hassles. You put up with a lot of mud a lot of rain and a lot of things happening on the rig. I had to stand by my husband because he needed my help to get through these tough times. We have met some wonderful people out of the oil patch and we still keep in touch with them.

Doug still goes out working. I love going with him because I do the books and the daily reports and I get to meet a lot of people. For me, this is part of the oil patch and I've loved every minute of it. I'll tell you, I know that some of these experiences I would never have had if I had not been around the oil patch.

Gerry Dunn (1997)

Irene Fyfe

Irene married George in 1942 and began a nomadic lifestyle, moving around Alberta and Saskatchewan. She is still active in "Oil Wives" and lives in south Edmonton.

I met my oilman in Calgary in 1941. We married in 1942 in Calgary and began a nomadic life style with a small touring trailer which was stuffed with my worldly goods. We pulled it with a Model "A" Ford which managed to transport us from location to location while wildcatting for oil. We traveled from southern to central to northern Alberta to such places as Tilley, Taber, Truax, Raymond, Kinsella, Minburn, Morinville, Vimy and Girouxville where mud was clay and children had to be rescued from ruts more than once. Our home later became a house on skids that could be hauled by truck or train.

In 1952, two camps of homes were loaded onto flatcars and moved to Camrose. That was the beginning of a more normal lifestyle for my three children and myself. George commuted to locations from there and the children enrolled in permanent schools. We bought a real house with running water and electricity. It was a great place to raise a family for such things as swimming lessons, Brownies, Cubs, Explorers and C.G.I.T.

I joined the Oil Wives Club and every third Wednesday I would join with three or four other oil wives to drive to Edmonton to an Oil Wives Dinner Meeting. We would meet there with other oil wives from many oil companies to exchange ideas on crafts, skits, recipes and knitting patterns, etc. It was always interesting. Besides, it meant being out for a dinner that didn't require bringing a casserole. There was always good entertainment usually put on by the various oil clubs.

We stayed in Camrose for seven years and then moved to Calgary. I transferred my membership to the Calgary Oil Wives Club where I enjoyed the many activities such as curling, golf and socials. Our children were now in elementary, junior high and senior high schools.

George went on a two year stint to Libya and I joined the "Learn to Paint" Artists Group of Oil Wives. It was something I had always meant to do. We transferred back to Edmonton when George returned. One week later he was sent to Norman Wells which was a drastic temperature change from 90 degrees in Libya to the deep cold of the north.

I transferred back to the Edmonton Oil Wives where I bowled, curled, played bridge and helped with all crafts such as decorating trees for the Festival of Trees.

Now that George is retired, we continue to live in Edmonton and I continue to enjoy my friends and activities in Oil Wives.

If I could do it over: I don't think I would change anything. It was a rough life at times. Other times it was quite a romantic life. I certainly learned my geography.

Irene Fyfe (1997)

Elsie Garstad-Rosenau

Elsie is retired now, living in Edmonton. She remembers the excitement when oil was found just outside of Leduc. The year was 1947. She was 16, attending school in Camrose and little did she know that this new development was to shape her destiny.

In the spring of 1947 the male population in Camrose began growing rapidly. The American/Canadian Rush was on as oilmen, all shapes, all kinds, arrived from all over the continent to get into the action. I remember the swaggering walk and the soft, slow speech that many of them used. They came in from Oklahoma, Kansas, Texas and Tennessee. Some even came in from New Serepta!

I remember one of the Americans in particular. His name was Dave and he worked for Baroid. He drove a new, or almost new, company car. When I expressed my admiration for his car, he replied in his slow drawl, "If you think this is a nice car, you should see my Daddy's car. My Daddy drives a Linc—oln." Back then I had never heard a grown man in Alberta call his father Daddy. And I had never been called 'honey chil' in my entire young life! But he did. It was an exciting time for all of us but we knew it wouldn't last.

Later, while working in an office in a small town in east central Alberta, I met a tall, blue-eyed man, age 21, who arrived in town with an oil crew. He was an ex-sailor, now a khaki-dressed, wellington-booted oil man and I was captivated. We were married the following year and I went into a most memorable experience that lasted 20 years.

The working conditions were very different then from what they are today. The living conditions were certainly different. In the post-war years work was not too plentiful and then suddenly, opportunities became available to earn twice as much money on one shift than ever was thought possible before.

There were humorous antics; especially those played on the 'green guys' or 'broncos', the nicknames used for the inexperienced men. Oh, these men had a different type of humour!

The men worked, sometimes driving for hours in the mud, only to arrive at the drilling site to work all day in more mud. These men worked in rain or shine, ice or snow, thunder or lightning.

One of the first places we moved to was Breton. It was early in the spring of 1953 and places to live were at a premium. We managed to rent one-half a house. The family had simply separated the house into two parts using plywood sheets, and left behind beds, bedding, dishes, furniture, lamps and ornaments. The owners moved in with their grown children.

The day we moved in, I went with two of the girls I had just met, to the pump across the road to 'fetch our pails of water'. A woman, looking like she had seen better days, came charging out of the house situated on the adjacent lot. She demanded $5 from each of us before we took any water.

My new friends and I didn't have $5, nor did we have the courage to confront her so we went away. We decided to wait until midnight to try to get our water. The plan worked until the screeching of the pump woke the woman, who came out the door in her nightgown, screaming at us and demanding payment. We ran with the pails we had managed to half-fill, over the road, across the ditch, losing most of the precious water.

Suddenly, I became very angry. I, who was usually so complacent and agreeable, loudly voiced my opinion. "This is a town pump and SHE does not own it! Let's go back." We marched back, filled our pails as the woman raved and ranted. We each took our turn telling her to shut up and go back into her house.

She stopped screaming but stood at a distance watching us. She was still standing there when we left the pump. After that we saw her occasionally; however, she avoided eye contact and would cross the street or walk right past us.

Another memorable experience was our move to Grande Prairie from Edmonton. We towed our 32 foot trailer with a pickup truck. It was mud all the way! Eventually the clutch went out and I was left with the trailer at the side of the road. I stood there with two babies under 19 months of age and waited for what seemed an eternity, while my husband hitch-hiked into town for the part he needed. The ride from Whitecourt to Valleyview, non-stop, took nine hours.

It was a nightmare for everyone! At one point, because the windshield became splattered right after he had cleaned it, Fred rolled his window down so he could see the road. A clot of mud covered his whole face and I, who had been silently weeping for sometime, burst into hysterical laughter! I'll always remember what happened next. He turned to me and roared, "Woman, I have never hit a female in my life, but so help me God, if you don't stop that damn laughing, I'll clock you!!"

I stopped laughing. There was neither tears nor laughter left by the time we finally arrived at Valleyview which was only a service station then and more mud.

There was such a scarcity of water! In Beaverlodge, a town near Grande Prairie, the 'water man' delivered water at five cents a pail. He drove a team of horses hitched to a sleigh in the winter, and a cart in the summer, hauling a huge barrel of water. He came on scheduled days, although sometimes it would be late afternoon if he had bumped into a party the night before.

We moved many times. One summer we lived on an oil lease, and then later in Wanham. We finally settled in Grimshaw for three years, before moving to Edmonton in 1961. My husband began working for Imperial Oil that year and worked steadily until 1972. Some of the locations he went to were Fort Nelson, Judy Creek, Swan Hills and the Arctic. The men were flown out to the drilling camps for three weeks and then flown back home for one week.

Now, at last, the health insurance was paid, the pay cheques were deposited directly into the bank, and we had a savings account. We bought a house and went on annual vacations. I thought I had died and gone to heaven!

The highlight of the year was the annual Imperial Oil Christmas party. These were always held in mid-December. The bar was open all evening. There were white tablecloths displaying a fabulous array of food, complete with appetizers and liqueurs.

There were good times and there were other times, but when I reflect on my life and times as an oil patch wife, I think I was fortunate to have been part of the 'rush', lucky to see the changes unfold. I can visualize almost every recollection printed in this book as I read them, because I was among the thousands of people who followed the rigs in the fifties.

Elsie Garstad-Rosenau (1995)

Katherine (Kathy) Jaster

Katherine lives in Edmonton. She moved around, in a trailer, to some very isolated places. In this story, she recalls some of her experiences, during the late fifties and early sixties.

I was married in the 1957, in beautiful Lacombe, and that was how I became involved in the oil patch. From there we moved to live in Red Deer, for a while. My husband worked in the oilfield and when we married, I had to resign from my job. I was working for Alberta Government Telephones and it was a promising job but I couldn't stay on as a married woman.

From Red Deer, we moved to Buck Creek, which was a real eye opener. It took us a long time to travel through the mud, and rough road. It rained a lot that year and the countryside was quite damp. We had difficulty in driving and had to keep cleaning the mud out from under the fender wells. We were practically swimming in mud. We found a one room place to stay in Buck Creek and we were lucky to get even that. Eventually we bought a mobile home. It was 8 feet by 24 feet and it was locally manufactured. It was quite compact and certainly a palace by comparison to what we had been living in. It was a used trailer and dirty but I cleaned and washed it up. My husband was away at work and I had a lot of time to scrub and clean and put it together. We stayed for some time but moved back to Red Deer in the fall of 1958.

Two months later, we moved from Red Deer back into mud country again. My husband was working at Lodgepole now, in a camp job, so I had to live in Buck Creek. It was quite an experience. Meanwhile, while we were living in Buck Creek Pembina Oil had a big complex built. There was a company town with all kinds of houses. I wondered, at that time, what it would be like to live in one of those company houses. I was living in a mobile home on the outskirts of Buck Creek. The mobile home didn't look quite as glamorous as what the houses did, but we met some people. I got to understand the value of having lady friends because they were always around. The men were always away working some place.

During that time, I adopted a surrogate mother. Her name was Laura Lindsay. She hosted a morning program on CFRN television and she cooked, sewed and talked with us every day. I tuned in every day. She was like my very special friend, helping me get through some very lonely times. For those of us who lived alone she became quite important in our lives since we were out in the country and very isolated. That was also the time when the babies began arriving. It was all hand laundry and no pampers. We had no dryers, only outside clothes lines.

One other thing that was really interesting in this mobile experience was, often we were told to park in areas where the grass was never cut. Every time the door was opened and closed, grass came in. We certainly didn't have much refinement around those places. One other thing that I discovered and I was unable too cope to easily with, was the distinction that seemed to be designated to people in mobile homes. We were almost in the same class as gypsies or wanderers. The name that I heard us being referred to, quite often, was gypsies.

We were not allowed to have a telephone unless we paid a huge deposit. Because we were in a mobile occupation, it was difficult to obtain good credit rating. This was quite hurtful too, because there was a great lack of trust. Yet, I always felt we were no different than the others. Later, I returned to Calmar and I spoke with some of the old-timers who lived there during the original oil rush. Most of them said that there were a lot of oil workers in the beginning that did leave debts behind when they moved on. Some of them even left through the night. This was very disturbing to the people who weren't used to seeing that happen and that seemed to brand all of us. I was careful and I worked very hard to prove that we were worth just as much as anyone else.

We stayed in this very mobile life for about five years. We came into Edmonton in 1962. The children were still little and they weren't in school. My husband decided that we would stop moving around and that I would stay in one place. By that time, we were in a 10 foot by 35 foot trailer. It was quite different then. We lived in a very large trailer court. It was definitely comforting to meet these women at the laundromat and through these meetings, I made many friends.

We bowled together, shopped together and if we didn't have cars, we helped each other. Most of us were without vehicles, but the odd person had one. That was a blessing, since the bus service didn't come to the trailer courts. They were all set up outside of town for some reason. There weren't any trailer courts in the middle of town, near amenities. The court that we were in was out of town, and we lobbied to get bus service. At that time, I remember speaking to an alderperson in Edmonton. I called because I thought there would be some sympathy shown to our cause. We needed a bus service closer to the trailer court. I was almost spat at, and was told that I was a gypsy, that I didn't need to ask for anything. They wouldn't consider doing anything for us. That, I must say, was quite another experience.

After awhile we started looking for a bigger place and we found a trailer which was built in Ontario. It was a superior product, better built, with thicker walls, a warmer structure all together. It had bedrooms, and a living room section, rather than a combination room. I was amazed to see how efficiently the space was used. It was a classic example of a well organized trailer. I thought of this one as my Cadillac.

Memorable recollections: There were some good times. We went to some good company parties at the Petroleum Club. The beautiful club in Calgary, on Center Street, was also open to us. We also had a lot of nice barbecues at the O.T.S. park. It was a such a pleasure to go to these and meet with other people in the same industry.

I think one of the biggest upheavals in my life, was when we had to sell everything, and leave Alberta to move down east. In 1972, we went across to the Hibernia field, off of St. John's, Newfoundland. That was certainly different. We had two children and we bought our first house in St. John's. From then on, we lived in houses, which was a blessing. St. John's was a real experience.

The highlight of our whole trip was when my two children and I were invited to come and dine at the captain's table, on a ship. I had called the R.C.M.P. and told them we were from the prairies and we would really like to see a big ship and that I didn't know my way around. They said, "OK, we'll see what we can do for you." I didn't expect a response because they were busy. However, they did call back.

They invited us to come and dine at the captain's table on a ship. We were accompanied by the ship's doctor and other notables of the crew. I was the only woman. My children and I came on board the ship and we had an eight course dinner and we were shown around the ship. It was marvelous to be there, to have this service when we didn't expect it. There were places where women weren't allowed on the ship, and they certainly pointed that out to me. There were superstitions, at that time, that they still believed.

Every Sunday was Harbor Day and we would go out there and visit the ships that were in port. They would let us on the ships and we also toured submarines. When we toured Signal Hill, we found that experience astounding. When you stand on the top of the rock, it's as if you can hear Marconi talking with you. This is the spot where the first radio wave was sent across the Atlantic. It gives you a sense of history. St. John's is a very historical place. This year St. John's is having its 500th anniversary and I would love to be there to celebrate.

We stayed in St. John's for a year, and then we came back to Edmonton. A short while later, we moved to Calgary for two years and then returned to Edmonton to stay.

If I could do it over: I wish that we could have been more accepted. Alberta is made up of a variety of working people. Not all of us can go to work in an office with a brief case every day. I remember when my children started school. The kids that lived in houses weren't allowed to play with the kids from the trailer court, because we were classed as transients, yet many of us were been long term residents.

I think the oil patch needed some of us to change it's bad image. By our perseverance, we managed to make the best of a tough situation, prove our worth and raise our kids to be responsible adults. I don't think I would change anything at all. I was glad to be, in my way, an "actor on the scene".

Kathy Jaster (1997)

Lorraine Jewitt

Lorraine is retired and living in St. Albert. During the '50's and '60's, she moved fourteen times in seven years. She worked many years as a Lab Tech in the Sturgeon General. It was a happy time when they moved back from Swan Hills to St. Albert.

I began to move around with the oil patch as soon as I got married in October, 1955. I met my husband at a dance at the Rainbow Ballroom in Edmonton. He wasn't in the oil business at that time. Sometime during the next few months, he went to work for Haliburton. We were married a year after we met and the first thing the company did, was send him out of town. You know, that's what they do. He was told that he was to be in Virden, Manitoba for the first of January. This was very disappointing to me because I worked and was making almost as much money as he was. To lose half your income was really quite a let-down, but then I wasn't going to work that long anyway. My husband worked out of Virden for a year and Steve was born in Virden.

Then we moved to Estevan, Saskatchewan - another lovely place. Suzanne was born there. We moved to Stettler. We're back in Alberta and it's OK. Ken, our third child, was born in Stettler.

When we moved back to Edmonton, I got my life really back in order. I liked it a lot. We had a nice house in St. Albert, and Steve was in grade three, Sue was in grade one, and Ken was my only kid at home and everything was really good.

I could get dressed up, go downtown with my little gloves on, and go to I.O.D.E. meetings and do good things. Everything was going just fine. Don came home one day in 1964, and announced, "I've been transferred again. They made me field man up in Swan Hills." I said, "So, are you going to run it from here?" He answered, "No, we will live there." "But," I said, "Bill and Darlene live there." He told me, "They're going to Whitecourt."

That night we went out to celebrate this. It didn't seem like a celebration to me but it was to everyone else. He took me up to see Swan Hills and we got up there and the sun was shining. There were no sidewalks or anything but the sun was shining. It didn't look that bad until he took me to our house. It was a very small house with no basement and two bedrooms. I said, "I can't live in this small house." Then he told me that he had permission to build on another room. He asked, "What did I want?" and I said, "A master bedroom." That was the plan so I didn't go up to Swan Hills again until moving day.

I'd get reports, "Oh yeah, it's coming along just fine." I'd ask, "Will it be ready when I get there at the end of June? He would assure me, "Oh yeah, definitely it'll be ready."

Well, moving day came and I made all these arrangements. Don came in to help with the final part of the move. He got a call to go to Red Deer for a day or two. I was just absolutely furious. Instead of helping me, he had to go to Red Deer.

I did what every woman should do. I went out and got my hair done. I had my little kids all dressed up in shorts and things, like every kid wore around St. Albert.

We started out on Saturday morning, it was beautiful here. The moving van was going to be in Swan Hills when we got there.

When Don found out that we had gone, he became quite concerned. He phoned Swan Hills and asked, "Is it raining?" and they said, "Yes." He said, "My wife is on her way up with the kids. I want two drivers to go and meet her at Barrhead because she doesn't know about gravel roads." I got there and I met this truck on the road. Oh, it was slippery! The truck came up behind me, and the driver asks, "Do you need some help? Don sent us out so one of us could drive you into town." "Oh good.", I said. At any rate, I thought, I looked nice because I'd had my hair done to go to Swan Hills.

We got up to Swan Hills. It was just a sea of mud. Grey, gloomy mud. They took me to the hotel and I checked in there. I got a phone call in the morning telling me that the moving van was there.

We went over and found the house. There was no third bedroom. There were only footings and the base floor for the addition. We're moving into this house! So they asked, "Where do you want your bed?" I said, "Right here." I had it put right in the middle of the living room because I thought I might get things done faster that way.

We were moved in and Don was on his way. At least a Haliburton car had been seen down the road. He did show up a bit later. He was not impressed with his bed in the living room but, too bad.

Swan Hills was very small and we lived very close to downtown. When I went out to get my groceries. I noticed that all the women wore men's rubber boots with gray work socks inside them. It didn't look very nice so I didn't want them.

Somebody said "You should buy yourself some boots, that's all you can do." I said, "Oh I hate them." I trudged around without boots. It rained every day and the kids couldn't ride their bikes because they got what Sue called 'plugs'. The wheels would just plug right up with mud.

One day I was cleaning my house and I found a whole porch full of muddy shoes that belonged to me. This is ridiculous, I thought, so I went out to buy rubber boots. I found little red rubber boots that were much more appealing to me than the other ones. They were fashion boots and they came right up to my knees. I was not about to turn them down and wear gray socks either. If I wore gray socks, then nobody was going to know it.

A story that was told around Swan Hills, and I don't know if it was true or not, was the one about when they were looking for the new townsite of Swan Hills. A couple of government officials were sent out in a helicopter. They were flying around and one of these guys said, "Put 'er down. Put 'er down, I have to go pee." They landed and he did whatever he had to do and then he looked around. He was on top of a hill and he said, "We'll build the town right here." There was all this muskeg and this scrub spruce and so they bulldozed all of that off and that's how the town site came into being. It was no small wonder that it was tar, because all the top soil was gone.

Then there was the story of a guy who had a whole lot of speeding tickets. He had lost his license because of these. I think this happened in the 1960's. He collected them, and as he did so, he thought they recognized his car and that he wasn't being treated fairly.

He was driving around in Edmonton for an hour or two before he noticed the police were following him. He couldn't get rid of them. He did everything he was supposed to, but they pulled him over. He asked, "What did I do? I saw you back there and I was trying to do everything right. What went wrong?" They answered, "Nothing, this is 'Safe Driving Week'."- he was the best driver that they had seen that day so he was the winner of a certificate for safe driving.

If I could do it over: Well, you have to remember that I got married in the 1950's and in the 1950's the husband's job was what was important. I had my own career but that kind of fell by the wayside. I didn't have a choice. If the circumstances were the same, I would go again. If it was now, I would have a lot more to say about it.

Lorraine Jewitt (1997)

Catherine (Kit) Johnson

Kit and her husband Cliff live in Wetaskiwin. When Cliff was working on the rigs, they moved around in a trailer to many locations. There were not too many trailer courts in those days. If there were any at all, there was room for only two or three. They usually lived on farms or on the lease.

I remember there were approximately eight families moving around from location to location. The day we moved, everybody rushed to get out on the road first. We wanted to get the best parking spot in the next place. Everyone had young families and we wanted to be as close to the wash houses as possible.

I didn't have to get up at five in the morning too many times. The porch had to come down first and it had to be loaded. Cliff liked to be the first one out on the road.

It was like a convoy. The first one to get there always made breakfast for the next bunch. We didn't always get into trailer courts. Sometimes it would be on farms. We wouldn't always be parked at the same place, we'd be split up but we still remained close and saw each other often.

We were parked in Stettler in a trailer court and Jim and Dorothy Werstiuk were parked right behind us. This big electrical storm had come up, and Dorothy was really scared She had a tiny, crying baby.

Jim was out working so she packed the baby up and came over to our place. It rained so heavy that on her way to our trailer, she dropped the baby bottle. We never did find the baby bottle. She was afraid to go home because of the lightning and thunder, so she stayed at our place for a long time.

Another time I remember is the time our trailer rolled near Whitecourt, we stayed in a hotel. The smaller hotels usually had one bathroom, down the hallway. During the night, I went in there and there was a guy, lying on the floor, passed out. I couldn't even get in there.

I moved around to the rigs with Cliff probably six or seven years. When the kids started school, I stayed in one place. We moved to Wetaskiwin, in the summer and that fall, Doug started school. Canbridge had their shop here. We have lived in Wetaskiwin since 1964.

We have three sons, all connected with the oil industry. The eldest is an oilfield consultant. The second boy works in the gas plant at Wizard Lake. The youngest son is a directional driller and works for Computalog. We have three grandchildren - two girls, ages four and thirteen, and one boy age nine.

Kit Johnson (1997)

Helen P. Kirkpatrick

Helen married George in 1937. Her husband was a roughneck working for Imperial Oil. He went up the ladder quickly. George was a toolpusher, taking him to many locations over the years. They moved around a lot - 28 moves in ten years. Helen has lived in Edmonton since 1947 with the exception of 2 1/2 years when they were in the Maritimes. She still plays in a band.

I was born on a farm near Little Chicago, which is now called Longview. We moved to the oil patch with a dance band and I played up until I got married. The dance band was made up of my dad, my brother, my two sisters and myself. We called ourselves 'The White Family Orchestra'.

I married my husband in 1937. There wasn't any place to live except this one woman let us live in her house with her, and she had the kitchen and one bedroom and we had the front room and another bedroom and we shared the kitchen. We did that more than once.

George was working in Tilley. He was roughnecking then for Imperial Oil, and for 40 years he worked for that one company.

We didn't live in Tilley very long. He came home one morning and said, "I have to be in Calgary by noon today." So we threw everything in the car, what we could get in, left what we couldn't get in, and then went back to Turner Valley. Then we went to Taber. There was quite a bit of oil activity around there. We lived in the hotel. We had a little apartment at the back of the hotel and to go to the bathroom we had to go through the hotel and up the stairs. That was a fun place!

When we went to Taber I was supposed to be met in Lethbridge by George's friend. This friend had just got a new girlfriend so he forgot to come and get me. So I landed in Lethbridge with two little kids, both asleep. I took the oldest one off, stood her on the platform and went back in the train and took the other one out. I went into the train station and waited and waited. Finally, they sent for someone from an office to come take care of us. She took us to the place and the next morning, I got word to George in Taber. The worst part was taking one child out in the middle of the night and setting that child down and having to say, "Don't move until I go back and get Joy."

It was about 1940 when George went wildcatting. We moved around 28 times with that in the next ten years.

We moved to Mannville in February or March in 1946. The weather was very, very cold. We moved into an old army hut that George brought in for us to live in. It was one long room. We had very little furniture - a couple of beds, a table and chairs and a stove, very little more than that. We hung our coats and clothes on nails on the wall and put our other things in suitcases and a large cardboard box. There wasn't a bathroom, we went out to an outhouse.

We had two children, Carolyn and Joy Anne, and I was expecting a baby who was born on March 31, 1946.

A few days after we moved in, there was a knock on the door. I went to the door and there were two smiling people, Lawrence and Doris Larcombe and their daughter Ardith. They said they had come to welcome us. I asked them in but didn't take their coats as we had ours on to keep warm. I made coffee.

We were having a nice visit when it started to snow. The snow sifted in from the ceiling all around us. They stayed until we drank our coffee. But we have been the best of friends ever since. I think it was my most embarrassing moment.

"It was awful. It was terrible. And you know, we had a dog and he was very well trained until we moved into this place where the snow came in and everything. Then he thought that it was OK to just go to the bathroom any place.

We moved to Edmonton in 1947 because Carolyn, our eldest one, had gone to five schools in grade two and we felt that it wasn't good for her. We stayed in Edmonton after that all the time except when we went to Prince Edward Island to drill.

We moved to Prince Edward Island with a new baby who was six months old. We travelled on a special train with four cars and I don't know how many dogs. We lived in P.E.I. only a couple of years. I enjoyed it in some ways - I had been used to people being poor. The people who owned the stores and businesses were rich. All the rest of the people were very, very poor. My cleaning lady had six children and lived in a garage with a dirt floor. Those things I found very hard.

So when we came back here, we came back to Edmonton and my husband worked out in the fields. He left again for three months and worked in Gaspe, Quebec.

If I could do it over: I don't think I would change anything. It was an exciting way to live and I didn't come from a rich family so I wasn't missing anything.

I went back to playing in a dance band about four years ago. We call our band "The Dots". I've gotten older now and I find my drums too heavy so I only play for dances and at the malls. The other band plays in senior citizen's lodges. That's where I started out, in senior citizen's lodges.

Helen Kirkpatrick (1997)

Dorothy Manning

Dorothy remembers the many moves during the time she spent in the oil patch. She was 17 when she married and began moving around with her husband to the various locations where he worked. Her husband was toolpush for Cantex Drilling, General Petroleum and Amerada Petroleum. She lives in Edmonton.

I wasn't even old enough to walk when all this moving around began. In 1920, we moved to Port Reve, Saskatchewan. My father was working for the Canadian Pacific Railroad and earning the princely sum of twenty cents an hour.

My husband, Joe Manning, and I were married the 25th of December and we left for Longview on the 26th. We had fifty cents when we landed in Longview. We didn't have a car so my father drove us down there. I remember my husband very generously went down and bought my father a twenty-five cent cigar so he could have something to drive home with. We then had twenty-five cents to last us for two weeks.

I walked into that little shack and I didn't know what to do. There wasn't much room to put anything but in the top drawer of the dresser, I found a four pound jam pail, a pail of peanut butter, a pound of butter and a loaf of bread. That was all there was and we were going to have to exist on this for two weeks. I thought, well, and I left a good home.

The manager at the Red & White Store in town gave us credit so things turned out all right. My husband started out digging sump holes for the drilling rigs with horses. His wages were fifty cents a day. He considered himself lucky to get a job, because there were fifty men standing right there to pick up the job if things didn't work out.

From this he started building rigs. That's when they were building them out of lumber, not metal. They used lumber and built them from scratch. We were in Hartell when he worked on his first rig. He built three more rigs before he went on to something else.

We had no chairs. We had four apple boxes to sit on and a home-made table. We had four orange crates, pounded to the wall. This was in 1937 and I thought, "What have I got myself into?" But time went by and we never starved. We didn't owe anybody. I couldn't even cook, believe it or not. My mother always said, "Get out of the kitchen, I can do it faster myself."

I had to learn to cook though. In February of that year, I found out I was pregnant. I had just turned eighteen on February 22.

The baby was born on October 30th, 1938. Joe took me to High River hospital in a Model A coupe car. I can laugh now, but it was no laughing matter then. We were going up the hill towards Little Chicago and then we would go down to Little New York. As we were going up this hill, we lost a wheel. It passed us on the road. I thought to myself, "This is it! This is where I'm gonna have this baby, right here."

Thank heaven for haywire and pliers! Joe went and got the tire, put it back on and away we went. We finally got to the hospital where our daughter was born.

We moved to Millerville later where a well was drilled west of there. After we got there, I got so sick I couldn't look after my baby so she went to my mother's. I was bound that I wasn't going to have an operation but I ended up having surgery and I didn't see my baby again until she was six months old.

Then we moved to Patricia in 1939. We had sold the little car with a rumble seat and had advanced to driving a Model A double seater with a trailer hitched on behind. We carried everything we owned, including a dresser, bed, bedding. We picked our daughter up and drove through sand, sand, sand. It was so hot, 110o F. We had a flat tire; before we got that one fixed, we had another one.

We eventually got to Patricia. The house we moved into was owned by a carpenter. When we put out the lights that night, there were bedbugs all over, even dropping from the ceiling. They didn't bother me but my husband was literally chewed to pieces. We decided to throw the mattress out, covered the springs with tar paper, put each leg of the bed in a can of kerosene, went back to bed and slept the rest of the night.

It didn't take long to find another place to live. One of the fellows gave us a granary. It was better than putting up with the bugs and we lived about a mile from the lease.

The following spring the rig blew in. What a mess! We lost one fellow. He had so many operations they literally killed him. The men stayed, trying to get the well under control. Another rig was put up and that one blew up.

We left the oilfields in 1942 and went to a homestead. In the winter of 1943, we went on a trap-line in Banff National Park. My daughter went to live with my mother in Strathmore. When we came back from the trap line, we bought a farm by Warburg. If my husband hadn't seen the red flares in the sky around Leduc, we'd have stayed on the farm!

The red flares were from Leduc #1 and Joe decided that spring of 1947 he was going back to the oilfields. I wanted to stay on the farm. I said," You go and follow the red flares and I'll stay here." By that time we had gathered quite a bit on the farm. Joe didn't agree. "No", he said, "it will be too much work for you." I replied, "Well, I don't know if it would be any more work than following you around all over the place." I did not like to stay behind. We had a sale, sold everything and moved to Calmar where we rented a house. We moved around for several years after that living in a skid-shack. We were in Redwater between 1948 and 1951.

This moving got to me after awhile. We moved to Stony Plain in 1953. Our daughter was just little then, Ideco Drilling had just brought a brand new rig up from the States. It was in January and 60° F below zero. Joe was pushing tools, and kept saying, "There is no possible way we can rig this rig up. With it being this cold, everything will just snap."

Orders came to set it up, and it was set up. Some men from Texas were coming up to see this rig and they were warned to bring warm clothes. Sixty below to a Texan didn't mean a thing. They don't know that when it's that cold your breath can even freeze as it comes out of your mouth. They came up wearing suits and oxfords!

The rig was about eight miles south of Stony Plain and Joe told them, "I'm not taking you out to the rig 'til you get some warm clothes on." The guy from the head office in Calgary had warned them about the cold as well but these men just would not listen. Joe wanted them to put on 'longjohns', a snowmobile suit and boots.

The Texans did not want to spend the money so Joe said, "OK, but I don't want to be responsible for you freezing." He took them out there but the rig wouldn't run. It was far too cold. They just stood there and froze. They couldn't believe that it could get that cold. They probably still can't believe it. They never ever came back!

Things started to open up in the north. We moved the skid-shack to Valleyview with Cantex Drilling Joe was drilling at that time. In

1954, we had a small trailer and then moved to Grande Prairie, to a well by Sturgeon Lake. Then on to Dawson Creek and Fort St. John in 1956.

Joe would come in and say, "You've got eight hours. Can you move?" I got so I could pack a trailer and be ready to move in no time at all. It got so it was automatic. We always kept boxes. Never threw the good ones out. Still don't.

While we moved around, our daughter managed to keep up in school. She went on to secretarial school in 1951 and got a job in a law office. She started working when she was sixteen.

We learned to look after ourselves and help each other. That sort of thing was done then, much more than it is now. I recall one time in Fort St. John, we had just moved our trailer into the trailer park. Joe was pushing tools and wasn't home that much. We all had oil furnaces in our trailers with a big barrel outside. The furnace would quit running when the oil was cold.

There would be about four or five of us women outside with a flashlight and a little can that we lit and held underneath the line to warm the oil so it would run. We would holler at each other across the way. It would always be in the middle of the night.

Most of us would be in our 'nighties' with just a blanket wrapped around us or whatever we could find. You could hear these women as they stood there struggling with the job of thawing the oil. "I'm not going to do this anymore. This is the last time." A man's voice would yell, "Oh, shut up. Keep quiet." Most likely he had probably just got home from work or a party. It was usually two or three in the morning.

After this happened four or five times, I decided that I didn't care whatever happened, I told them my plan. I said to the bulk dealer who filled the tanks, "I want a five gallon can of kerosene. I'm going to fix this once and for all, because I'm not coming out here in the middle of the —night anymore. I'm gonna put half of the kerosene in that oil tank."

I did just that and it worked. The rest of the women bought kerosene and we all were happy.

We had some good friends up there. We had some wonderful times together. But you know, when you begin to fall up the stairs drunk, that's where I draw the line. I don't need any more of that. No more bottles. I don't need them.

Something interesting to note about a bottle— I didn't even have a rolling pin to start out with. My first rolling pin was an empty whiskey bottle. Every time I moved, I threw that bottle out because I knew there would be another one around, wherever we landed.

Swan Hills, I don't want to think about it. It was 1959 or the early 60's. Joe was working for a rental company. I remember the mud was unreal. It stuck to your boots. Our trailer wasn't that far from the store. I couldn't walk more that a few feet without having to scrape the mud from my boots. It would stick that much. Swan Hills was the most godforsaken place I was ever in.

We, the women that were in this, are lucky though to have these experiences, not that we'd do them again. Some people just don't believe us when we recall some of what we had to go through. I've been in places where they threw up four poles, threw a canvas around the poles. There was a pole to sit on and THAT was your potty.

Yes, we went through some very hard times, but I learned to save twenty-five cents here and there. I can still save. The way some people throw money away really bugs me. We went through the thirties and that was probably the best damn training we ever could have had.

Dorothy Manning (1997)

Olga McBride

Olga married Dale in 1951. He was a toolpush, working for Regent Drilling. She moved around, living in trailers on leases for many years. She and her husband have made their home in Edmonton for 31 years.

Once, in 1954, we trailed our 26 foot trailer, leaving on Grey Cup Day. We were driving on the old Slave Lake road. That was the only road we could take to the Simmonette. The first night we made it as far as Valleyview, on that old winding road. On the way there, I remember, without checking the hill, up Dale goes and here was I behind with the car.

When he got stuck or had to stop, I had to run around, looking for a rock to put under the wheels so he wouldn't slide backwards with the trailer. We had chains on and he just kept diggin' till he made a hole so he could hold the trailer in one place, otherwise, it would have dragged us all down the hill. Luckily, a fuel truck came along then. He had chains on and so he helped us up that hill.

Once, on our way to Edson, we were parked beside a service station in Whitecourt. We slept in the trailer. It was so cold that Dale wore his fur hat to bed. We had our little girl in between us and even the cat got onto the bed. That was the only time it was allowed on the bed. The cat helped keep us warm.

In the early days, whenever it was wash day, I could get the clothes washed by noon. When Dale came in for lunch, he had two choices, either hang up the diapers while I made lunch or vice-versa. He would usually hang the wash.

Olga McBride (1997)

Editor's note: *At this point in the interview, Dale adds a comment, "Oh, I did that too? I must have been pretty house-broke in those days."*

Imogene Monks

Imogene moved up from Wyoming with her husband, John and their three children in 1957. She lived in a trailer for three years and then moved to a house. Her last child was born in Edmonton. She has lived in Beaumont for 17 years. She enjoys being around her 14 grandchildren and five great grandchildren. She's an avid swimmer and spends time doing quilting and crafts.

I was 17 when I met my husband, John. He was working in coal mines then, but shortly after he went to work on a rig as a pumper, checking producing wells. This was with Haliburton and later John went into the field on the rigs. John was going to be moving so we were married four months after we met. We didn't move for a few months but then we went to Worland, Wyoming. It was hotter than Hades there. I nearly died with a new baby. I was 18 when my daughter was born. Worland is just east of the gates into Yellowstone.

John started working on the rigs as a roughneck. He soon went working derrick, then he became a driller and then a toolpush. We made so many moves. We had Linda in Colorado, we went to Wyoming and then we moved to Vernal, Utah.

We just lived in whatever was available. For half the time, it was a motel room. In Vernal, we had a little teeny trailer house about 8 feet by 14 feet or something like that. No running water and no bathroom. None of those neat kind of things. It was in Utah that we had our second son. From there we went back to Wyoming and we had our third son there. Then we went to Denver and then from Denver back to Wyoming. And at this time, he stopped working on the rigs and went to work for a service company in 1955. It was D.N.S. Drilling and Service. He was away from home a lot more.

I had these three kids and I never had a washing machine until the third child was about six months old. Before that, I carted all the kids to a coin wash. When we started out, it was the old wringer washers. Dragging the kids along.

We moved to Casper, Wyoming three different times. By now we had a house trailer that was about 8 feet by 42 feet. We bought it in

Denver in 1957. The trailer actually had water and a bathroom in it.

Our oldest child was in kindergarten when we moved up to Canada. She started kindergarten in Wyoming and then we crossed the border on January 1, 1957. John had been up here three months before that. We pulled our trailer up here. We crossed the border on New Year's Day and everything was closed. They told us that we had to leave the trailer there until it could be inspected by Customs. And John said, "No, I'm not waiting for Customs to open tomorrow. I've got a wife and three kids here. We're going to Edmonton." They said, "OK, you call Customs when you get into Edmonton and have them come and inspect the trailer then." I'm sure they aren't that lenient now.

I remember my daughter, Linda who was about five years old at the time. When we crossed the border, her dad said, "Well here's Canada, we're crossing the border. We're going into Canada." And Linda said, "Oh, no. And they don't speak English there. And I don't speak anything but English." When Linda had told someone in school that she was moving to Canada, they had told her, "Oh, they don't even speak English there."

It was beautiful weather all the way up. We had a spot at the Allendale Trailer Park but we couldn't get into it yet. We parked the trailer in the parking lot at the Airlines Hotel. Two feet of snow fell that first night. The trailer sat there for two weeks in the parking lot because we couldn't move it. The kids thought that was great. They were really living it up. The hostesses and the waitresses in the hotel really catered to them. They never had so much freedom in all their lives.

Schaffer Tool sent John up to open up the company here. He was manager, salesman, did the servicing and the whole bit for a while. He wasn't home very much since he was on the road most of the time. And the kids were always sick when he was gone. That's par for the course. That's the way it goes.

When I actually got into the trailer court, we were hooked up to water and sewer and things like that. There was mud up to the eyeballs. It was a California built trailer and I'll tell you that we nearly froze to death for three years in it. Finally, we got rid of the trailer and just rented a house. We've been here for 40 years. We came for two years and it ended up being the rest of our lives.

Memorable recollections in the trailer court: We lived in the trailer court for three years. I would say that it was pretty miserable. And I stayed up many nights because I was so afraid that something would go wrong with the furnace. We would have to keep it turned so high to keep the trailer warm that I was scared to death that it was going to burn up. I would stay up at night to check on the kids and to make sure everyone was all right. I wouldn't even sleep. And then I would nap with the kids during the day and I would stay up during the night. Looking back, I don't know quite how I did it but you have to do what you have to do.

The window blew out of the trailer in the middle of one night in early spring. The trailer had huge picture windows and a window literally blew out. So here I am with three kids and freezing to death. Thank goodness I had good neighbors. Everybody looked after each other in the trailer courts because the husbands were always gone. Just keeping the fuel tanks full was a problem because it was turned on high all the time. The smell of the diesel fuel went through everything in the place.

My husband stayed with Schaffer Tool until the company sold out to Rucker. In 1973, John started his own painting and sandblasting company, Sahara Sandblasting. He sold it to two of his employees and it's still going strong. I think that Schaffer Tool was the first company in Canada with blow-out preventors. I think that they were being sent from the States before that. I don't know if there was anyone here who serviced them at all before.

John never had a day off since he was the manager. He never had a day off period. He took one here and there, but he was on call 24 hours a day, seven days a week for years. He was a workaholic and he just thought it would fall to pieces if he wasn't there all the time. I suppose that goes along with the type of guys that came from that generation.

We couldn't afford to go back home very much. I think we were here four years before I went home the first time. We had another child after we moved here. We had one everywhere we lived except New Mexico.

If I could do it over: I probably wouldn't change anything. It was tough times and they say it was the best of times for Alberta as far as the economics and everything but we sure didn't see any of that. The wages were a lot higher than what we were used to previously but still not in comparison with the cost of living. The cost of living was very high here compared to what we were used to. It was hard. The saving grace of the women in the oil patch was the friendship of other women in the oil patch. I never did join the Oil Wives but there were two people I met in the trailer court, the girl beside me was married to a trucker and he was gone a lot. She had four kids and I had three kids then. We were always there for each other when one of the kids was sick or if one of us had to take a kid to the doctor. That helped make life bearable.

Some of the women didn't drive. I had a car. The girl next door to me didn't drive so I helped her get her groceries. I taught myself to knit the first winter I was here. I'd never seen those Siwash sweaters until we came up here. All the kids wore them. I thought, "Well, my kids have to have them. This is where they are. They've got to have them. So I learned to knit.

It was hard moving up here a long way from family but I have never regretted it. I would have never had the experiences or gotten to know the people that I have if I had stayed in Wyoming. I've lived in Beaumont 17 years.

Imogene Monks (1997)

Mary Nazarenko

Mary was hairdressing at the O.K. Barber Shop in Leduc in 1947. She remembers the time when haircuts were 35 cents and shampoos and waves were 50 cents. Those were the days when she had to carry water from a pump outside and then carry it out again. Mary and her husband, Harry live on a farm near Leduc.

I was still downtown when the oil discovery was made near Leduc in 1947. I was at the O.K. Barber Shop. There was a private pump at the back of the shop. I would pump the water and carry three pails up to warm them up. There was be a tub under the sink. I would have to carry it out again. So when three pails were gone then I would have to carry in some more water.

I would average maybe at least ten or more customers every day. In the summer, the customers would average out. It would depend on what it was, whether it was hairstyling or whether it was perms. Perms were only $1.50 then. Haircuts with a shampoo and wave were 50 cents and haircuts were 35 cents.

I remember one Saturday night when a lady from Calmar phoned and said she was tied up. She asked me if I could do five perms that Saturday night. I said, "Sure I can." That was when we had the overhead spiral and overhead heated clamp machines. I told them to come in. I did all five perms. They came in about 6 o'clock and I finished about 1:30 or 2 o'clock in the morning. I had to clean the shop after but that's what you had to do. With the oil patch, we had a good chance to raise the prices a little bit with our perms averaging $4.95. That was a lot of money. It was better than $1.50.

Main street and 50th Avenue had no good sidewalks, no cement sidewalks. They were all wooden sidewalks. If you walked then you had to walk ahead of each other because one end of the sidewalk might come up and hit you in the face. We used to tell them to go ahead when we were walking together. We just had to say, "Walk a little bit ahead just in case one board is loose." Main street was just muddy. Right in front of our place, where the barber shop is now, there was a big pot hole. They used to put big tree trunks and things in the pot hole when it was raining. And it would always disappear.

It was almost like quicksand. I never thought that the pavement would stay there but it has.

The town of Leduc could have benefited more if more oil people could have moved into the town. The businesses that were there, flourished and new businesses started up because of the 'boom'. There were so many rigs around and the men had families who shopped in town.

When Harry and I got married, we lived in a two room house. I had a coal and wood stove and that little kitchen stove warmed the two rooms that we had. We burned coal for quite a while and then we changed it to gas.

Water came into Leduc in 1951 or 1952. We were one of the five people who first took the town water. They had five wells. I still couldn't understand people who wanted to stop progress and not vote to have running water. We were a little concerned because we thought we would be voted down.

I think that's where the oil people helped us. They wanted things to look better and people voted the sidewalks in. Of course, a lot of property owners paid for a lot of that.

There was mixed drinking in Leduc. I only went in once and that was on Halloween night. We weren't allowed in the pool room and women rarely went into the bar. My friend, Fran and I dressed up and went out in our costumes. We lived above the Post Office then and when we left the suite, we locked ourselves out. We knew the policeman, who was also the maintenance man, so we went to him.

We asked him to help us to get back into our suite. There were kids in the jail already behind the bars yelling, "Throw them in here, throw them in here. They're girls." Anyway, we got our suite opened. We went across to the pool room. That was a no-no in those days. Then we went to the bar. I still remember going to the bar. I think that we did drink a few beers but I never did care for beer. We barely sat down and our table started filling with beer. I said, "Let's get out of here." I might have drunk a half a glass more of beer and that was about all. I bet there were eight beer on the table. I couldn't drink any more. That was our experience in the late forties.

Mary Nazarenko (1997)

Faye Osborne

Faye married Bud in May 1953. Bud was a driller working for Regent Drilling working at Fort Saskatchewan. They moved to Ferintosh with their 1952 Pontiac car pulling a 28 foot trailer. Faye moved 49 times with her husband. Later they built a house in Peace River. They moved to Edmonton in 1975. She still lives in the same house.

I married Bud in May 1953. The rig Bud was working on, was at Fort Saskatchewan. We bought a house trailer and lived there until we moved to Ferintosh. My husband was a driller for Regent Drilling. When the rig moved we moved, hopefully, right behind the light plant, if we were going to be living on the lease. Being on the lease meant we would always have lights. I guess you'd say we followed the light plant.

Anyone who had a house trailer could live on the lease and we usually did. We had to haul our water in cream cans from the nearest farm or town. If we bought gas at the garage, they were happy to fill our water cans.

We had a little electric washing machine. It stood about 3 feet high by 15 inches square. It had a little hand wringer on it. There was a little wheel in the side of the washing tub that spun the clothes around. I had a separate tub for rinsing. It worked fine as long as you could get enough water heated to run the thing.

Some of the trailer courts we lived in had a wash house with two or three wringer washing machines. They were always busy. I don't know why we weren't electrocuted. The floors were always wet with water puddles and the power cords were hanging from the ceiling, some were even on the floor.

All the wells were shallow, which meant we only stayed about a month in each place. I have a list of all the places. We moved 18 times in the first two years. In March 1955 we went back into the bush with a new trailer. The trailer was 8 feet by 28 feet including the hitch.

Then my husband got set up as a toolpush in the spring of 1956. And it was back to a small rig again and more moves. Then Regent started going in to Swan Hills. There were lots of rigs there too and it meant lease hops which we did as well.

We went into Swan Hills in January 1959 which was our first stint there. We didn't take our trailer, since the company always had a shack for the toolpush. The kids and I went along and lived with Bud in this shack while the kids were under school age. Once they started going to school we had to settle down a little bit.

Our son Dale was born in October, 1954. On the first of December 1954 that we moved on to a place called Economy Creek, which was south of Goodwyn in the Grande Prairie area.

Bud didn't think he could make the trip pulling the trailer with the car, so he bought a one ton truck. We stopped to buy gas and the fellow said, "Oh, you're going to have trouble with the river hills." Bud said, "Oh heck no, I got lots of power. It won't be any problem." So we went hooting down the highway. We knew we had to turn off at Goodwyn, but we didn't find it. When we came to the Smoky River, we knew we had gone too far. We back tracked and stopped at a little store to ask if they could tell us where Goodwyn was. "This is it," the fellow said. We didn't make the river hills. They were like mountains.

A cat had left mounds of bush along the road when they bulldozed the road through. Bud backed the trailer into one of those to hold it with the vice grips on the trailer brakes. I made it with the car. I was ahead of Bud and I stopped because I thought he was never going to make it. I listened and I couldn't hear anything coming. I thought I better walk back. Sure enough, there he was. So we took the car and drove on into the rig. Bud went back out and pulled the trailer up to the lease.

We'd move into the lease in December moved out in March. It seemed we were there for quite a while. Towards the end of March when we moved to Kaybob. That move was a horror story.

Bud worked from November 1955 for 18 months straight without a break. The company gave us a week off when we were in Kaybob and flew us out. Regent would come out from the city in their plane which usually was for ferrying food and supplies. Roads weren't passable, so the plane was the only way.

We went to Judy Creek, we moved to quite a few places between that and Kaybob. We were in Blackfalds, Sedgewick, Chisholm, Kinuso, and even in Windsor, Ontario for six months. Some wells were drilled for Canadian Salt in the city dump at Windsor. That was an experience. It probably was more of an experience for the fellows on the rig than for me, because I had two small children to look after.

In January 1959 we moved to Virginia Hills by way of Whitecourt. We didn't take the trailer, instead we lived in a small one room shack with a couple of bunks on one end, a desk, and some chairs.

When our oldest boy started school in 1960, we stayed the winter at Fort Assiniboine. Bud was working in Swan Hills. Then we moved to Millet for spring break-up. In 1962, I stayed in Whitecourt for three years while Bud worked at Virginia Hills. We built a skid house with three rooms. It even had a bathroom. These skid houses were parked in the trailer court in town. We moved the skid shacks with one of the rig's high boy trailers. We only moved ours twice, once to Whitecourt and then to Peace River.

We went to Peace River in 1966 and lived there for 9 1/2 years. We built our own home in 1967. Bud was field superintendent when we moved to Peace River. He traveled the north to Rainbow Lake and Zama Lake country. I stayed in Peace River with the three kids who were in school by this time. I only made one trip up to Zama Lake with Bud.

There were so many roads going here, there and everywhere. It was dark by the time we got into the place. I didn't have a clue which direction was which; up and down were the only directions I knew. I was voicing my concern. Bud began leading me on. He came to a corner, stopped and said, "I think we better find the north star to make sure we know which direction we're going." He knew where he was going but I didn't. When we were at Whitecourt and Fort Assiniboine, the kids and I used to visit Bud on weekends. I got lost very badly once.

I kept going down roads which would run out or I would come to an oil battery. I would know then I was in the wrong place and I would turn around and go back. I would get mixed up not know which way I was going. Bud always said, "Just follow the best road." There were lots of best roads I thought. I finally stopped and a car came along. I flagged down the driver and told him what I was trying to do. He said, "You're going the wrong way. Turn around and follow me." I did and by the time I got to Judy Creek then I finally knew where I was. I lived in Peace River until 1974. On New Year's Day 1975, we moved to Edmonton.

Most memorable recollection: The mud is the thing I remember the most. Everything was always a sea of mud. I remember the wimpy, temporary clothes lines that had a habit of falling down. But I also remember the good things. Those were the people that you met. We made our own good times and did things together. We really stuck together, especially when we were in isolated locations We learned to rely on each other and we looked after each others' kids so there was a break to get into town.

Another memorable time was one of the first moves the first year we were married. October 31 we moved from Edmonton out in the bush west and north of Athabasca. As always it was dark by the time we to got close to the rig. We couldn't make the hill. There was a side road going off to what we presumed was a farm. Bud backed the trailer down that road and we spent the night there. We had to sleep with our heads at the foot of the bed because the trailer wasn't level. It was Halloween night and really spooky because it was totally dark and black. Bud got up in the morning, to go to work. He was going to leave me sitting there. That was one time that I protested. He said, "Well, my shot gun is in the closet." I said, "I wouldn't know how to use it anyway. I'm not staying!" The rig's water truck came and pulled us up to the well site. This move was a really bad move because it was one of my first moves in the bush and I wasn't used to it.

I quickly learned how to bake bread by trial and error. While living on the lease, we played a lot of cards and taught each other to play crib. There wasn't much else for entertainment

If I could do it over: I probably wouldn't change anything, knowing what I know now. I don't think those experiences hurt me much.

Faye Osborne (1997)

Dorothy Pickard

Dorothy's retired, living in Calgary. She remembers when the oil boom began in Leduc in 1947. She moved around Alberta and British Columbia and lived in many places, while her husband worked for various pipeline companies in the years that followed.

It was early 1947 when oil was discovered in Leduc. I was young and very much in love with the man I later married. We both worked for the City of Edmonton.

When the oil discovery was made in Leduc, close to Edmonton, nearly every truck driver around those parts equipped their trucks with 'oil tanks'. You see, there were no pipelines then to get the oil to the refineries.

One such truck driver was a fellow named Walter who had worked for the City and knew Ralph. He asked him if he would take his truck to Leduc to get two fill-ups of oil per night and truck it to Edmonton. I went along for the ride, of course, and what an experience to be in on the ground floor of the big discovery!! We'd take Walter's truck around 5 pm. after work, go to Leduc and line up at the wellhead.

As I recall, the wellhead was a little east of the town of Leduc. There was always a line-up at the welled. We'd wait our turn, talking with the other truckers, eat our lunch etc, load up, then leave for Edmonton.

The road was narrow then, two lanes with a dangerous curve right near Nisku. A lot of accidents occurred in those early days and with the oil discovery, that road became extremely busy with oil trucks. I really don't remember how long the oil was hauled this way before they built a pipeline into the oil refinery from the oil wells.

Alberta's oil industry opened up a few new towns, one of which was Devon. The men of that era were a lot of our soldiers, airmen and seamen who had come back from the war and found that there weren't too many jobs. They were all very anxious to get on the bandwagon and secure good-paying jobs which would provide their families with better living conditions and better education.

A lot of pipeline people moved into Devon, into 'skid shacks'. These were small homes, one room affairs, built on skids so they could be moved easily from one location to another as the warehouses moved along. They were the forerunners of the self-contained trailers.

Little did Ralph and I know, back in 1947, that we would become one of those 'oil patch couples'. We came after the original oil riggers and drillers and we were the pipeliners who worked jobs as they became available.

We moved about from place to place but the wages were very good and they got better. When we first started out in 1952, the wages were $1.75 an hour and when Ralph retired in 1984, if I remember correctly, the welders were being paid $23 per hour and had graduated to automatic welding machines. Of course, to make that money, you had to own your welding rig and every job you went on, you had to make a pressure test, plus the pipeliners were unionized.

Then, as the saying goes, "All good things must come to an end," and so the pipeline companies didn't do much work after 1985. There is still quite a bit of pipeline work available but no job has been quite as massive as the Trans-Canada Pipeline project. Those were the days!!

Dorothy Pickard (1996)

Shirley Roberts

Shirley married Jack in 1953. He was working as a locomotive fireman on the CNR. In 1955, he began to work with an oilfield wireline service company. Shirley and her husband live on a farm west of Stony Plain.

As a family, we never moved around much since Jack was with the service trucks. He would be gone two or three weeks at a time so I was left at home to raise our four kids. But we were independent and did lots of things even though dad was gone a lot.

Birthdays were a big deal in our family, we always had a cake, lit the candles and sang happy birthday. Even when dad wasn't home for his birthday, we had a cake for him and sang happy birthday to him.

Shirley Roberts (1997)

Dorothy (Dot) Rutherford

Dot was a war bride. She met Jim in England and married in 1945. They were both in the air force. She came to Canada in 1946. Her husband worked for Imperial Oil. In the eight years they moved around, they lived in 33 places. Dot and Jim live in Edmonton.

We met in England. We were both in the air force and we were on the same station. We were married in 1945. My husband came back to Canada in the fall of 1945. I came to Canada in the spring of 1946 with a boat load of war brides. Before the war, my husband worked for a short time in Turner Valley.

When he came back he was hired on by Imperial Oil. Jim worked for Imperial Oil all his working career. Of course, he changed from seismic work to working on small drilling rigs. They called them slim haul rigs. Eventually, when we came back to Alberta we were up in the Peace River country for a while and then he was transferred to construction work. And then we got our first house in Regina in 1954.

When I came over, he was doing seismic work. We bought a trailer and we lived in trailers for eight years. The first trailer was 8 feet by 16 feet and it wasn't insulated or anything. It was just like a box really. It was a home made trailer. We lived in 33 different towns that we lived in the trailers, mostly in Alberta and in Manitoba. We had two sons during that time. We lived in little towns and we would park in someone's back yard or a garage or a skating rink or any places like that. Of course, we had no conveniences in the trailer, no running water.

We had lots of funny experiences. We moved to Manitoba when my youngest boy was three weeks old. It was road ban at the time. We had the other little fellow who was three years old in the back seat. We had an old 1932 Buick which pulled the trailer all the way to Manitoba.

Our oldest boy was born in 1947 and he started school in Turner Valley because I was down there looking after Jim's mother. After she died, we went back up to Peace River where Jim worked and our son started school there. By the time he went into grade two, we were finished with trailer life.

I didn't know anything about the climate or anything because I had just arrived from England and I had no idea what I was doing half the time. I just thought this was the only way I could be with my husband and I had to live like that. The trailer wasn't insulated the first winter.

There were different things that would happen. When I first came, he was on shift work. He would work night shifts when they were on seismic work. One morning I woke up and all the trailer was white inside. And I couldn't figure out what it was. It was frost on the walls. I'd never seen that before because I was a city girl. Often, I've been thankful that I spent those years in the air force because I think it helped me to adjust better and to do what I had to do. It wasn't easy raising two babies. Getting the washing done, carrying pails of water in and out.

We've been in Edmonton since 1968. We went to Regina in 1954. I think we were there for six years. And then we went to Dawson Creek, B.C. By this time we were living in houses.

If I could do it over: I'd certainly make things a little more comfortable and I would have gotten Jim to insulate the trailer sooner.

Dot Rutherford (1997)

Beatrice (Betty) Smith

Betty married Tom in 1945. Tom was a driller working with Cantex Drilling, and this was the beginning of life in the oil patch for her. She and her husband live in Edmonton.

We moved to Taber in 1945. Our first home was a two room suite in a lady's house. We heard about people that lived in these shacks that later became trailers as the years went by.

This shack was 8 feet by 16 feet. The table was built over one wheel well and the clothes closet was over the other. We had a Winnipeg Couch for a bed and the stove was a two-burner coal and wood stove. The oven was on the stovepipe that went through to outside. Many and many a supper was either burned or uncooked.

When #1 son came along in 1947 and needed a crib, my husband built one on the wall above our bed. This little crib had three sides that folded. It was like a box, folded in, up against the wall, and that's where the baby slept.

In 1949 we moved to Calmar with this 8 foot by 16 foot trailer. By this time it had wheels on it and didn't need to be put on a truck for hauling. While at Calmar, Tom left Cantex Drilling and went to work with Regent Drilling. Experienced help was very scarce. Tom was put to work toolpushing two rigs. One on the west side and one on the east side of Calmar. I never saw him. I was just like a widow.

About that time, we answered an ad in the paper. Someone was selling a glider trailer. He was an American pastor. We went to look at it. It was 21 feet long! It had an ice-box and a chesterfield at both ends! It had a table with two chairs, a propane stove with an oven, and I thought I was in heaven. It cost $1,500. The bathroom, of course, was outside.

In the summer of 1951, we moved to Flathead, British Columbia. With three other families, we took four trailers pulled with pickups. We went down through Carway, Logan Pass and Glacier National Park, turned north at Columbia Falls and then through North Fork at the Flathead River into Canada. There was no other way across the mountains. It was close to Fernie but the mountains were between us and the town.

We were supposed to be in there for 17 months and we had to take our supplies and anything we needed to last us for that time. We had to go in there prepared. When we got in there we found that there was no place for the single boys to stay.

There was supposed to be a lodge there but it turned out to be just one room. The married people took the single boys in. The guide told us that we could use the lumber that was there. So while they were waiting for the rig to come in, the boys built shacks for the men to stay in.

We didn't stay the full 17 months but while we were there, all of us learned to bake bread. We all ate wild game, such as elk and deer. For entertainment, we would play rummoli twice a week. We had to stay in there, we weren't allowed to go back across the line.

One night it was too cold for the diesel fuel. We woke up to the cold. Tom woke up our son Barry and told him to crawl in with me. Tom put all the bedclothes on one bed. While Barry was running from his little bunk to my bed Barry yelled, "Its so cold my peeper froze up."

One time a group of women were cheesed-off because the men were going to have a party while they watched a World Series baseball game. The women decided to have a party of their own. I wasn't in on this because I didn't drink. After awhile, they called me over to rescue a little baby who hadn't been taken out of his crib since morning. I was green as grass and didn't know much about babies. We had a little foot tub and I was trying to bath him. Just as I was putting him in the tub, one of the guys came in, the baby slipped into the tub and there was water all over the place. You can imagine the mess, just from cleaning up this little guy.

We came out from Flathead just before Christmas in 1951, and then moved to Saskatchewan with our glider trailer. By early 1952, the General Trailer was being built in Ontario. We got acquainted with the fellow who was supplying our drilling mud. His brother was building these General Trailers. He said he'd like to bring one up into the oil patch and if we were willing to take one, 'sight unseen', just by looking at the pamphlets then he would bring one up. The price was $3,500 and we said, "Bring it!" It was 35 feet long!!

When he brought up the trailer, I had to write the cheque for it. In those days you put special stamps on cheques over $100 or the bank would refuse to process them. I didn't know how many to put on but he said not to worry about it. That cheque did go through with no stamps.

We got to know the fellow that had Barber Motors at Weyburn. He gave us an offer on a 42 foot Commodore trailer that we couldn't refuse. He told us, "If you let us use it as a showplace, we'll give you quite a cut on the price." This trailer had a "Youngstown Kitchen", a washer and dryer and a deep freeze. They had to convince me that the dryer really was a good thing. I thought it wore out the clothes because so much fluff came off them. There was a closet above the washer and dryer so Tom installed a reservoir tank so that I could use the rinse water more than once.

When Barry was five, I taught him correspondence. He did very well and he attended four or five schools a year in Saskatchewan. At one time, I drove him 35 miles back and forth to keep him in the same school. We had to leave him behind when we went into Swan Hills. He stayed with Tom's sister and went to school in Grande Prairie the year he was ten.

We were in Saskatchewan until 1956. When we left it was from Radville, Saskatchewan to Valleyview, in one big hop and then on to Swan Hills. It took us two days, going in on a logging road, to get to the lease. We finally arrived and stayed for four days. Then, because this was a 'tight hole', which meant the company didn't want information about the site getting out, the oil company wouldn't allow families to live near the rig. The trailers were all moved to Barrhead.

The last lease I was on was in 1986. Tom was consulting for C.N.W. We ate like kings, our shack had a jacuzzi and a television set, VCR and a washer and dryer!! Things really have changed!!

Betty Smith (1997)

Francis (Fran) Toner

Fran has been married to Pat for 44 years. They live in Beaumont. In the early days she moved, in a trailer, numerous times. Some of the locations were in bush camps in Northern Alberta and British Columbia. She lived in Fort St. John, High Level and Drayton Valley and places in Southern and Central Alberta. She has been a member of Oil Wives for 41 years, and still is actively working on the executive. She does volunteer work such as The Christmas Elves Organization as well as assisting with speech therapy in the local elementary school.

My mother was the cook in the restaurant and bar in Columbia Falls, Montana. One night, one of the cook's helper's challenged Pat to a squaw rassel in the middle of the dance floor. I asked, "Who is that?" Someone answered, "Oh, he's the Boss." "Oh, good going." I thought. Soon afterwards, we started going together and we were married in 1953.

The first place we moved to was Hoedley. We were in our trailer, a little 23 footer. Suddenly one night, one end of the trailer was tipped over, the door flew open and a whole lot of beer bottles and cans were thrown into the trailer. I guess this was supposed to be a 'chivaree' that the rig hands threw in our honor.

We moved around and lived on a lot of farms. This was better than the little auto courts in the small towns that had only space for three or four trailers.

When we moved up to Fort St. John, that first night we paid $5 for a cream can of water. After that, we bought it by the barrel. We carried our water, I used to carry two five gallon pails of water to do my wash.

We learned to be mechanics, plumbers or just about anything. I learned to take a diesel heater apart and put it back together again.

One time, moving around in the Fort St. John area, we were coming across the ferry with the trailers. I remember being pulled from one lease to another with a D9 Cat, the kids and myself sitting on a blanket spread out on the floor of the trailer, shutting the doors as they flew open.

I remember too, in Fort St. John, we lived on a farm and at night after the lights were out, you could see the mice playing tag on the kitchen floor in the moonlight. This little show stopped when we finally discovered that they were coming in through a hole under the sink.

We lived one whole winter with a broken front window in our trailer. I had dropped something behind the couch and without thinking, I reached down between the couch and window. My head hit the window, it was so cold that the window pane snapped. We were in Fort St. John and the closest window repair was in Dawson Creek. Until we could get it replaced, Pat took some paper, wet it and it would freeze solid to the glass. This worked as a good patch-job. We sure did learn to make do.

When we were moving to locations up and down the Alaska Highway, we patched up more heads and other parts just enough to get them to the doctor or hospital. There was never a dull moment.

One time one of the roughnecks was loaded and driving backwards down the street, in a jeep. The Mountie up there, who was nicknamed Red Head because of his red hair, stopped the roughneck, took the bottle away from him and told him to put the vehicle in the right gear. He did and went home. Red Head was pretty good but one or two warnings from the guy and the 'hammer came down'.

The only time Red Head got a little mad was when Pat and a couple of other guys stole a billy goat in Dawson Creek and took it in the car to Fort St. John. They tied it up to the hitching rail in front of the bar. Red Head lost it then and told them, "You take that goat back to Dawson Creek, to wherever you found him or I'll put you guys AND the goat in the same cell."

We had four children and they were in different schools throughout the years. They always managed to keep up with their school work. It wasn't too bad for them. There were usually four or five families moving from location to location. The kids stuck together and had their own friends.

Back then everybody had fun and it was all one big family. I joined Oil Wives. I've been a member for over 40 years. When we moved to smaller places, you could go out once a month while the men baby-sat, and you could socialize with other oil wives.

Something I will remember always, was my trip to Borneo. I went there for two weeks just before Pat left to come back home. It was a wonderful trip. In Singapore, we went to Boogie Street. It doesn't open until midnight and closes at six in the morning. You take nothing with you. No watches, rings or anything of value. There are people there selling all sorts of things. People are dressed up like nothing you've ever seen. They are called He-She's. See picture section.

If I could do it over: No, I wouldn't change anything. The experiences we've had have been a lot of good memories. Some were hard and difficult but it made people closer. There is a pretty strong bond between everyone that followed the rigs. It gave us all the satisfaction of knowing that if we had to do this, we could do it. Some couldn't. That's the way it is with everything. There's those people and then there are the survivors.

Fran Toner (1997)

Patricia (Pat) Weegar

Pat is the wife of Harvey Weegar. In her 21 years with Harvey, Pat has had many experiences: running the farm while he was at work, moving around with him in a small trailer, cooking for the men at times and doing up daily cost and time books. She enjoys her life and wouldn't trade it for the world.

If you just think about it, a catskinner; a foreman's wife, it takes a different kind of man and a different kind of woman to live those roles. Harvey and I were older when we got married and for the first five or six years, I ran the farm. We had a young son, so I didn't travel with Harvey then. He was gone a great deal of the time.

After we sold the farm and moved into a small place just outside of Grande Prairie, I got more involved in the business. We would take the holiday trailer and I would go with him. I still do that and I cook for the catskinners or laborers or whoever comes out. I enjoy it, there's always coffee on.

I try to take some of the load off of Harvey by doing his daily cost books and his time books. I've also done this for some of the catskinners or the labor men.

I've also been a truck checker, counting the trucks as they're going back and forth. We've been in some muddy places, where it rained for six out of seven days. There was another couple with us and we had a lot of fun. We played a lot of cards. Once I pulled the trailer ten miles from home just to be there on the job.

I recall one winter, he was traveling back and forth from home. He would leave at 5:30 in the morning in order to get to the job, and he wouldn't get home until 8 or 9 o'clock at night. He came home one night about 8 o'clock. It was November 20th and he said, "If I didn't have that trailer winterized then I would be pulling it down to the job." I asked, "How long would it take us?"

Harvey de-winterized the trailer and I loaded it. At mid-night, we were some two hours out of Grande Prairie, over bush road, down over terrain which I had never been over. We were down there three or four days and it started to snow really bad. Harvey moved the trailer up to the plant on top of the hill. The kids thought we were kind of crazy, going out in the middle of the night and setting up camp. We do enjoy camping!!

Catskinners are a special breed of men. Sometimes they work long hours at a stretch. The women at home do a lot of worrying, imaginations can run really wild. There has to be lot of trust when they come in at midnight, telling you they've been working on the cat.

I got a call at 12 o'clock one night from Fort Nelson from Harvey. And I asked him what he was doing, calling me at that hour and he said he was welding ice slugs on a cat. He told me that he had one track in the Northwest Territories and the other one in British Columbia.

They like to joke a lot. Their vocabulary is a little bit different, but they are very good men to live with. They like eating. The hours are very long. Five o'clock in the morning is normal time to get up and make breakfast. You have to get used to being alone all day. I think catskinner's wives are lonely women. At least the foreman's wife gets very lonely.

They get stressed out sometimes and you've got to listen to them. Sometimes I get very tired of 'shop talk' as we call it. Especially in our business, he's on call a great deal of the time. Phone calls can come in anytime from 5 o'clock in the morning 'til midnight or later. You're forever looking up phone numbers, addresses.

It's hard to live with these men because of the hours they have to work. The money is good but sometimes the women view the work as competition. Sometimes I feel as if I'm competing against Wales Contractors because they take a great deal of Harvey's time when I wish he could be with me.

Harvey missed out on a lot when Trevor was a small boy. He missed many hockey games and a lot of ball games but he's catching up on some of these times now with the grandchild.

This happened about ten years ago. With his job, Harvey doesn't really have to operate a cat. He is supposed to make sure that the job is done, he's a foreman.

This guy had started the job and Harvey goes out later and he's going to finish it. Now I had heard Harvey preach many times about doing a clean-up around the wellhead, "Do not go near it, stay so many feet back from it." I have heard this for years and years.

Harvey goes out there and he bumps into the well site! The catskinners love this story because the boss did it. The personnel people didn't have to come in and check it. He had dented it but he hadn't hurt it. It costs about $3,000 or $4,000 to have them come out and check the wellhead.

Harvey was on a job and he does trust his catskinners. And so Harvey had his lunch and he was parked back out of sight. And he decided to grab 40 winks. So he's parked there and a consultant came by and said nothing and Harvey didn't hear him. The consultant went down to the job to check things out and came back and Harvey was still sleeping. And the consultant at that time gave him the name 'easy money'. But it is a just a joke between the consultant and Harvey.

I've had different people tell me that what he does, he does very well. At his job, the men all like him, he's easy to work for but also if they do it wrong he'll tell them or show them. One company that we know of, won't hire on contractors unless Harvey is on the job as foreman. That's a feather in Harvey's cap, I think.

It's the long hours and it's trying to figure out where everybody is, the telephone contacts, the urgency of the job. The oil companies will phone him Thursday and they want all the machinery ready to start the next morning. That means a lot of coordinating and organizing. When they start a new lease there are all these new locations to send these guys to. I have got maps that he has drawn on my tablecloth. It started on a piece of paper and then off onto my tablecloth.

There's phone numbers all over on cigarette packages or on the back of a new letter. When a phone call comes in, I grab a pen and a piece of paper. I just have to be prepared to write down numbers and names.

On some jobs, we've had four or five trailers in camp. If there were two or three wives, then we all got together and had pot-luck.

So you learn to live without ice sometimes. We're usually close enough to town so we can get in and get our fresh meats and everything. When I'm out there, I don't feel as if I'm doing without anything. You find a place to go wash or wash up as far as possible and down as far as possible. We are usually parked by a creek.

You carry a lot of fly spray around with you and you keep the screen door closed.

If I could do it over: It's been interesting and I wouldn't change it. I like what Harvey does. You don't get any glory out of being the foreman's wife. I'm just a housewife like anybody else. I'm a grandma and a great grandmother. I wished I had done it when we first started, but I do like traveling with him now.

Pat Weegar (1997)

The Children

who moved around
with their parents

as they followed
the 'rigs'

or stayed in one place,
waiting for Dad

to come out on
'days off'

Dresdin Archibald

Dresdin was born in 1949. As a young child he moved with his family from town to town until he started school. His perception of those days shed some light on a child's view in the days of the oil patch.

I was born in 1949 as a child of the oil patch. My father was a roughneck for Imperial Oil. He had grown up in the oilfields, having moved to Turner Valley as a six year old in 1928. His father, Lewis Archibald, was once a blacksmith but switched to welding when technology dictated a change. He worked in the Royalite plant in the Valley. My uncles both toiled for Imperial, James as a driller and Lewis as a welder. My aunts also married oilmen. Gladys married Les Lake, who also worked at the Royalite plant. Ida married Imperial welder Samuel "Jimmy" Virtue, one of her childhood neighbours. Youngest sister Courteen, married Byron Brodner who worked for Gulf. As you might guess, all this made for very delicate family dinners!

WW II ended and so did my father's military career with the RCAF. Since Imperial was now drilling further afield from the Valley in order to find new fields, it was an ideal time for a young 'demob' to get away from home and build a life for himself. The life of a young roughneck was exciting and well paying compared to other options. While they didn't realize it at the time, they were participating in a major social change in Alberta's history. We were changing from a rural, agrarian society just emerged from depression and war and dominated by those associated values into a more prosperous industrial and materialistic one. One change associated with this was the new mobility of these industrial workers.

The post war years saw these men entering towns all over the province, drilling out in the farmer's fields, drinking in the hotel and mixing with the locals. On one such visit to the town of Provost in 1946, my parents were brought together. My grandmother ran the Club Cafe on the main street (There must be an obscure Alberta ordinance requiring all prairie towns to have a "Club Cafe"). Her daughter, after a wartime career in munitions factories down east, worked with her in feeding the single oil workers and the usual assortment of other coffee shop habitués. Meanwhile my future grandfather and uncle ran the family ranch south of town. They were solid cattlemen, very leery of city ways. People still often rode horses to town and tied them to hitching rails.

My parents married on December 21, 1946. For Christmas my mother got a radically new lifestyle. Instead of the stability of the farm with its seasonal rhythms she had to get used to moving every few months, night shifts and being viewed as a suspect alien at each new town. The "oil people" were viewed ambivalently. Merchants saw them as suckers ready to be fleeced through the infamous 'two-price' system - one for locals and another for oil people. Superfluous sons saw alternative careers for themselves in the Patch. Daughters were protected from the wild-eyed roughnecks. Farmers saw ways to make a few extra dollars renting out their machinery and themselves for road clearing, etc. In turn the oil people came into some surprises of their own as they came to towns where the main language was not the assumed English, but French, Norwegian or Ukrainian.

Our life was one of constant moves, about once every two or three months. During this regime we lived in the small one room skid shacks provided by Imperial. When it was time to move, the shack was just loaded on to the top of a highboy trailer, along with two or three others. Later we bought a trailer. It looked like the Taj Mahal in comparison. Over time we got to know many towns in this province. Today I can drive to a dozen towns and feel somewhat at home in each, as I remember where our trailer was parked. These include Lamont, Bruderheim, Morinville, Vimy, Munson, Provost, Stettler, New Norway, Leduc, Nisku and others.

This constant moving in small quarters militated against the accumulation of either a large amount of goods or any that were fragile. I remember us sliding down the road sideways with the trailer on Highway 9 west of Drumheller. We moved to a rented house in Edmonton not long after. For some years our trailer was parked in a lot near our new home. We would view it occasionally with great nostalgia - but not enough to want to buy it back and hit the road again. I remember my parents going to view the Lucille Ball film "The Long, Long Trailer" then, with only sardonic humour.

With limited housing and possessions, status seeking was difficult. Most people drove new cars while the women indulged in fur coats. We had both. But that was about it. With many others the rest went into a partying lifestyle.

Personal friendships were difficult for the kids since even other oil families came and went according to Imperial's whim. Parents kept in contact (there was an efficient, patch-wide gossip network) but kids could establish few long term friendships. We knew a family called the Donaldsons. Their two boys, Dwayne and Darryl were our friends. They would enter our life for a day when our parents visited, then disappear again until our paths crossed again. We would manage to pick up where we left off last time, but as many people know, it is the tough shared experiences that come to be valued most. Today after many years in the city most of the closest friends of my parents date back to their "on the rigs" years. No one else understands the early days so central to most oil patch people's memories as they get older.

A new respect for education emerged with the oil workers that was not present with the former farm lifestyle. This was due to learning that the engineers who visited the rigs occasionally were very highly paid and did not face a life on the road. They went to school in places like Norman, Oklahoma, had clean homes and kids with assured futures. None of this was familiar to any of the ex-plowboys on the floor. But as the novelty of high wages wore off and a ceiling to their future in the Patch could be seen many began look around. They broadened their outlook and began to absorb some new ideas. Some of those new ideas came from the wives who could see that this life might not be so fun with a few kids in tow, changing schools three times in a year. Perhaps if Joe learned how to do something in the company's office in Edmonton or Calgary.

In the camps you get to know your fellow workers intimately. Many, due to lack of skills in our people, were from south of the border. Americans were of two kinds - the bosses from New York and Dallas and fellow roughnecks like themselves who hailed from Texas and Oklahoma. The bosses were seldom seen but were known to look down their noses at the locals. The Okie roughnecks were of a different sort. Like their Canadian friends they were often ex-farmers themselves. People found that they were cut from the same bolt of cloth, that they had more in common than they first imagined. Soon many were learning the intricacies of hockey, curling, and Canadian beer. Many ended up making Canada their permanent home, becoming just as critical of their bosses' condescending ways as their Albertan counterparts. This daily contact with real life

Americans resulted in Albertans feeling little of the anti-Americanism that seems to make life worth living for so many eastern Canadians. We have quite a few such friends who have now spent a half century in Canada.

I have a peculiar Christmas memory which many oil patch kids may have experienced around this holiday season. We always used a Hughes-type tri-cored drilling bit as our Christmas tree stand. The bit was very heavy so the tree wouldn't tip over. The 'stand' immediately identified the occupants as oil people to all those poor benighted souls who had 'civilian 'jobs.

As I was approaching school age my father got a job in the safety sector of the business. This meant a move to Edmonton and eventually Calgary. It also meant a real home for all of us, especially my mother. I adapted well to city life in the new burgeoning suburbs, since at six adaptability is your main talent. I do remember wondering what life was like for the kids who were never part of the Patch. I couldn't believe that some people lived in Calgary all their lives, in the same house. I didn't feel envious. I just assumed that all people moved all over the place. I felt sorry for the poor beggars. At the adult level my parents then had to contend with another transition, that of small town to city as well as from transient to consumerist living. We settled in to Calgary in the 50's and 60's and did well economically but few memories developed there that would ever compete with those of the Patch in any future reminiscences.

Dresdin Archibald (1997)

Ian Archibald

Ian was born in Turner Valley in October 1943. He spent his formative years in the Valley and shares some recollections of what life was like as a child whose parents were involved in the oil patch.

I was educated mainly in Edmonton and spent one and a half years in Commerce at the University of Alberta. I quit Commerce to get married in January, 1964 and started articling as a C.A. in mid-1964. I finished my articles and graduated as a C.A. with Clarkson Gordon & Co. (Note: I resigned from the CA Institute a few years ago because I had never practiced publicly and never ever had any intention to do so.) I then went to work, briefly, for my largest client, the City of Edmonton (Finance Dept.). I became the volunteer Treasurer & a Director of the 1978 Commonwealth Games Foundation. After leaving the City at the end of 1972, I formed a small consulting group with three partners. Although I served short periods as the CFO or Treasurer of several companies, the majority of my time from 1973 through 1982 was spent consulting in nearly every industry that Alberta has to offer. In 1983 I became involved with a telecommunications venture that I am still a partner in. For the last year I have also been involved with a new Internet casino venture. At the present time I am Chairman and CEO of a U.S. public corporation that has invested in the Internet casino.

Being born in Turner Valley and having spent my formative years there has naturally instilled in me a special feeling for the `patch', a term that has never seemed new or unfamiliar. My father's ambition as a teenager in the Valley was to work on the rigs. He was lucky enough to have spent his career mainly with Imperial Oil and some of the 'legends' of the Alberta oilfields. He started in the cable tool days and saw the transition and growth from the front lines. Dad worked on some of the more interesting holes and in some of the most remote locations, in those days, that wildcatting had to offer.

Dad was a driller on the Golden Spike well which was the sister well to the Leduc Discovery well of February 1947. He drilled in the Northwest Territories. He also drilled on the Brazeau well. This well lost circulation and had to have a record one million pounds plus, of drilling mud flown in to the site. He worked on at least one well fire with that notoriously overrated braggart Red Adair. He maintained that the regular crews could have put out the blazes but the excitement was good for I.O.L. stock prices.

The production, or wildcatting, end of the oil business meant that the action was (by necessity) remote. And remote meant going further and further north. In the Alberta of the `40's and `50's this meant travel on bush trails, farm roads, gravel roads and perhaps even some two-lane highways. More and more it meant flying on company aircraft such as Beavers, Otters and DC-3's. But mostly it meant being away from home, family and friends. The camaraderie of camp life and shift work kept the men going. On the home front it was usually a different matter.

As a youngster in the Valley, this life was the norm. The entire community was steeped in oil. The whole place must have seemed like one giant support group for the oil patch widows All of this was created from the beautiful smell of the place, to my grandfather's welding shop, to the street names, to the presence of my uncles and to the crude oil on the streets which kept the dust down and kids shoes stuck.

Coming to Edmonton in 1950 was a dramatic but not a too traumatic change. Dad was working further and further north during that period and with the travel conditions this meant more long-change time wasted traveling to and from the well site. So we were to move north to a place I had never heard of, having just completed Grade 1. I remember asking an older neighbor kid about Edmonton and he gave me a typical 10 year old's line of BS, not knowing a thing about which he spoke.

It was not really like moving into a city when we moved to the far west end of Edmonton just north of McKinnon ravine. Consequently the move was easy: new friends, new surroundings, new and more varied things to do while still being close to the countryside.

The intent of the move was to allow Dad to spend more time at home. In those days they worked six weeks in the bush and had 12 days out. The drilling contracting companies would send their crews in for the entire winter, from freeze up until the road bans were off in the spring! Phones were not generally available except in emergencies. The basic problems were still there. For Mom and Dad it meant weeks of loneliness and longing with no supporting mate. Then a hectic reunion followed by a review of the activities of the kids and homey issues of the last 6 weeks.

One thing that an oil patch kid learns very early in life is the complete absurdity of the phrase “Wait ‘til your father gets home!” I never heard of a father who wants to lay a lickin’ on a youngster for teasing his or her sibling for some vaguely recalled incident after an absence of about five weeks. However, the count-down to Dad’s return was always filled with mixed emotions. It was nice to have this semi-stranger around but he had trouble remembering that he wasn’t on the job at home too. I would be given an assignment of jobs as if I were a floor hand, and I should add, without floor hand pay.

The lifestyle did have a profound effect on the family. This is not a whimper, just a statement that there must certainly be some mostly negative consequences of continual, periodic absences of the father from the otherwise traditional family unit of the forties and fifties. My Mother became increasingly affected by Dad’s absence, perhaps as most mothers were. The kids had their friends and school to keep them busy; they got by. Many marriages broke up, but those stories were not talked of in front of the kids. As a teenager it became apparent to me that my parents were having more and more difficulty relating to each other because of the continual physical distances between them.

The impact of the ‘patch’ on my life would probably be in my reaction to the life-long remoteness between my father and I and my belief in the family unit. We never knew each other. Even after I got my C.A. he still asked my brother-in-law (who sold machine tools at the time) to do his income tax. I had the opportunity to gain a small insight into my father’s working lifestyle at the end of my first year of university. I was employed by Imperial Oil on a camp job over the summer and worked on a well site in the remote bush of north-central B.C. Over the summer I met some of the `names’ that had been familiar to me over the years as Dad’s workmates. By then the camp jobs were three weeks in and a week out; I gained an increased respect for what my Dad and the rest of the men who had worked in far worse conditions.

Dad retired at the end of that summer when I was still in the bush; I only discovered this at summer’s end, when I returned home to an empty home. They had moved to Calgary. In his early fifties he had enough of going further and further north. The teenager that once loved the rigs now hated them. He had always preached his mantra to me "get your education." I watched with increasing dismay as my parents, in retirement, struggled and fought to get to know each other again after all those years. And I'll bet that this is a story repeated throughout Alberta.

Ian Archibald (1997)

Karen Bower

Karen was a child in the early days of the Leduc oilfield. She now lives in Edmonton and works at the University of Alberta. Two years ago she took up writing and this piece is a recent product.

When you are five years old bed time comes early, whether you like it or not. When I was five I remember being put to bed one day for a very long afternoon nap. The evening was to be special, because Mom, Dad, and I were doing something unheard-of, going for a drive after dark.

I don't remember what I was told would happen, but I knew it had to be special for me to be allowed to stay up so late. The sun had long since gone when we piled into the car and drove for what seemed like hours. Today I know the distance was less than five miles. We stopped on a height of land with a clear view of the western sky. Today that spot is at 75th Street and 45th Avenue overlooking the far northern edges of the Millwoods area of Edmonton. That spot is nowhere near the "country", which was where we felt we were.

The entire southwestern sky was alight with a pulsing orange-red glow. The horizon was dotted with dozens of fires, all of them flares from the Leduc oilfield. I had no idea what an oil well was, but what the flares did to the sky was mesmerizing to my young eyes. I remember Dad saying this was going to create huge changes in the world we knew. I had no idea what that meant, but anything that could make the night sky dance had to be exciting.

He was right about the magnitude of change and I was to feel the impact too. We moved to Leduc in the summer of 1949. We went from living in the city of Edmonton, close to my grandparents, with tree shaded streets and paved roads to a town that ended almost before it began and streets of nothing but mud.

Mud, mud, and more mud was an all pervasive factor of oilfield life. Around our house, where the streets should have been, there was mud. Houses existed in this new subdivision, but streets hadn't been built. Where sidewalks should be there was mud, or (perhaps) plank sidewalks that threatened to squish out from under our feet whenever we had a three-day rain. Where lawns should be there was also mud. No lawns had yet been planted.

On top of that there was no running water, no gas, and no indoor plumbing. All these were promised before we moved in. This was definitely a place of "Promises! Promises!" There were promises of city conveniences, promises of more and more jobs, promises of a new life, and always, promises of new opportunities.

After the first year in Mudville (alias, Leduc), water and sewer arrived. No party was held to mark the demise of the outhouse. Construction of the sewer and water bought with it more mud. During the no-water period all our water had to be gotten from a town well a block from our house. Whether you walked that distance or drove, it was a heavy trip, especially so on the way back. The water weighed a lot and the accumulated mud on our boots or tires made it seem even heavier. Well water in Leduc was, and still is, foul tasting and smelling, so Dad bought a galvanized barrel which he filled with water at my grandparents' house in Edmonton. That water was for drinking, and for the making of tea and coffee.

Well water, with its high iron content and smelly organic compounds was reserved for bathing and laundry. The iron deposits in the water had me thoroughly confused for years because I couldn't make sense of how it was possible for me to feel quite clean yet still produce such piles of red-brown silt in the bottom of the metal bath tub. Though I was confused I was still young enough to take this all as an adventure. My parents would have preferred far less adventure and much more convenience.

The end of WWII produced thousands of returning veterans and the oil boom brought in thousands more men eager for work. All of this created housing pressures of enormous proportions. Central Mortgage and Housing (CMHC) built "veterans" houses all across Canada in an attempt to relieve the pressure. My Dad was a "vet" so we were fortunate to have the luxury of a newly built house. Though, in the early period, it didn't have sewer, or running water, or gas, or a lawn, or sidewalks, or even a road in front. At least it wasn't a dwelling that had formerly been a chicken coop. There were many former barns, garages, and other farm buildings pressed into service as dwellings. People put up with whatever they could find.

It was difficult for families who followed the expanding activity in the oilfields. It wasn't much better for single men. Sometimes oil companies had their own camps. In other cases single workers lived in small town hotels and commuted to the rig sites by company bus.

One of those situations brought us George. Like others residing in the Leduc Hotel, George quickly attempted to find alternative lodging. Meals were monotonous. George's room was above the bar which didn't close until 2 am. George had to be up no later than five to ensure he got a chance at the shared bathroom. If he was lucky, he might have time for breakfast. It meant the night was very short.

Dad heard this story and others when he stopped at the hotel for an early coffee on his way to work at Henderson's Garage where he was Parts Manager. Henderson's opened at six and closed late in an attempt to handle the huge volume of work the oil boom brought.

George, a young man in his early twenties, was from a farm in Saskatchewan. Like almost everyone else he'd come seeking a good paying job in the oilfields and had no idea what to expect when he got there. He asked Dad if our family would take him in as a boarder. Dad told him the decision was entirely up to Mom. Dad said, since she would be the one to face the work of it, she should be the one to answer. He also told George the answer would likely be no. They had already talked about the subject. It seemed every family in town was being pressured with the same question. Oilfield workers had a poor reputation, and most families were very reluctant to take on something that might be difficult to continue.

But George decided to give it a try anyway and showed up on our doorstep to plead his case directly with my Mother. He talked with her and she was still very reluctant, though she told us later George seemed like a very nice young man. She gave him various reasons for her hesitancy, one of which was the need to share bathroom facilities. He said his need to be at the bus by six would ensure he was out of the house before anyone else.

The talk went on for some time until Mom began to weaken and she to showed George the room under discussion, thinking it would dissuade him. Perhaps she weakened because he reminded her of her youngest brother, George, who (in WWII) had been far away in Yellowknife in a similar situation and in need of somebody to take him in. Later she told me the telling factor had been the look on George's face when he saw the space. It was her sewing room. It contained a single bed, a dresser, a closet, a desk, and her beloved sewing machine.

George's eyes grew large and he looked even younger than his years. "It's so large," he said. She didn't think so, but he told her he had never had a room to himself on the farm. She gave in partially, but had him agree it would only be for the room. She would not provide meals.

I remember Dad laughing and saying he wondered how long that would last. I thought he meant how long would George seek meals at the hotel. What he really meant was how long would it be before my Mom's soft heart melted even further and George would join us for meals. He was right. It was only a few weeks before they were sharing breakfasts together, Mom was packing lunches, and weekend suppers meant there were four at the table.

I was very firmly told that the room was now off-limits. It was George's. He couldn't believe his good fortune. We all settled in to having a new member of the family.

Christmas was of 1952 was on the horizon and Mom intended to invite George to spend it with us. At the same time he'd been offered the standard oil company choice of a Texas Mickey (approximately 42 ounces) of liquor, or a turkey. For George it was no contest because he seldom drank and was always hungry. Unfortunately George's choice of turkey and Mom's invitation didn't come in the right order. George brought home the 36 pound bird after Mom had purchased one and before she gave out the invitation. The bird was so big it wouldn't fit in the oven. The butcher faced this with aplomb, suggesting he freeze the one Mom had reserved and split the thirty-six pounder in half. Problem solved. Except for my Dad, who ate turkey with reluctance.

That year I received the game "Monopoly" as a Christmas present and was rather distressed that I wouldn't get a chance to play it because there were no children my age in the neighbourhood. George became my hero by volunteering to play with me. Mom and Dad joined in too and we sat for hours waiting for the awesome bird to roast.

We played until we felt we knew Boardwalk, Park Place, Marvin Gardens in intimate detail. George and I felt we'd been there, though all we knew was Mom and Dad's stories of their own visits. We played until each one of us had been in and out of Jail enough to build a lengthy Rap Sheet. We played until we had labels for each other: Mother was the Shrewd Saver; Dad was The Negotiator; George was the Risk Taker, and I gained the label of Real Estate Tycoon, a phrase I barely understood but wore with pride anyway.

By four pm we were bottom weary yearning for the release of supper and Mom began to wonder why there was no scent of roasting turkey. "Gordon!" The tone was anxious. We all pressed into the tiny kitchen to see Mom place her hand into the stony cold oven. Dad tested the burners. They were working. "Oh, no! The fuses!" And we didn't have any to replace the burned-out ones.

Neighbours were canvased in rotation. Finally, the last one we tried was Roly Light, neighbour and hardware story owner, who responded by opening the store to supply what we needed.

Supper was very late that night and very, very welcome. By the time it arrived we had played Monopoly so long the money was beginning to show signs of extreme age.

George's sojourn with us continued for about a year until the company he worked for moved on to fields much further from Leduc. Commuting was no longer possible and he reluctantly left us to live in the company camp. We were sorry to see him go and I was sorry to lose my Monopoly partner.

Karen Bower (1997)

John Dreichel

John is the son of an oil worker. He was two months old when he began moving about in a trailer, with his parents. As a young child, he, like many others whose father was in the oil patch, struggled with the absence of a full time dad. John lives on an acreage in Spruce Grove.

It is with earnest expectation that I look forward to the completion of this conglomerate of stories. With the strength of granite, these people helped build this industry.

My father, Fred, had worked the oil patch for more years than I could remember. He had been a strong burly man, intense in purpose, but gentle in manner. Dad never spoke much about the oil patch, and usually when he did it was for instruction. He'd say, "If these knots aren't tied properly, unnecessary injuries happen.. Or it might be, "If you look after your feet, your feet look after you."

He was always a stickler for proper warm clothing and footwear.

Dad spent several winters at Norman Wells, in camp jobs, working for Imperial Oil.

I remember back when I was very young,, Dad spoke of working grave yards. I really thought he worked in the graveyards and I always hoped the ghosties wouldn't get him.

Through the years when everyone seemed to mention Murphy's Law, Dad would always say, "shit and two makes eight" and dig at the solution anyway.

The challenges presented to people in the oil patch were huge. The sacrifices these people made were too numerous to count. The years flew by quickly. To the stout hearted, determined roughnecks, derrick men, drillers, toolpushers, welders, etc., I salute you!

John Dreichel (1997)

Lynda Dreichel-Lee

Lynda was a small child in the fifties. She remembers how things were as a child of an oilfield worker in the fifties and sixties. The most difficult times were all the 'good-byes'. Lynda now has a family of her own and attending university working towards a degree in Special Education.

Our family usually celebrated two Christmas's because my dad always took advantage of the extra pay that could be earned on Christmas day. We would spend December 25th with mom's family and then Ukrainian Christmas with dad's family.

Christmas Eve, in 1962, stands out in my memory. This was different because my daddy would be home in time for Christmas day. We received word late on the 24th that he would be arriving later that night.

I had a fever and a headache that day but I felt better as soon as I heard he was on his way home. I was determined to stay awake until he arrived; however, I thought I was dreaming when I heard noises at the door. The snowflakes were gently cascading through the dark night as he and his suitcase came through the door. After hugs and kisses, he carried me up to my room and I fell asleep, feeling that this was a real Christmas.

Lynda Dreichel-Lee (1997)

Editor's Note: *The following is a copy of a letter written to Fred Dreichel from his daughter in 1961. Lynda was 6 1/2 years old and Fred was working as a motor man for Imperial Oil, in the Fort Nelson area.*

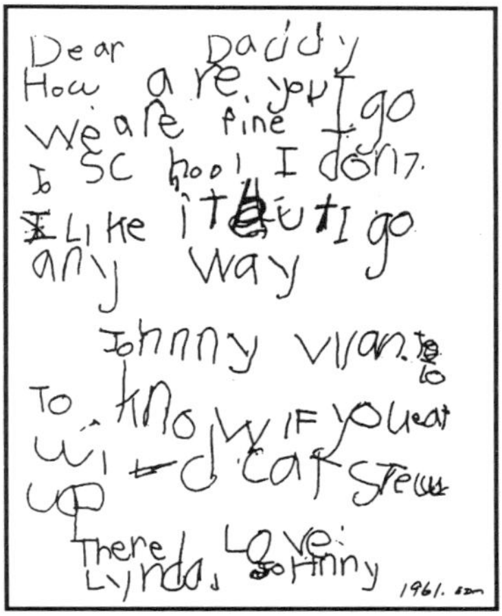
Dear Daddy
How are you
we are fine I go
to school I don't
like it but I go
any way
Johnny wants to
to know if you eat
wild cat stew
up
There Love:
Lynda, Johnny
1961.

Editor's Translation:

Dear Daddy:

How are you? We are fine. I go to school. I don't like it but I go anyway. Johnny wants to know if you eat wild cat stew up there.

Love Lynda and Johnny

Ione (Roblin) Scabar

Ione lived in Grande Prairie during the 'discovery' years. She now resides just north of Devon, not far from the Leduc #1 historic site.

OIL AND BRAN
(Not Necessarily the Ingredients for a Muffin - You Could Be Feeding Pigs! Or Drilling for Oil)

I hadn't really considered myself to be one of the oil patch generation of Alberta because we lived in the Peace River country - far from the Leduc #1. Upon reflection, however, I realized that I was there when the oil boom was happening in Alberta, and that I too was a part of the excitement and history that was created with the discovery of oil in Alberta. We lived in Grande Prairie and some of my experiences and some of my memories as a child are of those years - the good times, the boom times, the times that changed the lives of all Albertans.

My first impressions of the oil patch are linked to my mother's five brothers. They were born and raised in the Grande Prairie area, and when Imperial discovered Leduc #1, they discovered dreams of their own. They formed their own company around 1947 to 1948. I remember being very impressed at the sight of their name emblazoned on the sides of their trucks "Coopers Brothers Drilling". They had three rigs and three water trucks and the sound of any of them driving into the yard always created excitement in my young life. As a child, I was both impressed and fascinated by their stories and the oil patch lingo. They spoke of places I never heard of and talked of rigs, holes, toolpushes and roughnecks.

The drilling rigs, the water trucks and all of the equipment they carried also fascinated me. My favorite place to explore was up on the back of the tank of the water truck. That was where they stored all sorts of interesting tools and equipment, including sacks of bran. I loved the taste of the powdery material and considered it a treat to be able to grab a handful from one of the burlap bags. I munched on the stuff at every opportunity, always thinking that I was getting away with something, or that I was secretly taking some expensive or forbidden treat. Bran was a standard commodity for a shot hole drilling rig to have on hand. They used it like drilling mud to seal the oil when they lost circulation. I didn't know that. I just enjoyed it! To this day, I associate bran with drilling rigs.

Apparently there were others who didn't know what the bran was used for either. According to my Uncle John, on one occasion a farmer stopped by to see what they were doing out in the field. When he saw the bran, he asked, "What's ya doin'? Feedin' pigs?" In fact, they were dropping bran down a hole. I am told they also used corn husks and oat shells when the bran wasn't available.

Another visitor to one of my uncles' drilling sites happened along just after they had changed oil in the trucks. They had placed the empty oil cans down the hole. When the farmer asked if they had found any oil on that very nice April morning, the reply was "Yeah. We found about five cans in this hole."

The oil industry allowed many farm boys to become roughnecks, drillers, rig hands, and oil executives. It was economic freedom and it was a way to get off the farm, to see the world even if it was only as big as Alberta. It was also a way for many of them to be injured. If they didn't lose their fingers by catching them on the pipes or pipe wrenches, they broke fingers, or toes, or had toes cut off by falling drill stem. Two of my uncles lost fingers and another broke his fingers. Missing or damaged fingers seemed to be common for those working in the oilfield and I viewed them not as an oddity, but rather as a badge of service.

Working in the oil patch was probably more dangerous than most wanted to admit. Men worked with equipment that was new to them and with technology that was being developed as they went along. Our family chuckles when recalling the story of how my uncles decided to use some of the dynamite they carried on the rigs to blast out a stump in my grandfather's yard at the farm. It seemed like a quick and efficient way to remove the stump, while also giving the youngest of my uncles a demonstration of the power and use of the dynamite. The stump was removed all right. However, all of the windows in Grand Dad's house were also removed! When the dust settled, two very surprised and sheepish young men quickly clamored into their truck. As my Grand Dad appeared around the corner of the house to see what the commotion was all about, they shouted to him before he could say a word, "We have to go to town. We'll be right back." And back they did come - with all new windows for the house!

I remember there was pride in the industry, and in being a part of it. The pride showed up in things like drill bits, chromed or otherwise, that were displayed in homes as parts of lamps, ashtrays, coffee tables or simply as doorstops or desk ornaments. There was also a pride evident in the way the oilmen dressed. You could tell an oilman by his oilman's stetson, his aluminum hard hat, or from the matching grey work shirts and pants he wore. When it turned cold, many of them also sported hand-knit Siwash sweaters with oil derricks proudly displayed on the back. These things all said 'oil patch'.

And of course, there were the coveralls. I remember the endless pairs of coveralls that donned my mother's clothesline when my brother came home from the oil patch for a weekend. The mud was always everywhere but it seemed to gather in every pocket, seam and stitch of those coveralls. There were striped ones. There were also the white ones with the big embroidered capital "F" inside the red circle - the Failing coveralls. And there were the red ones! The red coveralls became fashionable after the internationally known oil well firefighter, "Red" Adair made them his trademark. My brother was 17 or 18 years old when he thought he would make himself a couple of pairs of red coveralls by dying some of his white coveralls red. To his dismay, the red dye didn't take all that well and he ended up with a couple of otherwise perfectly good pairs of 'pink' coveralls! It took a long time to wear them out as he rarely, if ever, wore them any place but around the yard to do oil changes and grease jobs on his vehicles. I liked to refer to him as "Pink" Adair when he wore them!

My brother started working as a roughneck at the age of 17. He worked first on the rigs, then on seismograph. The hours were long and the money good for the times. He bought his first brand new car in 1956. It was a 1956 red Ford Fairlaine. It was his pride and joy. The 'patch' provided many young men with the ways and means to make their dreams come true. It also made the mobile home business in this province one to be envied anywhere. When one of my uncles married, his first home was a very long mobile home. Friends and neighbors all came to admire the long, blue home on wheels as it sat in our yard awaiting the new bride and groom to come and haul it away to Blairmore. Moving about was part of the industry. It only made sense if you wanted your family to be with you that you had to buy a trailer. Trailer towns and trailer courts built up wherever the oil business went. I spent part of my summers with one of my uncles in their mobile home in Drayton Valley. My uncle worked for Mobil Oil back then. It took me a few moments to recall the name of the oil company, but I have never forgotten the image of the flying red horse that was their logo.

When the summers were over and cold winters set in, many men went to work 'up north'. The constant moving and traveling by the men left the women no choice but to become independent and self-reliant. If the water lines froze in the trailer, it was "The Mrs." that had to thaw them out. If the pickup had a flat tire, she learned how to change it. The women learned how to live alone. They raised their children in seclusion from their fathers and sought the company of other women in similar circumstances.

During these times, a unique and independent breed of people was created. Many of the men and women who lived these memories and who were challenged by these times are no longer with us. My brother is gone and so are two of my uncles, but their stories live on. I feel that the men and the women of the era have left an indelible mark in our lives and in the history of our province. Alberta and anyone who was touched by the lives and times of these men and women will always have a part of the oil patch embedded in their history and in their souls.

Ione Scabar (1997)

Anonymous Anecdotes

ANONYMOUS ANECDOTES

For obvious reasons, the following recollections must remain anonymous....

* * * * *

"Once, during the early sixties, before hard top at Drayton Valley, I went along for the ride to deliver some tools to a location near the town. Little did I realize the experience in store for me. It wasn't to bad when we drove out there but it started to rain during the day and when we headed back to Edmonton the road was a sea of mud.

A cat was pulling the cars through to the highway. We were about the 14th in line. We had been sitting in the car for about six hours.

The mud was deep - to the top of the boots - and me, with no boots on. I had to go to the bathroom. I waited some more. I was now in agony.

It was either get out of the car and sink in the mud or. Then, as luck would have it, I remembered that we always carried the hard hat in the car. OK, there was a choice here. So I said, "Well, what am I going to use, your boot or your hard hat.?"

And so, yet another use was found for the hard hat. We took a total of twelve hours to get back to Edmonton. I didn't go back to Drayton Valley for a long, long time."

* * * * *

"People had their own, somewhat weird sense humor. One time, after arriving home from a house party, a couple discovered a Billy goat in the trunk of their car. What a mess!! With a little detective work, — found out who the trickster was and decided to get even. The fellow had a birthday coming up, so she planned a party for him, complete with a birthday cake.

She scooped up the goat turds from the trunk of the car, put them in a little box and arranged this on a plate. Then she iced and decorated it, with a 'Happy Birthday' message.

At the party, the guy who had the birthday got to cut the cake. When the contents spilled out, he immediately knew why this special cake had been created just for him. The look on his face gave the hostess the satisfaction of knowing that this really was "pay back time." Every one laughed uproariously and continued on with the party.

* * * * *

"One of the most humorous things I seen around the rigs, was a time when we were in a camp, near Fort St. John. One roughneck was sitting drinking coffee about 8 pm, worrying about his wife sleeping around and he was kind of moping around.

Another bugger was watching this and he apparently was a bit of a smart aleck. He walked up to the table, put his hands on the table, in front of the worried guy and gave him this advice, "Listen, one can't hurt 'em, and two can't get on, so you got nothing to worry about."

Well, that bugger that was worried, just came unglued and they scrambled that kitchen up pretty bad. As soon as the instigator got loose, he broke out of the kitchen. He gave the worried roughneck plenty of leeway for two to three days so his emotions could settle a little."

* * * * *

I remember one of these jobs down in —. One night we all decided to go to the bar and watch the strippers. Pretty soon the bet was on which foreman could go up to the stage and see which girl could make the most money getting these dollar bills out of my mouth. The girl I was with, was just gathering the dollar bills up, taking them out of my mouth with her boobs.

Finally, I told this girl, "Well, see those guys over there, that real tall guy and that real short guy. Go over there and catch them two." Well, all you could see of the little guy, was the bottom of his moccasins. He never did touch the ground. He was just siftin' it, hittin' 'er for the bathroom. The tall, slim guy, made about seven steps and made it into the bathroom. The girl never caught up to them.

All these men were all broke in the morning because they just couldn't stop feeding down there. Early next morning, I phoned home and told my wife what had happened. She asked, "Why did you phone me with this story?" "Well" I said, "You might as well get it from me first rather than hear it from all the other guys because they're probably gonna be phoning."

* * * * *

We were cutting line in Whitecourt. One night we all stopped at the bar. They started talking about stealing the Budweiser barrel that was in the bar. The barrel was full of ice and stuff. Anyway, we had a few drinks and then we decided to go for supper. After supper, another guy and I decided not to go back down to the bar.

But down to the bar the rest of them go. They decided they were going to steal this Budweiser barrel after everything was settled down. One said to the other one, "Well, you pick up the barrel, one guy will be out there with the truck. We will have to get this barrel empty because it is too heavy to pack with ice in it." The one guy went up and told this girl to take the ice out of the barrel because they were going to steal it. So she told someone to take the ice out of it.

Anyway, it went on for a while and this other company that was in there, said, "Well, you guys are too chicken shit to do it. We'll do it." So our guys decided that they were going to steal this barrel. One guy went out and got the truck running, the other guy was going to hold the door open and the third guy was going to take the barrel. They managed to get away with it. When they got going, they threw the barrel in the back of the pickup, got in and took off. But they lost the lid off the barrel and they had to drive back to pick it up. By this time the cops were coming, but they finally got the lid back.

They got back into where we were staying about 3 or 4 o'clock in the morning with this Budweiser barrel. One guy took the barrel up to his room and the other guys were downstairs. About 4 o'clock, a knock came to my door and I got up. It was the R.C.M.P. He said, "We're looking for a guy short with a mustache." I said, "Well, what's happening?" He told me what they had done. The cop was standing outside, so I closed the door and asked my son, "T——, do you know anything about this?" He said, "No, I've been here all the time." So I went back out and told the R.C.M.P., "I don't know much about it. I don't know what happened or anything." He said, "Well, we found ice in the back of the pickup and it belongs to your company. And that's the company we're looking for. They stole a Budweiser barrel out of the hotel."

Anyway, I closed the door again and I asked this other guy about this. He said, "No, I've been here all night." So I woke my son up again and asked him again. And he said, "No, he didn't know nothing about it." The cop then said, "Well, there's a guy with a mustache, he's not very tall and he wears glasses."

I told the cop, "Well, he's over in the next room." The mountie went over the other room and asked this guy. They dithered back and forth and the mountie was told, "Well, the guy upstairs maybe knows something about it." So they went up there and found this barrel up in the other guy's room. He's a real tall guy with a mustache. The next morning, we went back to work. Everybody got off that night and, they didn't have to do anything then. J— came over and asked, "How old do you got to get before you quit being stupid?" I said, "Boy, you'll have to ask somebody older than me. Because I'm still the same way. It could have been me as well as the rest. Whatever happened."

Anyway, they stole this barrel using the company pickup. Two of them were my son-in-laws and one of them was my son. That was in 1987. When we had to go to court, I phoned a lawyer in Grande Prairie and I went in to see him. He said, "Well, I'll look after it." We got the short guy with the mustache to go in and plead guilty to the fine. The other two boys, who were my son and the tall guy with the mustache, paid for the $500 fine.

* * * * *

This following story happened in the sixties. This oil man is a fun loving fellow and he's leaving the beverage room in the Slave Lake Hotel one night. As he's getting into his car, a mountie stops him to question him about being under the influence of alcohol. The oil man is a pretty good sized man. He unlocks his car and picks the mountie up and puts him in the trunk of the car and shuts the trunk. It's pretty cold out.

Figuring he was going to get fined pretty heavy this guy thinks up a plan. He goes back in the bar and tells these guys that he has a tiger in his trunk. They don't believe him. With a bunch of drunks like that, he has about 20 or 30 guys betting him $100 a piece that he has no tiger in his trunk.

So then, he tells them to come out and he'll show it to them. He has 20 or 30 guys standing around the car and they all paid a $100 to see this tiger in the trunk. He opens the trunk up and, yes, there sure is a tiger in his trunk, and it comes out of there madder than a hornet.

The oil man made about $1,500 to $1,800 on side bets after his fine was paid. He was fined $1,000 and he probably got $3,000 in bets. In those days, money flowed pretty easy.

* * * * *

In our cluster of trailers, privacy was almost non-existent and we all knew of the 'hard' time one of the girls had with her husband.

He had a short fuse and would slap her around at the slightest provocation. One day she came running into my trailer saying, "Please don't let him find me." I hid her in the closet. Almost immediately there was a knock on my door. The door opened and the husband said to me, "I know she's in here. I saw her go into your trailer. Get her out here." "She's not here" I said. The guy became very angry and as he stood on the step yelling and making threats against his wife, the step was teetering.

Now my husband didn't fix things until he had no choice and so the step was only a wooden crate on uneven ground, by the door, outside the trailer. While this fellow was loudly voicing his threats, the step teetered to one side, and down — went, under the trailer into a shallow hole. He crawled out quickly and headed for the waiting carload of crew members. They were on their way to work. When they were gone, — came out of the closet. I made her promise to come over the next morning so I could see that she was OK. When she came over the next morning, she had no visible bruises, but she said to me, "I was lucky this time. He just slapped me a couple of times."

* * * * *

I heard about this guy who had a bit of a problem with 'binge' drinking. One weekend he very drunk but still very mobile. He had a little dachshund dog. This was a beautiful little dog and the guy was very attached to it. He realized that he couldn't drive but he wanted to show the dog the mountains around Banff. "Well", the guy said to himself, I'll just call a taxi." Now a taxi ride from Calgary to Banff and back costs a fair amount of money but — didn't care. He was satisfied that he had given his little dog some joy in it's life.